# Dallas Planting Manual

*Originally Compiled by*
*Mrs. Edward A. Belsterling*

2001
Fourteenth Edition

THE DALLAS GARDEN CLUB
of the Dallas Woman's Club

## Printing History

under the original title
### Planting Manual for Dallas Gardens
### within 100 mile radius

First edition 1941. Project of Group III of The Dallas Garden Club
of The Dallas Woman's Club. Compiled by Mrs. Edward A.
Belsterling. Second edition 1946, Third edition 1948.
Fourth edition, Copyright 1950 by The Dallas Garden Club,
Dallas, Texas. Compiled by Mrs. Edward A. Belsterling.
Fifth edition, Copyright 1952 by The Dallas Garden Club, Dallas,
Texas. Compiled by Mrs. Edward A. Belsterling, enlarged
edition. Sixth edition 1955. Seventh edition 1959.
Eighth edition, Copyright 1963 by The Dallas Garden Club,
Dallas, Texas. Compiled by Mrs. Edward A. Belsterling, new
enlarged edition, Mrs. R. Edgar Padgitt, ed.
Ninth edition, Copyright 1968 by The Dallas Garden Club of The
Dallas Woman's Club, Dallas, Texas. Originally compiled by
Mrs. Edward A. Belsterling. Mrs. R. Edgar Padgitt editor
emeritus. Mrs. George N. Aldredge, Mrs. Mark Lemmon, Mrs.
P. C. Lockett, Mrs. J. T. Montgomery, eds. Tenth edition 1970.
Eleventh edition 1981.
Twelfth edition, Copyright 1991 by The Dallas Garden Club of
The Dallas Woman's Club, Dallas, Texas. Originally compiled
by Mrs. Edward A. Belsterling, Mrs. Walton Grayson III, ed.
Thirteenth edition, Copyright 1998 by The Dallas Garden Club of
The Dallas Woman's Club, Dallas, Texas. Originally compiled
by Mrs. Edward A. Belsterling, Mrs. David H. Gibson ed.

## Cataloging in Publication

Belsterling, Louise B(abcock), (1877-1970)
Dallas planting manual/the Dallas Garden Club of the
Dallas Woman's Club; originally compiled by Mrs. Edward
A. Belsterling; Lorine Crenshaw Gibson, editor — 14th ed.
p. cm.
Includes bibliographical references and index
Rev. ed. of: Planting Manual for Dallas Area Gardens.
LCCN: 97-77688
ISBN: 0-9652349-1-6
1.Gardening—Texas—Dallas. 2.Plants cultivated —Texas.
3. Flower gardening—Dallas. 4.Landscape plants—Texas.
I. Title
SB453.2 T41998          635'097642812

*As with the Thirteen previous editions, the proceeds of this
Fourteenth Edition are dedicated to*

**The Belsterling Scholarships in Horticulture Research
and
The Belsterling Botanical Library**

# FOREWORD

## From The Original Edition

This little booklet was conceived with no idea of originality. It is
published as a project of the Dallas Garden Club, whose members
deemed such a manual highly desirable, in view of the fact that the
great mass of horticultural data already published has no application
to our climate, soil, and conditions.

When the actual compilation was undertaken, the editor drew not
only from the many articles published on the subjects treated, but from
the personal experience of many members of the Dallas Garden Club.

The articles on what to do and when to do it, on perennials, leaf
mold, cold frames, roses, soil, air-layering, and foliar feeding, were
compiled from the editor's personal experience.

With the hope that this work may in some measure meet the need
for which it was conceived, it is submitted to the public.

*Louise B. Belsterling*, 1941

# SHORT HISTORY
## Of The Dallas Garden Club

The Dallas Garden Club was founded in 1926 with Mrs. Gross R. Scruggs as first President. It was called "The Garden Club of The Dallas Woman's Club". Then, as now, members must be members of The Dallas Woman's Club. Fascinating programs and workshops through the years have encouraged members to learn flower arranging and to study gardening methods. Then, as now, Civic Beautification has been a major interest. Funds have been raised and donated to plant trees, flowers and shrubs in public locations to make Dallas a more pleasant place to live. The Dallas Garden Club was instrumental in the founding of the Dallas Horticulture Center at Fair Park and still contributes support. Daughters form a Junior Group so that they can benefit from the Senior group leadership.

Mrs. Edward A. Belsterling wrote her first Planting Manual in 1941. This is her legacy to The Dallas Garden Club. The Belsterling Foundation was established from a bequest by Mrs. Belsterling for the purpose of funding scholarships in Horticultural Research and supporting the Belsterling Botanical Library housed at the University of Texas at Dallas. Proceeds from the sale of the Planting Manual augment this endowment. Now in its seventh decade, the Dallas Garden Club continues its program of study and its involvement in Civic Beautification. In this newest edition, we have endeavored as always to make this manual useful to the beginner and to update the more experienced gardener on new ideas, trends and environmental concerns. Our goal, like Mrs. Belsterling's, is to help provide a better community for us all.

## The Planting Manual Revision Committee
Mrs. David H. Gibson, Editor

| | |
|---|---|
| Mrs. William L. Furneaux | Mrs. Donald Padgett |
| Mrs. G. Douglas Gill | Mrs. Kimball S. Watson |

Mrs. Lewis L. May, Jr.

## The Planting Manual Section Representatives

| | |
|---|---|
| Mrs. Frederick N. Scripts | Mrs. Stephen Sands |
| Mrs. P. Mike McCullough | Mrs. M. A. Ashmore |
| Mrs. Donald E. Bowles, Jr. | Mrs. Michael E. Bogel |

# ACKNOWLEDGMENTS

We proudly present the 14th Edition of the _Dallas Planting Manual._ In print since 1941, this useful guide endures because a chain of dedicated gardeners has continually provided written, up-to-date instructions for horticulture in our community. This is a statement of gratitude to the contributors to this newest edition.

First and foremost, we honor the book's originator, Mrs. Edward A. Belsterling, for her generous gift of the manual. During her lifetime she shared her amazing knowledge of gardening in all its phases. Second, we offer our thanks to the merchants and the public for their enthusiastic support of the manual through its 57 years.

For this on-going project we acknowledge many of the same author-advisors from the 12th edition: Dr. E. L. McWilliams, Texas A&M University, Professor of Floriculture; Dr. David Morgan and Chris Hager, both Belsterling Scholarship Recipients; Michael Cheever, Dallas Horticulture Center; Mrs. James K. Kerr, Bulbs; Howard Garrett, Organic Gardening; and Michael Shoup, Antique Rose Emporium. In the ninth edition, assistant chairman of the Planting Manual revision committee, Mrs. C. L. Lundell, illustrated the insects found in Chapter 6.

In the 12th and 13th editions two club members, Mrs. William L. Furneaux and Mrs. Lewis L. May, each an internationally honored specialist in her field, contributed "Herbs" and "Native Plants" respectively.

In the 13th edition, Dr. Michael Merchant at the Texas Agricultural Experiment Station of TAMU consulted on "Insects, Diseases, and Remedies." Dr. Sam Cotner, Head, Department of Horticulture Sciences, Texas A&M University, reviewed "Vegetables". The Lawn Grass section is adapted from a paper by Dr. M. C. Engelke, professor, Texas Agricultural Experiment Station of TAMU. Tina Dombrowski of the Dallas Horticulture Center and Ernie Ryan gave information on local butterflies. Steve Brainerd, Town of Highland Park, and Eugene Westlake at the Dallas Arboretum and Botanical Society advised on Azaleas.

Derald Harp, a Belsterling Scholarship recipient at TAMU, allowed us copyright for excerpts from his doctoral dissertation and the map on Metroplex hardiness zones.

Assisting the editor were Logan Calhoun, David Andrew, Charles E. Finsley, Molly Shelton Hussing, Bill Edwards, Sandra Lipe, and 1997-98 Club President, Carol Marsh. The superb design expertise of Cover Artist Philip Lamb and Graphic Designer Judy Hampel illuminated this valuable manual for the Millenium. The encouragement, support, and patience of my husband, David, was unlimited.

Like other members of this club, I resonate with beauty, nature and the soil. Early in my life, I was taught a belief in organization, tradition and the written word. The _Dallas Planting Manual_ was my first gardening guide. We share the same original publication date - 1941. My connection to this book is a joy in my life.

There will be more editions as our science and gardens evolve into a creative partnership with Nature herself. You readers are also an extension of this chain as you study, garden and pass on information. All of us must continue our commitment to raising our consciousness of the earth, to enhance our community's beauty and to thrive in this beloved area where we are planted.

*Lorine Gibson*, 2001

# TABLE OF CONTENTS

# Gardening by the Month

*This monthly calendar for practical gardening is the first and most used chapter in this historic manual. Many valuable tips are not found elsewhere. Read it carefully the first of each month to find what, when, where, and how to plant.*

# JANUARY

Cold winter weather is a choice time to hibernate. Rest, read, dream. Visualize your garden. Harmonize your attitude and intent with the space and the spirit of the land. In this quiet season, resolve to enjoy, align, witness and listen to Nature. Prepare the prime element in planting — the soil. Add compost, mulch and/or fertilizer. Winter rains will dissolve these nutrients into existing soil by planting time.

## PREPARE

**Soil ▪** Compost, add nutrients (see pp 31-41).

**Tools ▪** Clean and sharpen tools and equipment; use lubricant on metal, linseed oil on wooden handles. Organize your garden storage.

**Garden Design ▪** Create new gardens on paper. Read catalogues, estimate budget.

**Garden Techniques ▪** Learn about xeriscaping, organic gardening and composting.

## PLANT

**Trees, Shrubs, and Roses ▪** When the ground is not frozen.

**Seed in Flats Indoors ▪** Alyssum, Eggplant, Marigolds, Morning Glories, Peppers, Petunias and Tomatoes.

## WATER

**Evergreen Trees and Shrubs ▪** To a depth of 6" before a freeze.

**Herbaceous Perennials and Winter Annuals ▪** Should be kept drier during freezing temperatures to reduce freeze damage.

**Bulbs ▪** Even with rain, bulbs need extra water to develop good roots. Reduce irrigation but do not stop watering completely in winter.

**Sprinkler System ▪** Cycle should begin at dusk to protect planting from late night freezes. Do not water plants that are already frozen. Check system after freeze for breakage.

## PROTECT

**All Bare Ground ▪** Mulch to protect plants from cold *(see pp. 36-37)*.

**Less Hardy Species as Sweet Peas ▪** Cover with cloth.

**Pansies ▪** Blooms can be protected by covering during severe freezes.

**Evergreens ▪** Spray with anti-transpirant to prevent drying.

## FERTILIZE

**Wisely ▪** Choose organic forms when possible. Compost is the best and cheapest fertilizer *(see pp. 39-40)*.

**Trees ▪** A balanced fertilizer with trace nutrients.

**Iris, Peonies and Asparagus Beds** ∎ Balanced fertilizer high in phosphorus (Bone Meal).

**Pansies** ∎ Balanced fertilizer with urea or natural form as Blood Meal rather than nitrate.

## PRUNE
**Major Trees** ∎ Begin pruning if the job is large.

## CONTROL
**Caution** ∎ Follow directions with any and all chemicals. Cover your body. Do not spray in the wind. Lay in a good supply of plastic gloves, *(see p. 55)*. If scale is found on undersides of evergreen leaves such as Hollies, Euonymous, or over-wintering on trunks and branches of Fruit or Nut, Dogwood, Lilac or Japanese Quince, use Winter (Dormant) oil that suffocates insects and eggs rather than poisoning them. Commercial Winter-Dormant oil is available or make our recipe *(see p. 56)*. Shake repeatedly to mix contents of oil and water.

**Hand Pick** ∎ Bagworms on conifers and evergreens.

**House Plants** ∎ Check for Mealy Bugs, Spider Mites or Scale. Wash the leaves with non-detergent soap or Alcohol Spray *(see p. 54)*.

## DESIGN
To plan, list the attributes of your space: plants, soil, shape and hardscape. List your landscape desires: sun or shade, peace or activity? Live with an existing yard one year. Monitor carefully. Find hidden perennials, the vibrancy of existing planting, seasonal sight lines to hide or to open, and the shade of large trees impossible to replace. Know that starting an entire planting scheme from scratch is expensive. Use what you have.

## WINTERIZE
**Feed** ∎ The birds.

**Branches** ∎ Shake carefully after heavy snow to prevent breakage.

## BLOOMING
Bush Jasmine, Camellias, Calendula, Carolina Jessamine, Helleborus, Mahonia, Pansy, Primrose, Wall Flower and Winter Bush Honeysuckle.

## CELEBRATE
Bring the usually unseen part of the plant to your window sill. Watch the rooting of a hyacinth in a forcing vase or toothpick a sweet potato in a narrow glass. Dwell upon your own self-rootedness in the calm of this bare season.

# FEBRUARY

Buds swelling with promise on bright crisp days are symbols of pre-emergent spring. February days are wonderful for pruning just before new growth appears. Don't worry about winter-burned foliage on live oaks or other broad leaf evergreens. Unseen, the new leaves are preparing to replace them. It is Nature's way. Expect warm weather to alternate with cold fronts. Cultivate when dry, fertilize before the rain.

## PLANT

**Spring Annual and Wildflower Seed** ▪ Cornflowers, Gaillardia, Larkspur, Penstemons, Petunias, Poppy, Purple Coneflowers and Texas Bluebell (Eustoma). Sow seed outside after February 14th in prepared beds on top of loosened soil.

**Winter Vegetable Seed** ▪ Arugula, Beets, Broccoli, Brussel Sprouts, Cabbage, Carrots, Cauliflower, Collards, English Peas, Kohlrabi, Lettuce, Parsley, Radishes, Spinach and Turnips.

**Vegetable Starts** ▪ Onion Plants, Asparagus Crowns, Potatoes, Strawberries and Bedding plants. Flowering Kale and Cabbage.

**Spring Annual Plants** ▪ Alyssum, Dianthus, English Daisy, Forget-Me-Nots, Pansies, Primulas and Snapdragons.

**Gladiola** ▪ Continue planting every 2 weeks through July for continuous bloom.

**Nasturtiums** ▪ Plant 3" deep and 6" apart. They like poor soil.

**Bare-Rooted Plants** ▪ Roses or fruit trees, before the 15th.

## TRANSPLANT

**Hardwood Cuttings** ▪ Transfer to permanent site if roots are present.

## WATER

**New Plants** ▪ Daily
**Everything** ▪ If dry.

## FERTILIZE

**Trees and Shrubs** ▪ A balanced fertilizer with trace minerals, if not done in January, or an organic fertilizer which always includes trace minerals.

**Pansies, Winter Annuals and Spring Blooming Perennials** ▪ A complete fertilizer application.

**Grass** ▪ Delay on dormant grasses unless overseeded with Rye. Good time to fertilize Rye and Fescue. Not recommended are pre-emergent weed killing fertilizers as they may damage broad-leaved shrubs and trees.

## PRUNE
**Bush Roses** ▪ Mid month, just above buds that face outward. *DO NOT PRUNE* climbing roses until after the spring bloom.

**Summer Blooming Shrubs as Crape Myrtle** ▪ Cut suckers and seed heads.

**Spring Bloomers** ▪ *DO NOT* prune.

**Liriope, Mondo and Monkey Grass** ▪ Last two weeks of month before new growth emerges.

**Major Trees** ▪ As needed.

## CONTROL
**Scale** ▪ Dormant oil may be used until buds pop.

**Roses** ▪ After pruned mid-month, Black Spot or leaf mildew prevention is recommended. Soda Spray, Bordeaux Mixture or Dusting Sulfur may be used every two weeks until June *(see pp. 54-55)*.

**Peonies** ▪ When tip of buds first appear, use Bordeaux Mixture to prevent Botrytis Blight which causes bud blast.

## DESIGN
Bring branches inside to preview the spring outside. Saucer Magnolia, Japanese Quince and Forsythia are traditionally forced. If flowering branches aren't available, select Elm, Willow, Sweet Gum or any deciduous sprouting tree. For excellent results, cut in the warmth of the day before expected low night temperatures. To promote uptake of water, recut and split stem ends at least 2", then add one aspirin to water. Mist branches daily. Place in sunny window until flowers open.

## CULTIVATE
**Hint** ▪ *DO NOT* till or plant when soil is wet. Air is easily forced out of wet soil which loses its friability, an important facet of rich organic earth.

## BLOOMING
Andromeda, Azalea, Camellias, Carolina Jessamine, Chinese Photinia, Crocus, Cyclamen, Daffodil, Dogtooth Violet, Early Snowdrop, English Daisy, Flowering Almond, Flowering Apricot, Forsythia, Hyacinth, Japanese Quince, Loropetatum, Narcissus, Pansy, Photinia, Primrose, Senesia, Violet, Wall Flower and Winter Jasmine.

## CELEBRATE
Share the planting of a tree with friends or family. Speak of your commitment to the future of our Earth. Affirm the work of green plants in rebuilding our atmosphere and cleaning our air. Make the activity a corporate, hands-on event with each one present adding soil on top of the root ball and pressing it firmly to encourage root growth.

# MARCH

Daffodils welcome the equinox with promise. The Metroplex weatherman's last average day of killing frost, March 15, may be less exact than waiting for the Pecan trees to bud out. Most of March's weather is a gardener's delight, but old timers expect sporadic excitement of wind, rain, hail, sleet, snow and late frost.

## PLANT
**Summer Seeds** ▪ Ageratum, Alyssum, Asters, Balsam, Celosia, Coleus, Coreopsis, Cosmos, Dianthus, Impatiens, Lobelia, Nicotiana, Morning Glories, Periwinkle, Portulaca, Salvia and Sunflower.

**Vegetable Seeds** ▪ Beans, Cucumbers, Corn, Lettuce, Lima Beans, Mustard, Squash and Tomatoes.

**Potted Seedlings** ▪ Started in January can be set into open ground. Protect from frost by covering with heavy paper or burlap but never plastic.

**Bare-rooted Plants** ▪ Leafed out specimens will not live

**Gladiola** ▪ Plant every two weeks for extended flowering.

**Cannas** ▪ Divide and replant every 3rd year.

**Vegetable Seedlings** ▪ Tomatoes, Peppers and Cauliflower.

**Perennials** ▪ Plant toward end of month: Artemisia, Balloon Flower, Coneflower, Coreopsis, Daisy, Mealy Blue Sage, Petunias, Rudbeckias, Salvia Greggii, Texas Blue Bells and Yarrow.

**Asparagus** ▪ In year old bed, plant male asparagus crowns to replace any female crowns removed last fall. In 3rd year beds, harvest large stems when 8" tall.

## DIVIDE
**Daises and other hardy perennials.** Re-pot house plants.

## WATER
**Step up waterings** if spring rains are delayed.

**Sprinkler System** ▪ Be aware of sufficient rain and cut your sprinkler off during natural watering. More water is required in the spring when plants are actively growing.

## FERTILIZE
**Pansies and Chrysanthemums** ▪ Light application of fish-oil, liquid manure or commercial fertilizer. Water often. Good drainage is essential.

**Naturalized Bulbs** ▪ Fertilizer high in nitrogen after blooming period. Allow foliage to remain to bring food to the bulb for next year's bloom.

**Roses** ▪ First feeding with balanced fertilizer. Repeat every 6-8 weeks.

**Lawn and Grasses** ▪ At the end of the month, lower mower blade height to remove dead leaves, then fertilize with 4-1-2 or 3-1-2 ratio with sulfur and trace minerals or 1/2" well-aged compost. Scalping the spring lawn is no longer considered the appropriate procedure.

**Trees and Shrubs** ▪ If not done in January or February. **Hint** ▪ Do not fertilize spring-blooming shrubs such as Azalea, Camellia, Indian Hawthorn, etc. until bloom is finished. Rapid growth will cancel blooms.

## PRUNE

**Ground Covers** ▪ Asian Jasmine, Liriope, Monkey Grass, Trailing Euonymus and Vinca. Cut back early in the month to encourage new compact growth.

**Azaleas and Other Spring Blooming Trees and Shrubs** ▪ Cut errant branches for inside flower arranging during blooming period.

**Shrubs** ▪ Remove winter damage.

## CONTROL

**Fire Blight** ▪ While flowers are on Pyracantha, Pears and Hawthorn, use organic agricultural streptomycin to stop fire flight spread by insect pollinators. Any wood contaminated by fire blight should be removed and burned.

**Slugs, Snails and Pill Bugs** ▪ Place beer traps or mechanical traps. Spread diatomaceous earth. Protective masks should be worn when spreading this airborne material.

**Cutworms** ▪ Bury a cardboard collar 1" deep around stem of newly "set-out" tender plants.

**Fruit Tree Borers** ▪ One of the few insects against which chemical controls are often used. Chlorpyrifos is formulated for borer spray. Use again in August. The organic control is rotenone/pyrethrum. Stressed trees seem more susceptible, especially the newly planted.

**Aphids** ▪ Combat with strong water blasts with hand held garden hose or Tobacco Tea. *(See p. 55.)*

**Whiteflies** ▪ Use yellow sticky traps or Bug Burn. *(See p. 54.)*

## BLOOMING

Alyssum, Ajuga, Azalea, Bletilla (Ground Orchid), Crossvine, Candytuft, Crabapple, Daffodil, Delphinium, Deutzia, Dianthus, Digitalis, Dogwood, English Daisy, Forget-Me-Not, Hyacinth, Hawthorn, Lady Banksia Rose, Louisiana Phlox, Mexican Buckeye, Narcissus, Pansy, Pear, Phlox, Plum, Poppies, Primula, Pyrethrum, Redbud, Snapdragon, Spirea, Texas Mountain Laurel, Thrift, Tulip, Violet and Wisteria.

## CELEBRATE

Gardening is an activity that can cultivate your land, your mind, your soul and your body. Integrate aesthetic pleasures into chores. Watch the daily light dance through your garden. Touch the tapestry of textures. Breathe in the fresh, fragrant outside air. Feel the strength of your body as you till the soil. Delight in your artistic skill as you envision landscape transformations.

# APRIL

Emerging plants lift the soil. Springing forth, April fills our gardens, wildflowers cover the roadsides and blooming trees are alive with migrating birds. The weather warms to a safe degree and almost anything can be planted in Dallas after April 15.

## PLANT

**Summer Annual Seed** ▪ Balsam, Candle Tree, Celosia, Cleome, Cockscomb, Cypress Vine, Hyacinth Bean, Marigold, Morning Glory and Zinnia.

**Vegetable Seed** ▪ Cantaloupe, Cucumber, Okra, Peppers, Pumpkins, Scarlet Runner Beans, Squash and Watermelons.

**Second Vegetable Plantings** ▪ Sweet Corn and Green Beans.

**Plants Started From Cuttings** ▪ Plant outside.

**Seedlings** ▪ Eggplant, Peppers, Sweet Potatoes and Tomatoes.

**Herbs** ▪ Basils, Thymes and Rosemarys.

**Summer Flowering Bulbs, Corms, and Rhizomes** ▪ Amaryllis, Canna, Crinum, Elephant Ear, Gladiola, Montbretia, Tigridia and Tuberose.

**Dahlia Seedlings and Tubers** ▪ Place in permanent location. Set stakes for support at time of planting.

**Bedding Plants** ▪ Perennials *(see p. 116)*. Also Begonias, Coleus, Ferns and Salvias.

**Container Grown Shrubs** ▪ Can be planted year round if properly watered after planting. Because of this month's heavy rainfall, it is a good time to plant.

**Lawns** ▪ Start from seed sprigs or sod.

## WATER

**Crape Myrtle** ▪ Soak the ground. Water on leaves causes mildew.

**Sprinkler Systems** ▪ Cut off during spring rains.

## CULTIVATE

**Spring Weeds** ▪ Easily pulled after rain; add to compost if not seeded.

## FERTILIZE

**New Bedding Plants** ▪ Wait until they show some growth, usually about two weeks. Then apply 10-20-10 ratio fertilizer.

**Vegetables** ▪ Balanced ratio needed every 6 to 8 weeks.

**Azaleas** ▪ First application of Azalea-Camellia type food applied after blooming. Add 2" to 3" mulch to insulate roots from approaching hot weather.

**All Established Trees and Shrubs** ▪ Apply 3-1-2 or 18-6-12 ratio in a circle well away from stems and leaves followed by a good soaking.

**Lawn** ▪ Mow and fertilize, if not done in March.

## CONTROL

**Thrips, Mealy Bugs and Aphids** ▪ Every two weeks release Lady bugs at base of plants when cool, possibly at night or after watering. Green Lace Wings released have larvae that are voracious eaters of Aphids, Red Spider Mites and Thrips.

**Pecan Case Bearers** ▪ Release Trichogramma Wasps.

**Fire Ants** ▪ Use broad application of Logic in April and August. This takes two weeks for results. Updated controls are published in local newspapers.

**Cutworms** ▪ Bury a cardboard collar 1" deep around stem of newly "set-out" tender plants.

**Snails and Pill Bugs** ▪ Place beer traps or mechanical traps. Spread diatomaceous earth. Protective masks should be worn when spreading.

## DESIGN

**Planning and discipline** hold the key to a spectacular orchestration of garden design. Full, flourishing flowers in April encourage garden artists into a buying frenzy. The many markets selling blooming plants tempt the most casual enthusiast.

**Each year evaluate** the number of flower beds, container plants and hanging baskets you can effectively maintain. Clarify color schemes. Recall past successes. Estimate quantity, height and width of mature plants; then shop. When purchasing, vary from the original list by substituting available varieties and healthier species. Trust your judgement to choose the best plants for your garden.

**Consider** digging tulip bulbs and filling hole with summer annuals. Place bedding plants in front of daffodil foliage to camouflage their decline.

## BLOOMING

Ajuga, Azalea, Begonia, Bluebonnet, Candy Tuft, Columbine, Delphinium, Dogwood, English Daisy, Foxglove, Gladioli, Iris, Larkspur, Lilac, Louisiana Phlox, Lychnis, Mealy Blue Sage, Pansy, Peony, Petunia, Rose, Snowball Viburnum, Snapdragon, Spanish Broom, Spirea, Strawberry, Tulips, Verbena and Wisteria.

## CELEBRATE

Usually just about everything is blooming around town. Aren't you glad you live in Dallas? The Farmers Market overflows. Open yourself to the abundance of Lady Springtime. Every culture has important rituals rejoicing at the signs of a new year in nature. Make time to participate fully in yours, Earth Day, Passover, Easter or make up your own. Choose to bring April's floral bounty into your home. Celebrate Spring's presence by placing one blossom in a vase in every room. Nestle a small bouquet on a table beside the chair of your beloved. Inside rooms can release Spring's rejuvenation with a fresh blooming plant.

# MAY

May is the perennial flower gardener's month. Flora is at her finest. Mild spring weather has a short season, moving rapidly into Metroplex heat. With enough water, plants have a burst of growth. It is a picturesque time to photograph your home among flowers and leafy trees.

## PLANT

**Summer Annuals From Bedding Plants .** Cleome, Coleus, Cockscomb, Copper Plant, Impatiens, Marigold, Melampodium, Portulaca, Vinca and Zinnias. Plan to rotate species yearly to prevent Nematodes and soil problems.

**Caladiums .** Wait for warm days and nights.

**Tropical Color Plants .** Allamanda, Bougainvillea, Firecracker Bush, Hibiscus, Lantana, Mandevilla, Mexican Heather, Penta and Plumeria.

**Vine Seeds .** Hyacinth Bean, Gourds, Morning Glory, Perienial Sweet Pea.

**Ferns**

**Balled and Burlap Specimens .** Can still be planted. Use root stimulator. Water often.

**Water Plants .** Water Lily, Pickerel Rush and Louisiana Iris.

## WATER

**Sprinkler .** Adjust to morning starting time to discourage fungus on lawns.

**Compost .** Keep it moist and well-aerated.

## FERTILIZE

**House Plants .** Sink pot to the rim in a shady place outside, top dress with a complete balanced fertilizer to renew plant vigor.

**Ground Covers and Lawns .** 4-1-2 or 3-1-2 analysis.

**Blooming Shrubs, Color Beds and Roses .** A fertilizer balanced for bloom, such as Azalea-Camellia type every 6 to 8 weeks until August.

**Roses and Lilacs .** At the end of the bloom.

**Yellow Leaves .** Use Iron Chelate.

## PRUNE

**Blooming Shrubs .** Forsythia, Hawthorn, Quince and other spring flowering shrubs. Re-shape after flowering to encourage compactness and side branching.

**Climbing Roses .** Immediately after flowering remove all wild, weak and non-blooming canes, cutting back to the main branch.

**Fall Blooming Perennials .** Aster, Chrysanthemum. Lightly pinch back to encourage side branching and a more compact habit. Begin at 6".

## CONTROL

**Spray fruit trees** and succeptable tree trunks for borers now and in

August with organic Rotenone/Pyrethrum. Use a chemical control formulated for Borers called Chlorpyrifos.

**Bagworms,** especially on Conifers, can destroy large shrubs or trees in one season. Pick off and destroy. An alternative measure is *Bacillus thuringiensis* (Bt).

**Pick off Squash bugs and destroy.** Refer to organic recipes *(see pp. 54-55)* to fight Aphids, Spider Mites, Whiteflies, Scale and Scab. Release beneficial insects.

**Use Pyrethrum products to control** Fleas, Ticks and Chiggers. Dust yourself and grass with Sulfur against Chiggers. Do not use Sulfur Dust if temperature is above 90°. Use it in the cool of the morning or evening. Spray for Pecan Nut Casebearer and Scab at times recommended by county agent. Timing varies each year. Spraying is for the pecan crop. It is not necessary for the health of the tree.

**Treat Roses and Crape Myrtles** with Soda Spray or Bordeaux mixture to prevent mildew *(see pp. 54-55)*.

## DESIGN

For more continuous, solid summer color, plant variegated leaf plants in semi-shade; use Caladium, Coleus and Syngonium (Angel Wings). In sun, try Copper Plant, Amaranthus and varigated Ginger.

## CULTIVATE

**Pecan Seedlings** ■ Beginner gardeners, learn to identify these plants early. After the first year they are difficult to remove. Dig entire root after rain or watering.

**Volunteer Seedlings** ■ Identify before weeding. The plant in question emerging may have been purposely planted, but now forgotten.

**Mulch** ■ To retard weed growth, help retain moisture and insulate soil from temperature fluctuation.

## HARVEST

Radishes, Snow Peas and Lettuces.

## BLOOMING

Alyssum, Ageratum, Amaryllis, Begonia, Button Bush, Coreopsis, Crinum, Daisy, Daylily, Dianthus, Golden Rain Tree, Iris, Madonna Lily, Magnolia, Nicotiana, Petunia, Purple Coneflower, Rose, Salvia, Viola, Wine Cup, Yarrow and Yucca.

## CELEBRATE

**Mother's Day** ■ Rejoice in the fecundity of the Earth. Honor your own nurturing spirit. Recall and repeat stories of your maternal gardening mentors. Let memory speak. Remember your Grandmother staking tomatoes, the neighbor sharing her roses and Mother Earth radiant in springtime.

# JUNE

Memories of the forest primeval are recalled in June as Dallas becomes lush with leaves. Trees in savannas, along every creek and in backyards on the Blackland Prairie grow canopies in shades of green.

## PLANT

**Summer Annual Seed** ▪ Balsam, Cockscomb, Columbine, Cosmos, Globe Amaranth, Marigold, Periwinkle, Portulaca, Salvia and Vinca. An optimum time to seed is after pulling up Cornflowers and Larkspur.

**Summer Vegetable Seed** ▪ Squash, Pumpkin, Okra.

**Other Planting Options** ▪ Spider Lily Bulbs, Ground Covers, Warm season lawn grasses. Bargains on spring perennials.

**Water Plants** ▪ Tropical water lilies and bog plants.

## DIVIDE

**Narcissus** ▪ Separate when foliage is brown. If in a bed by themselves, they may remain in ground until blossoms show signs of crowding.

## WATER

**Soak** ▪ Don't sprinkle.

**Newly Planted Shrubs, Perennials and Trees** ▪ This time is critical for water.

**Newly Planted Grass** ▪ Perhaps as much as twice daily

**Mulch** ▪ With grass clippings, ground pine bark or cotton seed meal, the organic way of conserving moisture – a most important step this month *(see pp. 36-37)*.

**Sprinkler System** ▪ New growth may block original watering patterns. Check for wilt or less than prime plants, add heads, reposition or prune blocking foliage. As plantings reach mature heights, reposition head to spray under shrubs.

## SEASONAL

**Lawn Mower** ▪ Raise mower blade height.

## FERTILIZE

**Trees, Shrubs and Color Beds** ▪ General balanced fertilizer every 6 to 8 weeks until August.

**Roses** ▪ Each month except October, November and December.

**Azaleas, Gardenias, and Acid Loving Plants** ▪ With Sulfur, Iron Sulfate or Iron Chelate when Chlorosis appears.

**Lawn Grass** ▪ With 4-1-2 or 3-1-2 fertilizer.

**Vegetables** ▪ Every 6 to 8 weeks with a 10-20-10 ratio.

## PRUNE

**Coreopsis, Crape Myrtle, Petunias, Roses and Long-Blooming Perennials** ▪ Remove spent flowers to encourage continuous bloom.

**Begonias, Coleus, Copper Plants, Chrysanthemums, Fall Blooming**

*Dallas Planting Manual*

**Perennials** ▪ Pinch back to encourage branching.

**Daisies, Lilies, Hosta, Lance Leaf Coreopsis** ▪ After blooming, cut back old bloom stalks to basal rosettes, the short leaves next to the root.

**Wisteria** ▪ Cut shoots to buds to encourage flowering.

**Violet and Columbine** ▪ Cut foliage if brown. New growth will appear. Don't keep red spider mite infected leaves in compost.

**Shrubs, Trees and Roses** ▪ Prune any erratic growth.

## CONTROL

**Spider Mite** ▪ Cut foliage off when "burned". Do not compost these leaves. Use Bug Burn *(see p. 54)* or soap and water. Spray every three days for nine days.

**Webworms** ▪ Found primarily in Pecans and Persimmons. *Bacillus thuringiensis* (Bt) can be used. Do not use if you are trying to attract butterflies as it will also kill the larvae.

**Black Spot** ▪ Soda spray *(see p. 54)*.

**Heat & Dry Winds** ▪ Anti-transpirant sprays prevent leaf margin dehydration that later turns brown. Use on fragile non-natives as Dogwood, Japanese Maples and newly planted shrubs.

**Lace Bugs** ▪ A chewing insect different from the beneficial Green Lace Wing. Use Bug Burn, which is also good for Elm Leaf Beetles.

**Grubs** ▪ Release beneficial nematodes.

**Chiggers** ▪ In grassy areas apply fine Dusting Sulfur *(not Soil Sulfur)*.

## DESIGN

Creating order after spring bloom and leafing out is imperative. Transplant invasive species, clear paths of loose soil and active branches. Reclaim lost design features such as garden sculpture and rocks.

## HARVEST

Cucumbers, Lettuce, Onions, Peaches, Pears, Potatoes, Radishes, Snap Beans and Squash.

## BLOOMING

Ageratum, Althea, Balloon Flower, Begonia, Buddleia, Canna, Celosia, Copper Plant, Coreopsis, Cosmos, Crape Myrtle, Crinum, Daisy, Dianthus, Echinops, Gaillardia, Heliopsis, Hemerocallis, Hollyhock, Hypericum, Lilies, Linaria, Lythrum, Magnolia, Maypop, Mexican Heather, Mimosa, Monarda, Nierembergia, Petunia, Phlox, Purple Coneflower, Plumbago, Rose, Salvia, Texas Bluebell, Vinca and Zinnia.

## CELEBRATE

Summer nights are full of magic and fireflies. Stroll through your garden on mid-summer's eve, the shortest night of the year. If you want more light, use votives or hurricane lamps. Listen to the garden. The simplest city yard under darkness becomes a flute melody in another world. Enjoy yours.

# JULY

This hot, humid month is good for gardens but may wear out gardeners. Early Dallas plant people learned to take advantage of the weather by incorporating colorful summer species that originated in the tropics into their landscape. Cannas, Impatiens, Caladiums, Marigolds, Zinnias, Hibiscus and Crape Myrtle adore torrid July. Vacation in the jungle of your own backyard. Take on native habits, garden early and late in the day. Leave the midday sun to mad dogs and Englishmen. Indoor pot plants will enjoy an outdoor vacation in the shade. Stand back, fan yourself and watch your plants thrive.

## PLANT
**Summer Annuals** ■ Still time to plant: Marigold, Portulaca and Zinnia.

**Gladiola** ■ Plant for last time this year. They will bloom in about three months.

**New Lawns** ■ Only by sodding. It is too hot for sowing seeds except with proper irrigation.

**Fall Vegetables Seeds or Plants** ■ Tomatoes, Peppers, Summer and Winter Squash, Melons and Pumpkins.

## WATER
**House Plants that are Summering Outside** ■ Check daily.

**Hanging Baskets** ■ Soak every few days in addition to regular daily waterings.

**Azalea, Camellia and Dogwood** ■ Give adequate moisture.

**Sprinkler System** ■ Check each head on each station before leaving on vacation.

**Mulch** ■ All plants to conserve moisture and protect from heat stress.

## FERTILIZE
**Hint** ■ The chemicals in fertilizer can burn a plant, roots, stem and leaves. Dry specimens are more likely to be damaged. After fertilization, wash leaves. It is best to avoid fertilizers with herbicide because of potential damage to underlying tree and shrub roots.

**Trees, Shrubs, Color Beds, including Azaleas** ■ A balanced 10-20-10 fertilizer every 6 to 8 weeks.

**Water Lilies** ■ Add fertilizer tablets.

## PRUNE
**Dead Head, Pinch Back** ■ All spent flowers (see June).

**Branches with Web Worm Nests** ■ Cut off and burn.

**Azaleas** ■ Don't prune after this month.

**Chrysanthemum** ∎ Complete cutting back to encourage multiple branching by July 15.

**Poinsettia** ∎ Pinch tips to produce bushy plants or root if want more plants.

## CONTROL

**Aphids** ∎ Do cars parked under your trees get sticky? If so, you have Aphids. The Aphid dropping, called honey dew, is sweet and sticky. Crape Myrtles, Oaks and Pecans are Aphid choices. When it is rainy in the summer, the honey dew's sugar content will host black mildew. Releasing Ladybugs is one way to control Aphids.

**Black Spot and Powdery Mildew** ∎ Check Crape Myrtle and Roses. Treat with Soda Spray *(see p. 54)*.

**Scale** ∎ For uncontrolled scale on shrubs, use summer weight horticultural oil.

**Slugs and Snails** ∎ Beer traps.

**Fleas, Ticks, Chiggers, Bermuda Mites and Chinch Bugs** ∎ Diatomaceous earth or pyrethrum products.

**Leafrollers and Bagworms** ∎ *Bacillus thuringiensis* (Bt).

## DESIGN

Add a water feature to your garden visible from inside your home. A simple bird bath can be made by filling a large bowl, tub or planter with water. Place a rock or a brick in the center above the water line to give birds a perch. To inform your birds of this new water source, hang a hose to drip from a tree for the first hours to show its presence.

## HARVEST

Vegetables and Herbs.

## BLOOMING

Allamanda, Althea, Begonia, Canna, Crape Myrtle, Dianthus, Geranium, Gladioli, Hemerocallis, Impatiens, Jacobinia, Lantana, Lythrum, Oak Leaf Hydrangea, Papaya, Petunia, Phlox, Physostegia, Plumbago, Rose, Rudbeckia, Salvia, Tithonia, Vitex, Water Lily and Zinnia.

## CELEBRATE

July is vacation month. Become your own tour guide. Explore. See spectacular horticultural displays at the Dallas Arboretum and Botanical Garden. Go to the zoo. Summer safari to Pegasus Plaza, Pioneer Plaza, public prairie parks and garden shops. Experience the award winning urban water gardens in downtown Dallas at Fountain Place and those at both ends of downtown Fort Worth. Pretend you are a tourist; wear a hat and dark glasses.

# AUGUST

August has teenage energy. The birthing of spring has developed into an abundance of wildlife activity. Ground yourself and enjoy the high level of life around you. All the insect action foretells a transition. Observe the cycle of the noisy cicada and June bugs. Large striped black, bristled caterpillars on the passion vine will become the Gulf Fritillary butterfly. Bird parents initiate their young in your garden.

## PLANT

**Wildflower Seed** ▪ Last week of month: Bluebonnets, Coreopsis, Cosmos, Drummond's Phlox, Gaillardia, Larkspur, Mealy Blue Sage, Mexican Hat, Poppies, Purple Coneflower and Yarrow.

**Fall Vegetable Seed** ▪ Arugula, Beans, Broccoli, Brussel Sprouts, Cabbage, Carrots, Collards, Lettuce, Mustard, Parsley, Spinach and Watermelon.

**Fall Blooming Bulbs** ▪ Spider Lilies and Fall Crocus.

**Fall Vegetable Plants** ▪ Broccoli, Cauliflower, Peppers and Tomatoes.

## ROOT

**Tropical Plants** ▪ Begonia, Coleus, Croton, Jacobinia, Plumbago and other foliage plants for winter pots and next year's garden. Rooting is more successful in hot weather.

## WATER

**Water** deeply and frequently. August is the driest month.

**Mulch** ▪ Conserve the moisture available. Use 3" of bark for shrubs and ground covers, compost for annuals and perennials.

**Native plants** grown in appropriate areas may require no extra moisture. Xeriscape is an answer to August.

**Leaf texture** can show need for water. Recognize the need before wilting occurs.

**Azaleas, Camellias, Dogwoods** ▪ Mist the foliage while plants are in shade. This is the season they set bloom.

**Fish Pools** ▪ This month city water may have higher levels of purifying chemicals. Be sure the pH level is acid enough for fish survival and health.

## SEASONAL

**Newly Emerged Plants** ▪ Shade from the hot afternoon sun.

**Compost Bin** ▪ Build, prepare for end of summer pruning and fall leaves.

## FERTILIZE

**Last application** of fertilizer for everything except the lawn and roses.

**Yellow Leaves** ▪ Need Iron Chelate.

## PRUNE
**Crape Myrtle** ▪ Extend blooming time by cutting spent blosoms. New bud stems will produce a second flowering and a third.

**Hedges**

**Roses** ▪ Reshape before fall bloom.

**Chrysanthemums** ▪ Time to allow growth, stop pinching back.

**Other Perennials** ▪ As Phlox. Cut seed heads.

**Herbs** ▪ If leggy, cut back to promote new growth.

**Annuals** ▪ Trim now for best fall look. Pinch back height for fuller growth, e.g., Copper Plant. Cut fallen or floppy seed heads, e.g., Purple Fountain Grasses.

**Poinsettia** ▪ Stop pinching back.

## CONTROL
**Hint** ▪ Healthy plants and fertile, aerated soil will tolerate some insect population. Instead of concentrating on the remedy, enrich your soil with compost and organic fertilizers. Chemical pesticides not only kill the pests, they also destroy beneficial organisms that build soil.

**Use Lucinda's Fishy Food** ▪ To strengthen plants (see p. 55).

**Grubworms** ▪ Good soil culture is the best control. Add beneficial nematodes and milky spore.

**Borers** ▪ See March. Remember mulching roots makes healthier plants.

**Beneficial Insects** ▪ Release more.

## DESIGN
Make a small garden space of plants you have received from friends. The friendship garden concept is the way our ancestors acquired plants. This eclectic memory garden is a style of country design coming into favor.

## BLOOMING
Begonia, Caladiums, Cosmo, Crape Myrtle, Crinum, Dahlia, Fall Blooming Clematis, Helenium, Hibiscus, Lantana, Marigold, Ornamental Grasses, Periwinkle, Petunia, Plumbago, Portulaca, Queen's Wreath, Rose, Rudbeckia, Salvia, Shrimp Plant, Tithonia, Verbena, Water Lily and Zinnia.

## CELEBRATE
Offer a friend a walk through your garden, despite the heat, no matter the maintenance. Guests will be grateful with your gift of time and space. They will find joys you had not seen or had forgotten. Sit down, serve a cold drink and simply be with them there. Recall a gentler era. Notice the vitality plants have in summer. Witness the effects of nature on your peace and friendship.

# SEPTEMBER

The Texas gardener counts September as a summer month. Fall usually begins with a "norther" or a "cool snap" around the third week. It will get warm again in October, but never with the consistent intensity of September.

## PLANT

**Seeds** ▪ After the first soaking rain, prepare beds by spading, adding sharp sand, humus and fertilizer. Mix well, rake smooth and sow. For even better results, sow seeds during rain. The rain will incorporate seeds into the soil. Alyssum, Bluebonnet, Calendula, Coreopsis, Dianthus, Larkspur, Poppy, Snapdragon, Sweet William and any wildflower seeds not planted in August.

**Fall Vegetables** ▪ Cold hardy varieties, both seeds and starts as onions.

**Perennial Seeds** ▪ May be planted in flats and pots to be held in cold frames until spring.

**Iris, Hemerocallis and Lilies** ▪ Plant now.

**Bulbs** ▪ Force or plant inside for Christmas bloom, Amaryllis, Cyclmen, Grape Hyacinth, Narcissus (Paper Whites particularly).

**Perennial Plants** ▪ Coreopsis, Columbine, Salvias, Purple Coneflower.

**Lawns:**

    **Sod** ▪ Do not plant after the end of August.

    **Seeding Fescue** ▪ Sow where St. Augustine thinned from lack of light.

    **Winter Rye** ▪ Over seed existing grass.

## ROOT

**Foliage House Plants** ▪ Make cuttings and root.

## DIVIDE

**Iris, Hemerocallis** and spring blooming perennials.

## WATER

**September May be Wet or Dry** ▪ Monitor and water accordingly.

## SEASONAL

**Poinsettia** ▪ To have color by Christmas, place in darkness from 6 P.M. to 8 A.M. for 5 to 7 days. Water sparingly before closeting. Then give light and water as normal.

**Roses** ▪ Stop feeding to harden before frost. Prune spent flowers for more bloom in fall. Do not cut if you want rose hips, especially on Rugosa Roses.

**Amaryllis** ▪ Bring in potted specimens that have summered outdoors.

**Spring Flowering Bulbs** ▪ Purchase and save in refrigerator crisper. Store in mesh type bags. Do not store with apples which give off ethylene gas and cause blossom blast.

## FERTILIZE
**Lawn** ∎ This last fertilization will help grasses survive winter.
**Trees and Shrubs** ∎ Stop fertilization to allow to harden for winter.
**House Plants** ∎ Re-pot overgrown plants and feed established ones. Then in November they will be primed to return inside.

## PRUNE
**Wisteria** ∎ Root prune to stimulate flower bud setting.
**Spring Flowering Trees** ∎ Do not prune or cut back flowering trees as you will be removing potential flowers. Wait and cut for inside forcing in early spring.
**Perennials** ∎ Deadhead spent blossoms.

## CONTROL
**Aphids** ∎ Use control methods listed in March and April.
**Webworms** ∎ May appear in Mimosas, Pecan and Honey Locust Trees. Treat with *Bacillus thuringiensis* (Bt) or mechanically prune out. Release Trichogramma Wasps.
**Fire Ants** ∎ See April controls.

## DESIGN
For a seasonal transition, add Ornamental Grasses and Copper Plants to a bed of summer blooming perennials, converting it into a fall garden.

## HARVEST
Corn, Figs, Herbs, Okra, Persimmons, Peppers, Tomatoes and materials for dried arrangements, .

## BLOOMING
Ageratum, Autumn Joy Sedum, Aster, Cardinal Flower, Chive, Cockscomb, Colchicum, Crape Myrtle, Cypress Vine, Dahlia, Eupatorium, Fall Blooming Aster, Four O'Clock, Helenium, Heliopsis, Hyacinth Bean Vine, Lantana, Marigold, Moonvine, Morning Glory, Ornamental Grasses, Pavonia, Physotegia, Portulaca, Queen's Wreath, Rose, Rudbeckia, Salvia, Solidago, Spider Lily, Staghorn Cactus, Sumac, Sweet Autumn Clematis, Texas Bluebell, Turk's Cap, Verbena and Zinnia.

## CELEBRATE
History changed when the first seedling was planted. The nomad existence was no longer necessary. As you witness the lush growth of September, remember inspired gardeners, past and present, professional and amateur. Recognize your own participation. Continue this horticulture heritage. Share your gardening knowledge with another. Gather and offer seeds, cuttings or current organic thought.

# OCTOBER

The gifts of good husbandry through the year come to fruition this month. Majestic maturity crowns the cycle of life. Pleasant temperature and even moisture may cause a confluence of late perennial bloom and early colored leaves. October is a golden time in the Metroplex.

## PREPARE
**Tulips and Hyacinths** ▪ Pre-cool for 45 days at 40° to 45° prior to planting. It is possible to purchase pre-cooled bulbs.

**Caladiums** ▪ Dig, store in dry dark areas.

**Dried Material** ▪ Collect for fall arrangements, wreaths and door decorations.

## PLANT
**Winter Annual Bedding Plants** ▪ Alyssum, Chrysanthemums, Pansies and Wallflowers.

**Strawberries** ▪ Install bedding plants in sunny location.

**Perennials** ▪ Divide all spring bloomers, especially Iris and/or place new plants in ground now to establish better roots for winter growth.

**Winter Herb Seeds** ▪ Borage, Caraway, Coriander, Dill and Lovage, as well as Poppies. Replant in February if necessary.

**Peonies** ▪ Transplant and set out now. Renew bed if replanting.

**Bulbs** ▪ Amaryllis, Crocus, Dutch Iris and Muscari.

**Herb Plants** ▪ Garlic, Parsley and French Sorrel.

▪ Divide and replant chives, garlic and multiplying onions.

**Shrubs and Trees Container Grown Plants** ▪ Fall is the best time to plant in the metroplex because roots have time to establish before spring.

**Winter Rye Grass** ▪ If not sown last month.

## FERTILIZE
**Lilacs** ▪ Super-Phosphate.

**Chrysanthemums** ▪ Organic.

## CONTROL
**Scale** ▪ Watch Hollies, Euonymous and Camellias. Treat scale by washing leaves and stems with mild soap or non-detergent solution. Scale may also be controlled by Logan's Spray (see p. 55).

**Brown Patch in St. Augustine** ▪ Treat with Soda Spray *(see p. 54)*.

**Cabbage Loopers on Cabbage, Broccoli, Brussel Sprouts** ▪ *Bacillus Thuringiensis* (Bt).

**Peach Tree Curl .** Use Bug Burn or Soda Spray *(see p. 54).*
**Web Worms .** *Bacillus thuringiensis* (Bt).

## DESIGN
Missing the fullness of summer perennials? Fill in the barest area with a group of pumpkins. Need height? Stake a shock of sugar cane and a scare crow. Have a throw away basket? Fill it with autumn gourds and place it effectively in your landscape. Bird feeders, bird houses, plant labels are attractive additions. Garden sculpture need not be limited to permanent materials of wood, stone or ornamental iron. Ephemeral, seasonal decorations can be charming.

## WINTERIZE
**Motorized Tools .** Lawn mowers, weed eaters and blowers. Sharpen blades, drain gasoline, change oil and replace spark plugs.
**Container Gardens .** Gradually accoustom plants summering outdoors to less light.

## HARVEST
Green Beans, Nut Crops, Peppers, Pumpkins, Squash and Tomatoes.

## BLOOMING
Aster, Calendula, Camellia Sasanqua, Candle Treep, Celosia, Chrysanthemum, Dahlia, Elaeagnus, Fall Blooming Aster, Hearty Cyclamen, Marigold, Maximilian, Narrow Leaf Sunflower, Mexican Hat, Mexican Mint Marigold, Ornamental Grasses, Pansy, Queen's Wreath, Rose, Salvia, Snapdragon and Sweet Autumn Clematis.

## CELEBRATE
We give thanks for the bounty of a successful harvest. The State Fair of Texas is a civic expression dedicated to high rejoicing for completion of another year's growing season. Attend, see exhibits of the finest in agriculture and home economics. Explore acres of blooming, native water plants at the lagoon across from the Dallas Museum of Natural History. Return to the Dallas Horticulture Center during the State Fair to see "Butterflies in the Blachly". Plants of Africa on view all year are mesmorizing with live color in graceful flight. Reward your own year of hard work with Fair food and a ride on the Midway.

# NOVEMBER

Tree transitions are the delight of November. Dallas leaves color late. This year, stand in your garden amid leaves floating down gracefully. As the foliage thins gradually, one can see the basic design of the garden. Admire bare branched silhouettes that emerge through short winter twilight skies. Mauve sunsets appear regularly. Fertilize and water less to allow plants a natural winter dormancy.

## PREPARE
**Soil Testing** ▪ Optimum time to determine balancing needs.

**Asparagus** ▪ In year old beds, remove all female crowns (those with berries). Begin plans for an asparagus bed next year. It is not too early to start preparing the bed.

**Tuberoses** ▪ Lift and store tubers.

**Leaves** ▪ Rake and compost.

**Lawn and Beds** ▪ Mulch with manure or sewage sludge organic fertilizers to aid in over-wintering.

**House Plants** ▪ The first week of November begin to move indoors.

## PLANT
**Bulbs** ▪ Anemones, Daffodils, Grape Hyacinths and Crocus.

**Tulips** ▪ Plant Thanksgiving to New Year's Day.

**Perennials** ▪ Lilies, Thrift, Lythrum and spring blooming perennials.

**Seeds** ▪ Radishes, Spinach, Turnips, Mustard Green, Onion, Coriander and Parsley.

**Bedding Plants** ▪ Pansies, Pinks, Snapdragons, Iceland Poppies and Escholtz, a California Poppy.

**Container** grown Trees and Shrubs.

## ROOT
**Winter Honeysuckle, Crape Myrtle, Japanese Quince and Forsythia** ▪ Make pencil size cuttings and stick in moist, protected location outside. In spring transplant to desired location (see p. 49).

## WATER
**Sprinkler System** ▪ Reprogram cycle to start at dusk to protect from light freezes.

## FERTILIZE
**Peonies** ▪ Bone Meal

**Louisiana and Japanese Iris** ▪ Manure, fresh if possible, if not, substitute a low analysis fertilizer.

## PRUNE
**Major Tree Pruning** ▪ For easy spotting, remove dead limbs before leaves fall.

**Perennials** ▪ Cut back after frost or at the end of their season.

## CONTROL
Use Logan's Spray *(see p. 55)* for Scale, Mites or Fungus on Fruit Trees and Flowering Loquats. Alcohol Spray *(see p. 54)* for Aphids and Mealy Bugs before bringing in house plants. Watch house plants for root rot. Do not overwater. Watch roots of removed annuals for Nematodes which form nobs on roots. *(See p. 61)*. Application of beneficial nematodes can control.

## DESIGN
In a bare spot make a small Japanese garden. Accent this negative space with vacation-gathered rocks or driftwood. Highlight with a few tufts of Monkey Grass. Add a few small bulbs, Grape Hyacinth, Chionodoxa or Galanthus.

## WINTERIZE
**Tomatoes** ▪ Pick the night before first frost.

**Urns, Jars and Empty Containers** ▪ Turn over. Freezing water will cause breakage.

**Birds** ▪ Feed.

**Bird Bath** ▪ To prevent cracking when water freezes, place a piece of unpainted wood in the water to absorb expansion and contraction. Birds will need water in winter.

**Outside Fish** ▪ Do not feed in winter. Cold temperatures inhibits the digestive system action of fish.

## BLOOMING
Aster, Camellia Sasanqua, Calendula, Chrysanthemum, Fall Crocus, Mexican Mint Marigold, Rose and Sternbergia. Look for coloring foliage and fruiting plant color.

## CELEBRATE
The dormant season begins with the lowering of the sap in trees. This causes trees to drop their leaves. Plan a family work day. Gather on a perfect fall day to rake leaves and build or repair the compost bin. Then decorate your home and/or dinner table with colored leaves and bare branches. Celebrate the autumn and maturity in the cycle of life. Realistic workers in nature know there is no end to energy in a "dead " leaf. Its use and beauty continue in compost and will make new soil.

# DECEMBER

Two traditional weeks of good weather encourage gardening. This is the time to look at your basic garden design. Evergreens are the foundation of most winter gardens. Our native selections are limited and many marginal horticultural varieties have been introduced. A mild temperature can suddenly drop and shock less hardy plants. Listen to weather reports and respond.

## PREPARE

**Amaryllis** ▪ Bring container plants to light and warmth. Water moderately.

**Asparagus** ▪ If foliage has turned yellow or brown, and you have none left with berries, cut the foliage to the ground. Then (very shallowly, to protect especially the young roots) rake in some compost and fertilizer. Give it a rest until spring!

**Christmas Trees** ▪ Select early. Recut the end and soak outside until ready to decorate. Spray with anti-transpirant to help retain moisture. Keep watered.

**Hollyberries, Mistletoe and Poinsettias** ▪ Poisonous. Keep out of reach of children.

**Mulch** ▪ Do not cultivate.

**For gifting**, choose natural and plant-oriented presents:
- ▪ The updated version of the *Dallas Planting Manual*,
- ▪ A basket of organic fertilizers,
- ▪ A homemade herb wreath,
- ▪ A membership to a Metroplex gardening organization.

## PLANT

**Bulbs** ▪ The perfect month for planting.

**Sweet Peas**

**Trees and Shrubs** ▪ When all leaves have fallen from deciduous plants, it is safe to plant bare-rooted stock or to transplant Arizona Cypress, Atlas Cedar, Austrian Pine or Eldarica Pine.

**Living Christmas Trees** ▪ Choose Evergreens hearty to the Metoplex. Leave inside for no more than 10 days. Protect from extreme cold after moving outside. Excellent options include:

**Arizona Cypress** *Cupressus arizonica* ▪ Drought and cold tolerant. Xerophyte, conical shape.

**Atlas Cedar** *Cedrus atlantica* ▪ Open branching, broadly conical, slow growing, cold hardy.

**Austrian Pine** *Pinus nigra* ▪ Slow growing, densely branched, dark green, best for traditional form.

**Eldarica Pine** *Pinus halepensis* ■ Easily grown in Metroplex, irregular, open branching.

**Japanese Black Pine** *Pinus thunbergiana* ■ Easiest grown in Metroplex, irregular, open branching.

## WATER
**Bulbs and Evergreens** ■ When scant water is available.

## FERTILIZE
**Beds** ■ Maintain a three-inch mulch of composted organic material to protect from cold weather and drought.

**Pansies** ■ Blood meal or fertilizer with high phosphorus content.

**House Plants** ■ Light application of general fertilizer.

## PRUNE
**Live Oaks**

**Shape Hollies and Evergreens** ■ Use prunings for decoration.

**Peaches**, Plums and other fruit trees.

## CONTROL
Not necessary to spray this month. Jack Frost is the champion pest eradicator. Cut Mistletoe out of trees and remove infected limbs.

## DESIGN
Foundation plantings anchor the garden in winter. Do your evergreens flow together or is the vision spotty? Ground covers can extend the drift or even out the edges into a graceful curve.

## BLOOMING
Camellias, Christmas Iris, English Daisy, Pansy, Rose (if no freeze) and Snapdragon.

## CELEBRATE
We observe in our fellow creatures, both animal and plant, the great cycle of birthing, maturation, flourishing, declining vigor, death, decay and reconstitution in changing form. This cycle is worthy of honor.

Recycling and recording are year end activities that give a gardener continuity. Celebrate the end of the year. There will never be another like this. Next year keep a gardening diary. View your recycling as an offering to the earth. Compliment yourself for every effort you make towards conservation. Compliment the earth for her restorative powers.

# Chapter 2

# THE ENVIRONMENT
Geology ❧ Geography ❧ Climate
Plant Hardiness Zone Map ❧ Dallas Plant Organizations

## IDENTIFY AND RESPECT YOUR GARDENING ENVIRONMENT
The type of plant that grows well in a space is determined by the overall environment including geology, geography, water, climate and light. Our habitat in North Texas is a prairie ecosystem located in the transitional zone between the tallgrass and shortgrass prairies. This area is the first native grassland west of the southern forests. We are the southeastern extension of the Great Plains of North America. While predominantly a prairie, this grassland is crossed by timbered areas particularly along its creeks. Several *plant associations* exist in the Dallas/Fort Worth Metroplex. In limestone uplands like Oak Cliff with shallow soils, Ashe Juniper, Shumard Red Oak and Texas Ash thrive. In riparian bottomlands native stands of Pecan, Persimmon and Cedar Elm colonize. Wildflowers, Plum thickets and grasses naturalize on flat deep soiled sunny prairies like Plano. Beyond these generalizations each homestead may have one or more micro-environments. Often plants native to East Texas will grow here in sandy soils or well amended deep organic soils where supplementary watering and some shade are plentiful. In other locations plants particular to the Southwest will flourish in well-drained sunny spots. Prairie plants may be the best horticulture to raise in windy, treeless plains with unammended clay soil.

## GEOLOGY
Plant communities are affected by the nature of the rock from which the soil is formed. Eighty million years ago Cretaceous seas covered North Texas. Our geology and thus our soils originated from these fossilized sediments. Over eons, an accumulation of the shells of microscopic sea creatures were compressed into a white, crumbly limestone. In shallow water muddier deposits of silt contained more clay and transformed into shale. In time the limestone and shale were uplifted. After the Cretaceous period the seas retreated. The soft rock of the old sea beds was converted into the soils we have today by wind, rain with its dissolved gases, floods, decaying organic matter and the action of microscopic organisms.

Rock is scientifically named by its composition. Generally, the Taylor Limestone surfaces on the far eastern side of Dallas County; the Austin

Chalk outcrops through the center of the county; and the Eagle Ford shale is exposed in western Dallas County. Sands and gravel occur sporadically along the river and underground. The land becomes generally higher on the west. Soft shales erode faster than the harder Austin Chalk leaving a steep rocky ridge known as the White Rock Escarpment. This escarpment claims the highest elevations of the county at Cedar Hill. The rather flat Dallas area topography is defined by these cliffs and the terraces of the Trinity River.

## GEOGRAPHY

Sited at Lat. 32°58', Long. 97°16', Dallas County's elevation above sea level ranges from 382 to over 800 feet. Today three branches of the Trinity River converge around the Metroplex. The West Fork, including waters of the Clear Fork, comes from Fort Worth. The Elm Fork flows southeast from Gainesville parallel to Interstate Highway 35E. The two meet near Texas Stadium. The main river then flows south passing downtown and the Great Trinity Forest. The East Fork skirts the east county line and enters the Trinity in neighboring Kaufman County.

White Rock Lake is formed by another major water shed. White Rock Creek cuts the county in half diagonally, beginning north of the Galleria. It flows through the lake to its juncture with the Trinity below Fair Park. These rivers and creeks and their various tributaries have developed flood plains in the middle of the prairie, encouraging miniature timber areas, i.e. the deep alluvial soil surrounding White Rock Creek nurtures stands of large Chinkapin and Bur Oaks.

Circling the metropolitan region, more streams have been dammed to form a lake system that serves as the water district for Dallas-Fort Worth and outlying cities. The many regional lakes have increased the Dallas humidity. Gardeners nearer bodies of water often find a warmer micro-climate .

## CLIMATE

The Greater Dallas Chamber of Commerce in their 1997 brochure "At A Glance" describes local weather as follows: "Dallas has a mild year-round climate with a normal average daily minimum temperature of 54.6°F and an average daily maximum temperature of 76.3°F. The average number of days with a minimum temperature of 32°F or less is 38 days a year. Snowfall in Dallas area averages 2.6 inches a year. Winds average 10.7 miles per hour. Dallas averages 62 percent of sunny days a year ranging from 52 percent in December and January to 75 percent in July. There are clear skies in Dallas 135 days a year, partly cloudy skies 97 days, and cloudy skies 133 days per year. On average, there are 235 frost-free, growing days in the Metroplex."

Dallas has erratic highs and lows in temperature. The first freeze stops plant growth. The average date of killing frost is November 17, however it was as late as February 8 in 1907. The earliest fall freeze recorded was on October 22, 1898. Dallas usually has a late spring freeze. The earliest last freeze recorded was January 4, 1972. Warm weather is expected in February and March, but the exact timing of the last freeze is eccentric. The latest spring freeze on record is April 13, 1957. Gardeners usually count March 14 as the average frost free spring date.

## HARDINESS ZONE MAPS

Weather data has been organized and codified to assist horticulture. Low temperature, the most brutal judge of plant life, is the basis of one scale of measurment. The United States Department of Agriculture publishes a cold hardiness map of our country. The coldest region is Zone #1. As the zone numbers get larger, the average low temperature rises. Today eleven zones with increments of 10°F are sub-divided into categories "a" and "b" with 5°F increments. The map, found on the back of seed packages and in gardening tracts, is based on the average cold temperatures of years past. The simplified USDA hardiness map to the right details the U.S. with zones 7, 8 and 9 labeled. The half zones are not seen on the U.S. map opposite but are found on the close up enlargement below.

In the 1990 USDA map, the majority of the D/FW Metroplex was categorized into the Zone "8a" with winter minimum temperatures typically between 10° and 15°F. Since its publication, new weather science has indicated updates in the Metroplex hardiness zones. Research conducted by Derald Harp, (using data from 1984-95) indicates an even warmer zone in Dallas and Fort Worth. Placing these city centers in "8b", with the average low temperatures of 15°F to 20°F, which is 5° higher. The second change is the inclusion of virtually all of Tarrant County in zone "8a". Previously the 1990 USDA map included the western half of Tarrant County in zone "7b". In the Harp map, this line is moved west into Parker County.

The effect of urban warming can be seen in first and last freeze dates. Local weather authorities have found that first and last freeze dates in urban areas of the Metroplex may differ from outlying areas by as much as 10 to 15 days. This type of change may allow the urban gardener an additional 20 to 30 growing days than the gardener in the country. This could allow the urban gardener to plant tender crops earlier and grow them later into the fall.

Remember, these maps do not predict future winters, and plant damage may occur during severe winters such as we saw in 1983 and '89. However, hardiness zone maps give us our best representation of what the temperatures average. With the hardiness zone map, local gardeners can select those plants most likely to survive our North Texas winters.

# USDA HARDINESS ZONE MAP

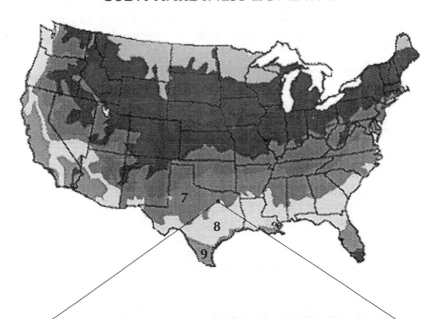

## 1998 HARP D/FW HARDINESS ZONE MAP

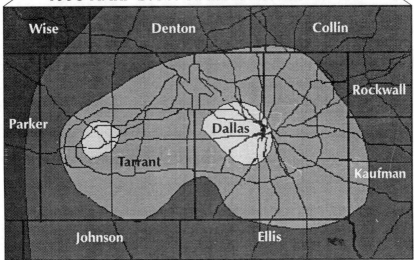

| 7b₁ | 8a₂ | 8a₁ | 8b₁ |
|------|------|------|------|
| 7.51°-10.00° F | 10.01°-12.50° F | 12.51°-15.00° F | 15.01°-17.50° F |

# LOCAL BOOKS OF REFERENCE

*Neil Sperry's Complete Guide to Texas Gardening*, 2nd edition, Neil Sperry, Taylor Publishing, Dallas, Texas, 1991.

*Native Texas Gardens: Maximum Beauty, Minimum Upkeep*, Sally and Andy Wasowski, Gulf Publishing, Houston, Texas, 1997. *One chapter: "Our Nine-Season Garden" has 9 color photos of a Dallas garden.*

*Plants of the Metroplex* by Howard Garrett, University of Texas Press, 1996.

*The Southern Living Garden Book*, edited by Steve Bender, Oxmoor House, 1998.

# LOCAL GARDENING ORGANIZATIONS

**Botanical Research Institute of Texas** (BRIT)
509 Pecan Street
Fort Worth, Texas 76102-4060
(817) 429-3200 (metro)          (817) 332-4441 (Fort Worth)

**Dallas Arboretum & Botanical Society** (DABS)
8617 Garland Road
Dallas, Texas 75218
(214) 327-8263 -- Horticultural Hot Line -- extension 134

**Dallas County Agent**
Texas Agriculture Extension Service, Horticulture Section
10056 Marsh Lane -- Suite B-102
Dallas, Texas 75229          (214) 904-3053
Master gardening classes begin in August each year. Call for information.

**Fort Worth Botanic Garden**
3220 Botanic Garden Blvd.
Fort Worth, Texas 76107          (817) 871-7686

**Texas Discovery Gardens** (formerly Dallas Horticulture Center)
3601 Martin Luther King Blvd. -- Fair Park
Dallas, Texas 75315          (214) 428-7476
Free admission -- Environmental and Horticulture education.

**Texas Garden Club Inc.**
3111 Old Garden Road
Fort Worth, Texas  76106          (817) 332-6602


See specific local plant organizations listed at the end of each chapter.

# Chapter 3

## SOILS, AMENDMENTS & BEDS

*Soil Components ᦥ Local Soil Types ᦥ Soil Amendments*
*Mulching ᦥ Bed Preparation ᦥ Compost Bins*

### DALLAS SOIL

In North Texas, the original farmers considered the local soil good. In fact, when cotton became king, our prairie was considered some of the best land in the state for cotton production. The deep Blackland soil still reaped the benefits of the thick humus and gave back economic riches. Farmers at that time might complain about drought or wind, but not about the soil. Today however, urban horticulturalists may want to nurture a private Eden that requires considerably more than just "turning over the dirt". Whether you dream of a native prairie habitat or an English flower garden, basic soil information will be as important to the success of your effort as knowledge of the plants you intend to grow.

### SOIL COMPONENTS

Soil is a living dynamic system. A maximum-fertility soil contains five essentials: sand, air, water, living organisms and humus. Sand or small rock particles allow water to drain. Air enables oxygen and other nutrients to come in contact with the roots. Water dissolves minerals and nutrients for plant roots to receive. Living organisms consist of small plants, bacteria, small animals and micro-organisms. Their presence, life processes and by-products enliven the soil. Humus is decayed organic material. Common forms of humus, plant compost and rotted manure, hold water and food in soil and increase porosity.

### LOCAL SOIL TYPES

Metroplex soils can generally be described as transitional combinations of Blackland Prairie Clay, Eagle Ford Shale and Woodbine Red Sandy Loam. Where these meet, rocky ravines with rapid surface drainage occur. Generally we can tell what kind of soil we have by looking at its texture and color or by digging down to the rock below. If the soil is black, heavy and sticky when wet, with white rock below it, that is Blackland Prairie. If the soil level is very shallow and the rock gray and flaky, that is Eagle Ford Shale. Red, sandy dirt indicates the Woodbine strata found mostly in the mid-cities section of the Metroplex. A soil test will give you scientific information about your terra firma. Obtain a soil testing mailing kit without cost from the County Extension Service (214-904-3053). The testing itself requires a fee and is returned to the Extension Soil and Water Section of TAMU, College Station, Texas 77843-2474. Commercial soil testing for other organic percentages is also available.

## BLACKLAND PRAIRIE CLAYS

Metroplex soil tests often contain a higher percentage of clays. Clay by its nature has a measurable "shrink and swell" capacity and ours is no different. The cracks that come and go in Dallas homes are evidence of the extremes of expansion and contraction found in both the Blackland Prairie and the Eagle Ford. Old timers speak of the soil's "noonday plowing" properties, meaning that it is too damp and sticky to plow in the morning and too dry and hard to plow in the afternoon. This attribute is significant to city gardeners as well. Not only is it difficult to dig wet soil, doing so will cause the clay to lose structure, produce clods and hamper drainage in our beds.

Our black gumbo soil derives very little of its dark color from organic matter, but instead from magnesium oxide, a metallic compound that exudes black pigment into the clay. This dense soil is rich in nutrients and other trace minerals, but they are not readily available to plants. By adding organic material, we can optimize the properties of the soil. The organic acids reduce the alkalinity and break the colloidal bond holding in the minerals and release them for plant use. Organic additives also help counteract the clay's resistance to oxygen and water absorption.

## ACIDITY AND ALKALINITY

Among the ways horticulturalists describe a plant's soil preference is by the pH, a measurement of acidity and alkalinity. The pH scale refers to "hydrogen potential" or the concentration of hydrogen ions. This scale goes from 1 to 14 with 7 being the neutral position. Dallas and Tarrant County soil is usually about 8.0 or alkaline. Optimum growing soil is 6.3 to 6.8. Consider soil amendments to lower your garden's pH. There are few lime or alkaline loving ornamental plants *(see p. 167)*. The majority of ornamental plants prefer slightly acid soil.

## SOIL AMENDMENTS

An ideal soil mixture for growing plants is 33% sharp sand, 33% humus, and 33% ordinary soil which contains some clay. This soil will be crumbly and not sticky when damp. Unfortunately, we in the Dallas area can achieve this ideal only by means of soil amendments.

A soil amendment is anything added to soil to make it a more productive growing medium. If your soil is Blackland Prairie, it will need additives that increase the acidity. If it is sandy, it will need supplements that hold in the moisture and add food for the plants. If you have shallow soil you will need more earth and mulch to add depth and bulk.

Amendments may be natural - often termed organic - or chemical. Natural amendments include plant matter (compost) or animal matter (earthworms) or processes like aeration through which air is added to the soil. Chemical supplements include lava sand and commercial fertilizers.

## NATURAL AMENDMENTS

Healthy soil is balanced soil with just enough minerals, air, water, organic matter and living organisms. In the Metroplex, soil tends to be deficient in air and organic material. These organic amendments provide a more complete set of nutrients and minerals than do chemical fertilizers and they lower the pH and make the nutrients in soil more available to plants.

**Air ▪** Aeration is a mechanical process of getting air to the feeder roots of plants. Punching or cutting holes in the soil allows the air to move below the surface. Adding air with its elements of oxygen, carbon, and nitrogen to tightly compressed soil is the goal. Good aeration improves drainage, nutrient absorption, microbic activity. The same greening effect is achieved as with a heavy application of nitrogen fertilizer. Air holes 2" to 6" deep may be made by a simple garden fork or expensive power equipment. Yearly aeration is recommended for all beds and turf areas. *(See p. 107.)*

**Compost and Leaf Mold ▪** "Nature's fertilizer" can be used on any and all soils and plants. From the forest floor, homemade or purchased commercially, the best are made from a variety of plant sources. See Compost Bins later in this chapter.

**Manure ▪** Obtained from animal droppings (cow, sheep, horse, or poultry). When "green" or fresh, more nutrients and trace minerals are present, when rotted, many of these have leached out. Use green manure only in winter when plants are dormant. Top dressing all beds in December with green manure gives extra heat to soil through cold weather, increases survivability of marginal plants, and gives a nice flush of spring growth. Do not use fresh manure on vegetable root crops either as a soil amendment or a top dressing because of the possibility of disease and contamination. Dried manure may be purchased. Do not use on Azaleas or Camellias because it is too alkaline. In compost, manure may be added up to 30% of the total bulk. While some gardeners reject animal waste in any form, generally herbivore manure is acceptable. However, some health problems could occur if mishandled. Carnivore waste may attract insect and rodent pests. Use appropriate cleanliness procedures when working with animal residue.

**Liquid Manure ▪** Use 1 gallon fresh cow or sheep manure in 4 gallons water. Let soak 2 or 3 days. Use 2 quarts of this liquid in 3 gallons water. It will be the color of weak tea. Apply 1 pint to each plant or more according to size. The residue will make a good mulch.

**Earthworms ▪** Aerate and bring minerals to the surface. Purchase them and encourage them to stay in your garden by eliminating harsh chemical pesticides and fertilizers. A healthy garden has nearly 200 worms per square yard.

**Lava Sand ▪** Facilitates aeration and provides accessible minerals. Apply 30-40 pounds per 1000 square feet. Use around sick trees.

**Chips and Bark ▪** Pine bark, shredded hardwood bark and tree chips are all good bed preparations and mulches. They break down slowly and help neutralize alkaline soils. Avoid applying sawdust directly as it can deplete nitrogen; instead add it to your compost heap.

**Peat Moss ▪** *(Sphagnum peat recommended)* Partially decayed vegetable matter of swamp origin. It is acid and acts as a sponge to retain water in the soil making it an excellent mulch for a dry climate. Ground bark mulch can be substituted for peat with some success.

**Cotton seed hulls and peanut hulls ▪** Use the ground version as mulch or as another source of humus.

**Cotton Seed Meal ▪** A good additive with trace minerals and neutral pH, 6-2-1 and 7-2-2. Use 10-20 pounds per 1000 square feet on lawns and beds.

**Bonemeal ▪** A source of calcium and phosphorous, 1-12-0 to 4-12-0. Bonemeal is always used for bulbs, releasing slowly. Its drawback is that it will attract dogs, squirrels and other rodents who will dig up your plants. Best used where no digging pests are present.

**Gypsum ▪** A naturally occurring mineral of calcium sulfate. Excellent for improving clay soils, it should be applied at a rate of 9 to 28 ounces per square yard often before laying new sod.

## CHEMICAL AMENDMENTS

Nutrients necessary to healthy soil are: nitrogen for leaves, stems, weight, bulk and color; phosphorous for flowers, fruits, roots and crop maturity; and potassium to resist cold and heat damage, disease and insects. Plants deficient in nitrogen are light green in color and stunted in growth. In the Blackland clays, potassium can usually be omitted but iron should be added to combat chlorosis or yellowing of leaves. We supply these by the use of fertilizers — either the organic amendments listed above or the chemical products that follow. Whether you use organic or chemical amendments, humus must be added continually as the high temperatures in Dallas cause fast breakdown of organic materials, thus making soil less productive.

**Balanced Fertilizers** ▪ Always contain nitrogen (N), phosphorous (P), and potassium (K), which comes from potash ($K_2O$). Percentages are listed on the label in that order. 5-10-5 means 5% nitrogen (N), 10% phosphorous (P) and 5% potassium (K). These numbers are referred to as the fertilizer analysis. They may come in the form of granules or slow release pellets that have a longer feeding period. Read directions on container for amount of fertilizer per size of plant container or garden square footage. Generally, dig in lightly and keep away from the stems, as plants can and will be burned if you are careless. Always water plants first, later fertilize and water again. Never fertilize a dry plant. Refrain from fertilizing in late fall. Let plants harden before frost. *(See Chapter One, Gardening by the Month for specific times to apply.)*

**Super-phosphate** ▪ Use any time of the year. A thin snow-like coating on the soil around the plant worked in gently provides better blooms, berries and fruits.

## ADDITIVES TO CORRECT CHLOROSIS

An iron deficiency called Chlorosis can cause plant leaves to turn yellow or lose their normal green color. The veining on broad-leafed evergreens often appears pronounced.

**Iron Chelate** ▪ Corrects iron deficiency, restores vitality, gives new vigor, better color and induces more buds and flowers. Use as a spray or by soil drenching application. See Foliar Feeding. It is sold under many trade names, so follow instructions on the package.

**Sulfur** ▪ Spread thin coat around plants. Common pelleted sulfur is called soil sulfur. Add to acidify the soil annually in the fall.

**Iron Sulfate or Copperas** ▪ Use as above for sulfur, or as a spray - 1 tablespoon to a gallon of water. Apply monthly April to September. May stain concrete.

**Epsom Salts** ▪ Magnesium Sulfate. Use like sulfur. Not usually needed in Blackland Prairie which is rich in Magnesium but good for potting soil mixtures.

# FOLIAR FEEDING

Foliar feeding is spraying liquid fertilizer on the leaves. Use the spray attachment to your hose. This process supplements the regular root feeding to produce healthier plants and more perfect blooms though it should not substitute for root feeding. Foliar feeding is valuable to feed plants where tree roots compete for food in the soil. It also helps to rescue some very sick plants. For maximum results, foliar feeding, once started, must be continued every ten days until growth slackens (about September). This feeding should be done in the morning when the leaves tend to absorb more than they do in the afternoon. Cover the whole leaf, upper and under side, with a fine spray. Insecticide may be mixed with the fertilizer to save an extra spraying. Do not foliar feed if temperatures are above 85°.

**Organic Foliar Fertilizers** ▪ During the growing season plants can be sprayed with a solution of any or all of the following: Fish Emulsion, Liquid Seaweed, Blackstrap Molasses or Natural Apple Cider Vinegar. Mix one tablespoon per gallon of water.

# MULCHING

Traditional horticultural advice told gardeners to clear and till the soil. The current organic movement, however, advises against this practice. Healthy soil develops a complex system of layers from surface to sub-soil which consists of mineral, organic and microbic materials. Exposing it to the elements can be very damaging. Tilling disrupts the layers and upsets the healthy balance. Direct sun and ultraviolet rays kill beneficial microorganisms. Bitter cold penetrates deep into exposed soil killing roots as well as microorganisms. Rain compacts and erodes bare soil and reduces aeration, minerals and humus. Organic gardener or not, if you want to build healthy beds which you can improve each year then mulching, not tilling, is your best route.

## SUMMER MULCHING

A 2" to 3" mulch placed around garden plants during the months of May and June before summer heat arrives will conserve moisture by reducing evaporation, break the force of heavy rainfall and allow deeper penetration of water because of improved soil condition. A good mulch retards heat penetration from the sun, permitting plant roots to benefit from a more even temperature. A mulch discourages the growth of weeds and makes weeding easier.

Mulch material may be either organic or inorganic. Some suitable organic materials usually available in the Dallas area are pecan hulls, shredded bark, cotton seed hulls, sphagnum moss, peat moss, leaf mold or compost, straw, crushed stone and marble chips. Peat moss should be thoroughly wet before it is applied and should be maintained in a moist condition throughout the summer. Organic mulch has the advantage of adding humus as it decomposes. The decomposition process does require large amounts of nitrogen, therefore it is necessary to increase the supply of nitrogen in the soil at the time the mulch is applied by using a fertilizer high in nitrogen content. Sawdust and straw particularly require this treatment. Break them down in the compost bin before using. During the summer, the depth of the organic mulch should be checked and material added if necessary to maintain a cover of 2" to 3". Do not let any mulch cake on top.

Some inorganic mulch materials are newspaper, aluminum foil or sheet plastic.

## WINTER MULCHING

Gardens that are well mulched through the winter months are less susceptible to freeze damage, erosion, and compaction. To ensure that plants re-emerge in the spring, and that the soil is inviting to new plants, a 2" to 11" mulch should cover your beds. Green manure is especially helpful over the winter because as it composts the chemical changes produce heat which warm the roots. Fresh manure also produces nitrogen that can break down clay and help aerate the soil.

# BED PREPARATION

Blackland Prairie, Eagle Ford Shale, Sand, Perennials, Azaleas, Summer Annuals - whatever your soil, whatever type flower you wish to grow, your beds will need special preparation before you plant.

## ORGANIC BEDS

If you are considering beginning an organic program in your garden - be it an existing bed or one built from scratch - the most important step you can take right now is to begin composting. Even if you don't plan to depart down the organic path for an entire year, your compost (and composting skill) needs to be accumulating in the meantime. Compost is the foundation of a rich, healthy, organic garden. It's simple to make, but costly to buy. So begin the process now, before you build your organic bed.

### An Easy Organic Bed

A simple means of bed preparation consists of adding 4" to 8" of compost and organic fertilizer to existing soil, tilling it, then top dressing it with 3" of bark mulch after planting. Dig 4" for ground covers, 6" to 8" for shrubs and perennials. Maintain your bed annually with a fresh addition of compost, fertilizer and mulch.

## The Optimum Organic Bed

1. Carefully remove all unwanted plant matter from the top 3" of the soil. This includes weeds, grasses, root systems, rhizomes (underground stems), and stray pecans or acorns that might later sprout unruly saplings. Even something that is brown and dead-looking should be removed. It may look like compost, but it could miraculously spring back to life mid your perennials. Herbicides to kill existing plants are no longer recommended because of accidental kills to shade trees and/or water pollution.
2. If bed is to be raised or if grade needs adjusting, add native top soil as needed.
3. Spread four to six inches of compost over entire bed. See introductory paragraph.
4. Add rock minerals such as lava sand, glacial powder, granite sand, soft rock phosphate or other recommended by a local nursery, at a rate of thirty to forty pounds per 1,000 square feet.
5. Add organic fertilizer such as liquid biostimulant at label rates over entire bed. Again, consult your local organic nursery for recommendations.
6. Mix it all together to a depth of between six and nine inches.
7. Moisten bed before planting anything.
8. Mulch! Blanket all bare soil with a three to five inch layer of an organic mulch such as rough compost or leaves (good for annuals and perennials) or shredded native woods and hardwoods (good for shrubs and ground covers).

## How To Maintain An Organic Bed

1. Aerate twice yearly, in early spring and late fall.
2. Add compost at least once in the spring. You can't add too much or too often!
3. Mulch all bare soil at all times - even when the bed is empty. If possible, mulch with partially finished compost. This not only mulches, but also continually feeds as the compost matures.
4. Feed plants monthly with a foliar organic fertilizer spray such as fish emulsion, liquid seaweed, black strap molasses or natural apple cider vinegar. If you have the time, you can spray each of these monthly. They all dilute at one tablespoon per gallon of water.

## DOUBLE DIGGING (Also known as the 12-Year Bed)

The new gardener just starting out, as well as the old hand, about to do over an existing garden will do well to consider making a 12-year bed. By following these instructions, cultivation will be unnecessary, watering and fertilization both greatly reduced and the usual nuisance of replenishing the soil each year eliminated.

Remove all the soil in the bed to a depth of 36". If the top soil is acceptable, pile it aside to use; otherwise discard and bring in new topsoil. Should the sub-soil be clay, hardpan or limestone, drainage must be provided. To do this, fill the bottom 4" of your excavated bed with coarse pebbly rocks and follow with 2" of pea gravel. This 6" provides drainage as well as a reservoir of water which is drawn to the surface by capillary action when needed. Over the gravel, spread alternately 3" of top soil and 3" of manure. Repeat to within 12" of the surface of the bed. It is not necessary to spade these layers. The pH of the last twelve inches of soil should meet the acid or alkaline requirements of plants to be grown in the bed.

**Alkaline Top Layer ▪** Use 1/3 sandy loam or compost and 1/3 a mixture of sharp sand (builders' sand with no loam or silt in it) and 1/3 portion of native top soil.

**Acid Top Layer ▪** Use equal parts of native topsoil, leaf mold, peat moss and sharp sand. Both top layers should be blended. Add this special mix to your bed until it crowns surrounding soil (higher in the middle, sloping to the edges). The bed should stand 3" to 6" higher than the ground; rake smooth, set a garden sprinkler at the edge of the new bed and soak until pools of water appear on the surface. When these pools stand for 15 minutes, no more water will be needed for a week. If watering causes bed to sink below surface, add additional blended soil.

**Now plant your** shrubs and perennials. After this, the only maintenance required is the addition of a little commercial fertilizer and good mulch spread on top.

## MODIFIED 12 YEAR BED (The Rent-a-Rototiller Special)

If unable to undertake the 3' excavation, remember the minimal excavation for any good bed is 18". Put a layer of manure (1"), then a 2" layer of sand for drainage. Add 3" of regular soil and fork this 6" together. The top 12" should be composed as above in the Double Digging bed. All beds should be mulched with any form of humus. If using fresh manure, add only in winter months. Rotted manure may be used until July 1st in this area.

## MRS. BELSTERLING'S ACID BED FORMULA

For extreme acid lovers like Dogwoods, adapt your bed in the following way. Remove soil 18-24" deep. Place 4 to 6" of gravel in the bottom, fill with equal parts Canadian peat moss, leaf mold, rotted cow manure and loam, to which has been added 4 lbs. of sulfur and 3 lbs. iron sulfate for each 100 sq. ft. of surface. Keep a mulch 2" thick at all times.

# THE COMPOST BIN

The most important soil building technique is making compost and using it. First, one recycles garden debris that is otherwise expensive and troublesome to remove. Secondly, vibrancy of the soil is enriched. The waste vegetation from a lot, 100' x 175', will convert into six 55-gallon barrels of finished, screened compost each year. A casual leaf pile will turn into humus eventually. but composting with a commercial container or either of the two following systems will achieve faster results.

## THE WOOD FRAMED BIN

Using 1" x 6" rough redwood boards, construct a bin 10' long, 5' wide and 5' high, then divide in the middle to give two bins 5x5x5. The bottom should be open to the soil for microorganisms to enter. Throughout the year, fill one side. When leaf mold is ready to be taken out, it is only necessary to throw the top layers into the empty side until the decayed layer is reached in the first bin. Labor in handling is thus saved and the partly decayed material contains the living organisms to start disintegration of the new lot.

The side planks should have a small space between each one as ventilation is necessary to accomplish quick decay. Decomposition may be obtained in one year if a chimney is placed in the center of the bin. Make this of four 6" boards with lots of holes drilled in them. The bin should be partly shaded and protected from the wind by surrounding structures. Keep material in the bin damp but not soggy. Proper placement will help prevent rapid drying out in hot weather.

The bin will almost overflow at times, but green vegetation wilts quickly. Fork occasionally as you add vegetation when available. Soil, chemical and bacteria compounds may be incorporated to hasten decay. Avoid sticks, heavy stems and branches. Do use lawn clippings, leaves, faded flowers, tops of spent plants, vegetable tops and even weeds. Many things that go down the disposal could help make humus with a little extra effort on your part. Care should be exercised not to put in diseased materials since this might infect the mass. When ready, use as is for mulch or sift through quarter inch mesh wire for potting soil, half-inch for general garden needs.

## THE SIMPLER OPEN PILE SYSTEM

Select a sheltered spot any desired length and about 4'-6' wide. Set in the bare ground 3 or 4 chimneys at least 4' high made of wire netting rolled into cylinders. Start your pile around these. Make a layer of wilted green material (grass cuttings, leafy materials, faded flowers, vegetable tops, etc.) about 6" deep. Cover with 2" fresh cow, sheep or chicken manure. Add a sprinkling of soil, a light covering of soil sulfur and top with 1/2" layer of bio-stimulant. Repeat layer by layer to height of chimney tops, watering lightly during the process of building the pile. Keep it loose, not packed so the bacteria will have the needed air to work. Keep the pile moist but not soggy. In a few days, hot air will be coming from the chimneys. This is as it should be. Let the pile settle for three weeks when it will be ready to turn inside out with a fork. A second turning should be made about five weeks later. Twelve weeks after starting, you will possess lovely sweet-smelling humus.

## REFERENCES

*Gardening with Difficult Soils* by Scott Odgen,Taylor Publishing Co.

*The Dirt Doctor's Guide to Organic Gardening: Essays On The Natural Way* by J. Howard Garrett, University of Texas Press, 1996.

*Don't Waste Your Wastes, Compost 'em: The Homeowners Guide To Recycling Waste* by Burt Whitehead, Box 851971, Mesquite, Texas 75185, $10.95, 1971.

## MAP OF DALLAS COUNTY SOILS

Dallas County surface soil patterns are made clear in an elegant, large, terrazzo map in Court House Plaza on Main Street in front of John Neely Bryan's log cabin. Creeks, waterways and early communities are also labeled.

## ORGANIZATIONS

**Dallas Organic Garden Club**
Dallas, Texas
(972) 272-0097
Lesley Nittler

**Nature Conservancy of Texas**
North Texas Land Steward
P.O. Box 26
Celeste, Texas 75423
(903) 568-4139

**Texas Committee on Natural Resources**
5952 Royal Lane, Suite 168
Dallas, Texas 75230
(214) 368-1791

# Chapter 4

## WATER & WATERING
*Sprinkler Systems ᐱ Xeriscaping*

Water is the single most important element for plant growth. Water actually transports life-giving nutrients in the soil to the roots of plants. It comes to our gardens naturally through rainfall or deliberately through irrigation. Water is one of Texas' most precious resources.

## PRECIPITATION

Rainfall in North Texas is distributed throughout the year, reaching a slight peak in the spring. The thirty-six inches of average precipitation in Dallas is adequate for prairie plants and native trees. The trend is more rain in the east and less rain in the west. Fort Worth to the west receives 20% less rain. Rainfall of 20 inches (over 57% of our annual precipitation) occurs between April and September, the growing season of most perennials and vegetables.

Precipitation in the form of snow may come as early as November and as late as March, but is rarely as harmful to plants as freezing rain or hail. The average seasonal snowfall is 2+ inches.

Severe thunderstorms occur about 40 days each year, more frequently in the spring and summer. Usually these are spotty and of short duration. Old timers tend to ignore the TV weathermen's excitement and take thunderstorms in stride. Hard rains often create run-off in many watershed drainage systems, but flooding is rare. With conservation more of the excess moisture can be retained.

Precipitation should not accumulate in low spots or flood away, but move downward slowly to ensure a proper oxygen-nutrient-water balance to support plant and microbial growth. The Dallas area receives sufficient rainfall for growing native flora unless the area is in a drought. However, traditional home landscape plants such as Azaleas, St. Augustine grass and many broad leaf evergreens, require roughly double the normal rainfall with irrigation.

## HOW MUCH TO WATER

Maintaining moisture four to six inches deep in soil is the goal of watering. Check your soil with a screw driver or trowel, one to one-

and-a-half inches of water per application will usually soak down four to six inches, even in the heavy clay soils of Dallas.

Light, frequent applications of water produce weak, shallow-roots that cannot withstand heat and drought. By watering at the proper depth when your plants need it, you encourage deep, healthy roots.

## WHEN TO WATER

Use your lawn as an indicator of when to water. Look for discoloration and wilting. Your grass may take on a gray, dull appearance or the leaf blades may begin to roll or fold. A sure sign that your lawn needs water is when footprints remain visible after you've walked across it. While lawns require more water, in certain instances other newly installed plants will need even more water. Do not allow new plants to wilt before watering. *(See "Hand Watering" later in this chapter.) During your specific grass' dormant period do not water.*

Conditions that affect the need for water vary, so it's best to water when your lawn shows stress. In general, these grasses need water at these schedules.

| GRASS | HOW OFTEN |
|---|---|
| Buffalograss . . . . . . . . . . . . . . | Every two to three weeks |
| Bermuda . . . . . . . . . . . . . . . | Every seven to ten days |
| St. Augustine . . . . . . . . . . . . | Every five days |
| Tall Fescue . . . . . . . . . . . . . . | Every four days |

## GENERAL WATER MANAGEMENT - XERISCAPING

Currently water conservation in gardening is called xeriscaping. This common sense method is an environmentally natural way of landscaping that requires little or no supplemental water. Saving time, money and energy, this watering plan prevents pollution and water waste. One main tenet is to grow plants that thrive on local conditions including the soil, temperature and average precipitation. The City of Dallas has a North Texas Xeriscape Demonstration Garden at the White Rock Pump Station at 2900 White Rock Road.

### GUIDELINES FOR XERISCAPING

**Evaluate your site .** Be in your garden at various times of the day. Where and when is it sunny or shady, windy, wet or dry? Regard the high and low areas. Make a list of the microclimates in your own space. Make a plan considering the aesthetic effect desired in these spaces.

**Place Plants in the Correct Place** ∎ If water tends to stand in the lower back corner of your lot, use moisture loving specimens such as Eupatorium, Louisiana Iris or Primula. Where high and dry, plant appropriately. Roses are thirstier than Zinnias. Do not plant them together; both will suffer. The best solution for this is "hydro-zoning" which means grouping plants with similar water requirements together.

**Grow Plants that Thrive on Local Conditions** ∎ Select native or naturalized plants for drought tolerance appropriate to our prairie precipitation. A flowering Dogwood in the East Texas woods is adapted to that area. It needs no supplemental water there. In the Metroplex it is not native or naturalized. It cannot thrive without special treatment which includes supplemental watering. For a better choice in a small, spring flowering tree try Mexican Plum or Redbud.

**Eliminate Some Lawn Areas** ∎ The most water-needy landscape plant is lawn grass. If grass is your choice, plant ones that need less moisture. Use alternate solutions for broad areas such as ground covers, shrubs, decks, or patios. Use your parkway as a flower bed. Raise xeriphitics on the hot side of your house, plant ground covers on the shady side.

**Improve Your Soil** ∎ Organic matter like compost will increase the moisture penetration and capacity of soil to hold water. Mulch to reduce soil erosion and water loss. In clay soil water tends to drain either too slowly - pooling around and suffocating plants, or too quickly - leaving plants thirsty. Correct these problems with aeration and the addition of compost.

**Use Efficient Irrigation** ∎ Dallas Water Utilities has coordinated a series of free seminars to introduce xeriscaping. Telephone 214-670-4022 or 214-670-3155.

## IRRIGATION

Any supplemental water given to plants by hand watering, a rotating sprinkler, drip irrigation or a sprinkler system is known as irrigation. Each irrigation system is needed for different garden situations and has different techniques.

**Water Without Creating Run-off** ∎ If run-off occurs, you're applying moisture faster than the ground can absorb it. Texas A & M Horticulture Department says more plants are killed by over watering than under watering. Check for depth of moisture to decide if water is needed.

**To Calculate Water per Month on Your Garden, Use a Rain Gauge** ∎ Rain falling on full leafed trees will be consistently less than that on open land. If your garden landscape varies into open and sheltered spaces, use two or more gauges at various heights in your garden. (Sprinkler system output measurement follows.)

## HAND WATERING

Apply supplemental water with a garden hose or a watering can, two pieces of equipment essential to an active gardener. A pliable garden hose should reach to every corner of your cultivated land. Hand watering is necessary when adding new plants. Bedding plants should be hand watered before placing in the soil. The excavated hole for plants may be filled with water first. Immediate watering after planting is essential when encouraging new life. For the first two weeks, newly installed plants need supplemental irrigation. Mini greenhouses made from an upside down jar or a plastic bag may hold moisture for young plants. Perennials need extra water their first summer.

Hand watering is the preferable choice of irrigation for container plants. Because chemicals added for city water purification are alkaline, gardeners often collect rain water or gutter runoff to use for hand watering. One can add acidifers, e.g., acid water (1/2 cup natural apple cider vinegar to 1 gallon of water), liquid manure *(see p. 34)* or water soluable fertilizer when hand watering.

## SPRINKLER SYSTEM

An electronic underground sprinkler system can help with garden maintenance. As all tools, it must be monitored, repaired and used with discretion. Sprinkler system schedules should be monitored to reflect changes in weather, season and plant needs. Each zone should take in account its plants and the proportion of sun and shade. Timing for each station in the system will be different.

Irrigate one to two times per week for grassy areas and annual beds. For herbs and perennials, less is needed. Irrigate lawns early in the day during summer months in North Texas to avoid fungus. Time winter irrigation for late in the day to protect from freezes. Refer to Chapter 1 *(See pp. 2-22)* for more sprinkler techniques. Don't water on very windy days because of major evaporation loss. In watering your lawn, don't apply water to the point of run-off. If the sprinkler is applying water faster than the soil can absorb it, wait until after the water has soaked in (usually 30 minutes or more). Or turn the sprinkler off, and then repeat until enough water has been applied. Water that runs off your lawn to a sidewalk or street is wasted.

Install the sprinkler system before initial planting when possible. We recommend that you use professional services for installation. Local permits, electrical systems, measuring water pressure and back flow devices can be daunting. Save costs on labor by filling in trenches and doing the final cleanup.

If your digital system is not functioning properly, one way to alleviate the problem may be by unplugging the system and disconnecting the battery. Then, plug it all back in and re-program your system using the instructional manual.

## HOW TO MEASURE SPRINKLER OUTPUT

It is difficult to know how long to leave a sprinkler system on. You must measure each zone's output to see how long that zone must run to receive one inch of water. Then multiply as needed.

Here is a procedure: On a windless day, set a few empty cans or glasses of the same size in a straight line at various distances from the sprinkler (make sure all cans are within the spray pattern). Run the sprinkler long enough to put an inch of water in your containers.

This experiment establishes your future watering habits. By timing how long your sprinklers were on, you'll know how long to run them to get the right amount of water on your lawn.

## DRIP SYSTEMS

Irrigation that is subterranean or that lies on the surface of the soil is the most efficient method of adding supplemental water for horticulture. Drip irrigation provides more even moisture for shrubs and beds than any other type of sprinkler system. Evaporation may rob 70% airborne sprinkler moisture before it hits the soil. Also moisture resting on foliage has a tendency to breed disease, molds and fungus.

Soaker hoses with minuscule holes covered by mulch is the most inexpensive installation. Buried systems are costly and awkward to monitor, but can be effective.

## SPECIFIC DALLAS NEEDS IN WATERING

Dallas tap water has an average 8.0 pH but can occasionally increase to 10. For optimal plant cultivation of favorite traditional home landscape plants, a pH of 6.5 is recommended, *(see p. 32)*. Acid amendments will help. Some soil amendments can be added to your home irrigation by an injector system.

Clay soils are difficult to water deeply. Only 5% of organic matter is present in most non-modified soils. In clay soil water tends to drain either too slowly, pooling around - suffocating plants' or too quickly - leaving plants thirsty. Slow trickle drip irrigation is best, but expensive.

## REFERENCES

*Common Sense Landscaping*, Bonnie Arnold Reese, 1848 Oates Drive, Dallas, Texas 75228, (214) 224-1179, 1994.
*Xeriscape Gardening: Water Conservation for the American Landscape*, Connie Ellefson, Tom Stephens, and Doug Welsh, MacMillan Publishing Company, New York, NY, 1992.

# Chapter 5

## PROPAGATION & PLANTING

*Division ❧ Germination ❧ Transportation & Storage of Plants*
*Choosing Best Location*

## PROPAGATION

Increasing the number of plants in your garden is rather easy in a climate with a long growing season like ours. Plants can be propagated in a number of ways. One is by Division, cloning the parent plant using small sections (cuttings) of its roots, stems, or leaves. Another is germination, growing a new plant from fertilized seeds. Either type of propagation benefits from proper soil mixes, root hormone, and an appropriate "nursery" environment.

## AIDS TO PROPAGATION

**TEXAS A & M ALL PURPOSE PROPAGATION MIX**
Mix thoroughly:
1/2 bushel of Perlite
1/2 bushel of sphagnum moss
3 tbsp. ground limestone
3 tbsp. 5-10-5 fertilizer

Add to this 1 Tbsp. 5-10-5 fertilizer dissolved in a gallon of water. Keep plants moist but not wet.

**ROOT HORMONE**
Available at nurseries. Initiates cellular changes in plants to encourage root buds in cuttings. It often includes fungicides, which guard against rot in the cutting.

**MINIATURE GREENHOUSE**
Use for rooting cuttings *(cutting instructions appear later in this chapter.)* Work water into potting soil so that when the soil is squeezed, only a few drops come out. Place enough of this mixture in a pint size plastic bag to make 4" of rooting soil. Set cuttings in soil, sprinkle lightly just to dampen foliage, seal with a rubber band or twist-tie, and place in a bright location, preferable with a northern exposure where there is light but no direct sun. Do not disturb until roots have formed. The bag recirculates its own moisture. Check at the end of one month. Any dead or rotten cuttings should be removed immediately. When roots have formed, transplant plants to pots.

## MRS. BELSTERLING'S COLD FRAME

If the writer could only have either a greenhouse or a cold frame, her choice would be the latter. Experience gained in its management is invaluable in preparing for the management of a greenhouse. However large or small the cold frame may be, it demands much less care than a greenhouse, and as an adjunct to a greenhouse, it is indispensable.

A cold frame may have "under heat" by the use of electric heating cables placed about 2" below the surface, or it may be solar-heated. Glass, fiberglass, plexiglass, polyethylene sheeting or any other coating used for greenhouses may be used. In the frame may be grown flats of seedlings, pots of seedlings or cuttings and pots of not-too-tall plants to be kept over the winter. With the electric wires giving bottom heat, it is an excellent place to root cuttings of all sorts.

The walls may be made of cypress, redwood or concrete, with the back (26") higher than the front (18"). The size should always be 3 feet by 6 feet, or multiples of 3 feet, in order to utilize stock-size glass sash. A 3-sash frame will hold 800 or more 2-1/2" pots. If built against a shed or wall, the sashes may be let up or down by means of window pulleys and ropes. The best exposure is facing south.

In planting seeds, I prefer flats placed in the frame. These flats can be shifted or removed for potting or transplanting, and they are altogether more satisfactory than planting directly in the frame. Plant cuttings directly in the frame, in 3" layer of potting medium since they root better if close to bottom heat.

The sashes should be opened on all possible days, as plants need plenty of fresh air. If the weather is cold, open the sashes only an inch or two. Plants in the cold frame also need water, but they do not like wet feet. All the little pots of seedlings raised in the greenhouse may be grown cool in the cold frame before being transplanted to their permanent positions.

In the summer months, the frame, with a portable lath cover, is useful for starting perennials from seed since here they can be protected from wind, washing rains and sun.

# PROPAGATION BY DIVISION

## ROOT DIVISION

Involves digging up a clump of the plant and breaking or cutting it into several pieces, each containing roots, stems and leaves. These are then replanted. Divide plants the opposite season from their bloom (i.e. spring blooming perennials should be divided in late summer and fall).

## CUTTINGS

**Hardwood Cuttings** (deciduous plants as Crape Myrtle and Japanese Quince) ▪ Propagate in November. Make pencil-size cuttings, and place in moist soil in a protected location outside. In spring, transplant to permanent location. Root hormone is suggested.

**Semi-hardwood Cuttings** (evergreens like Azaleas) ▪ Propagate in late spring. Start with cuttings of mature stems from the current season's growth. The cuttings should be 4-6" long and cut diagonally just below a leaf bud. Strip off most of the foliage, dip the cut end in a root hormone and insert the lower several inches into a container or flat of moist, sterile growing medium: potting mix, sand, perlite or vermiculite. The container or flat should be placed in a bright, cool and moist location for several weeks. Place in a clear plastic bag to increase humidity, but not in direct sunlight. Bag must be opened periodically for air exchange.

**Softwood Cuttings** (Geraniums, Chrysanthemums or Coleus) ▪ Start anytime vigorous stock plants are available. Take cuttings when the stem is firm enough to snap when bent. Remove leaves except for the top whorl of mature foliage. Dip the cut end in root hormone. Plant the bottom of the cutting in moist, sterile potting mix. Protect the cutting from direct sun, but it will still require light to make food for growing roots. Place in a plastic bag, as discussed above, or a miniature greenhouse or terrarium. Roots may take two weeks to one month to appear. Some plants rooted this way may root in water alone, but suffer from shock when transplanted to soil. *(See pp.112 and 118).*

**Root Cuttings** (perennials) ▪ Dig sections of root from the parent shrub in the late winter or early spring before rapid shoot growth. Cut root sections 2-6" long, tie in bundles, pack in damp peat moss or sand and store at 40°F for three weeks. Then plant 2-3" apart in a well-prepared nursery soil with the tops of the cuttings level with, or just below, the top of the soil. Cold frame recommended for this procedure.

**Leaf Cuttings** (seasonless tropicals as African Violets, Sedums and Gloxinias) ▪ Remove fleshy leaf from the parent plant, place on moist potting soil or sand and anchor with pegs or bobby pins. If a part of the stem adheres to the leaf, it should be buried and the leaf itself held flat on the rooting medium. A cut at the large veins encourages development of roots at that point. Leaves should be protected from strong light until roots are formed and then transplanted to pots.

## LAYERING

The surest way to increase the number of plants is by layering. This can be done any time of the year. It is done by bending a branch of a vigorously growing plant to the ground and pinning down with a stake, brick, etc. until rooted. Cut the stem and transplant after sufficient roots have formed. For woody plants such as Azaleas, this usually takes one year. For Roses, it takes three to four months.

**Air-layering** ∎ Is useful when a plant is too tall. You can make a new plant out of the top of the old one or from a branch, so long as you make your cut below a node (joint). Cut the stem approximately 1/3 of the way through at a diagonal. Coat the cut with rooting hormone and place a toothpick in the cut to keep it open. Wrap the section of stem around the cut with wet sphagnum moss. Secure the moss by crimping aluminum foil around it and, to retain moisture, wrap the area with plastic wrap using twist-ties or waterproof tape. It may take several months to root. Periodically check the sphagnum and re-moisten as necessary and monitor root growth. When sufficient roots have formed, cut the stem below the root mass and plant.

## PROPAGATION BY GERMINATION

Hardy annuals may be sown outdoors, some in early spring, others in the summer, fall or winter. Check time for planting in alphabetical listing under *Annuals*. If perennial and biennial seeds are to be planted, they should be sown as soon as they ripen and seedlings carried through the summer in partial to full shade in flats or pots. Place the plants you have grown or purchased in permanent quarters in the fall.

**Plant Seed Outdoors** ∎ Prepare the soil properly. Never dig black waxy soil when wet. Remember the top inches of the soil should have a sifted feel so that tiny plants can push through. Sow seeds in rows or group in drifts. See directions on seed packet for spacing and depth as well as information found under *Annuals, Biennials and Perennials*. Mix very fine seed with sand before broadcasting to allow even distribution. Very fine seed should not be covered with soil. Just press in with the back of the hand or a board. Good soil contact is important. Water in with a spray mist to prevent washing them away. For stronger growth and better flowers, thin when true leaves appear. True leaves are the second set of leaves to grow and they are the first typical of the specific plant.

**Plant Seeds in Flats** ∎ Fill crates within 1/2" of the top with growing medium and tamp down soil to make a firm seed bed. A good planting medium consists of a mixture of equal parts of sterilized potting soil, peat moss and vermiculite, sand or fine bark mulch. Mix well and sift through a screen. Sow seeds in rows at least 1" apart, barely covering with the same sifted mixture. Remember, very fine seed just need pressing in. Set flats in a shallow pan of water until thoroughly wet, then remove and cover with glass or plastic wrap.

Flats should be labeled and dated. In all probability no more water will be needed until germination, i.e. when first leaves appear. Keep flats in shade until that time. If watering is necessary, use a fog nozzle or mist sprayer to moisten the soil without disturbing the seedlings. After germination remove plastic or glass, but keep from intense sun.

**Transplant Seedlings** ∎ Watch for the second set of leaves (the true leaves) to appear. Then transplant the seedlings to small pots. These may be clay, peat or plastic. Fill containers with potting mix to within 1" of the top. Using an old table fork, make a hole in the center and carefully transfer seedlings from flat to pot. Gently press down soil around the seedling. Stand the pots in a pan of water until top of soil is moist, then remove pots from water. Keep pots moist but not wet for 1-2 weeks until a good root system is formed. At this stage the plants need higher light levels for proper growth. After danger of frost is over, move plants outdoors to acclimatize or harden them off at least one week prior to planting. When planting plants grown in peat pots, remove the peat pot from the rootball. When removing plants from plastic or clay pots, hold your hand over the top of the pot with fingers on each side of the plant's stem, invert the pot and tap gently on a hard surface to remove soil and roots intact. After planting, put out snail and slug bait if needed.

# PLANTING

Installing a new plant into the environment is for many gardeners the beginning of their fascination with horticulture. Whether it be seeds or an established plant, success is more likely when the gardener creates an appropriate environment of soil, sun and shade and water.

Guidelines for transportation, storing, and the placement of new stock are basic for the ultimate existence of your new plant.

## TRANSPORTATION & STORAGE OF NEW PLANTS

1. Protect plants on trip from nursery (cover with tarp if open vehicle). Don't leave plants in the high heat area of the trunk or car.
2. If plants are to be held before planting, inspect daily and water.
3. If root bound with a mat of roots on the outside of the root mass ball (especially container grown shrubs), soak root ball. Cut 3 or 4 vertical lines 1/2" deep, using a sharp knife.
4. Don't expose newly purchased protected plants to full sun immediately. Gradually increase amounts of sun at the planting sites.
5. New plants added to the garden should be watered immediately when planted.
6. Many gardeners water the excavated hole, place the plant, and water additionally from soil level.

## CHOOSING NEW LOCATION FOR PLANTING

**New Building Sites.** Complete all fabrication, discard all construction debris, remove all contaminated soil. Brick, mortar, stone, and sheetrock particles are all extremely alkaline and toxic to most plants.

**Protect Existing Structures .** Wooden structures such as homes, garages, or fences have significantly shorter life spans when organic materials are placed against them. Do not raise beds adjacent to these areas but remove soil and place beds below building levels.

**Protect Existing Trees .** Leave trees a radius of undisturbed land, two thirds of the canopy coverage. Do not cover above ground roots. If necessary create a bowl of original level soil around the base of the tree with rock edge. During construction install a temporary fence to protect trees using the two-thirds of canopy size.

## STARTER SOLUTION OR ROOT STIMULATOR

Use with newly installed plants to stimulate root growth. Take a fertilizer that is completely water soluble and high in phosphate which stimulates root growth. An example is 1 lb. of 12-24-12 fertilizer dissolved in 5 gallons of water. Use a cupful (more or less) of this mixture according to the size of the plant.

For additional information see specific plants.

# REFERENCE

*Know It and Grow It III: A Guide to the Identification and use of Landscape Plants* by Carl Whitcomb, 802 pp. $60.00, Lacebark Inc., P.O. Box 2383, Stillwater, OK 74076, (405) 377-3539, 1976.

*Garden Flowers from Seed* by Christopher Lloyd and Graham Rice, Timber Press, Portland, OR, 1995.

# Chapter 6

# INSECTS, DISEASES & REMEDIES

*Pest & Disease Control  ✒  Dusting & Spraying Chemicals*
*Insecticides  ✒  Pesticides  ✒  Fungicides*

## BENEFICIAL INSECTS

Adapted from an article by E.P. Cheatum, Ph.D.
Retired Chairman, Biology Department, SMU

There are many ways to combat invaders in your garden. Before you resort to harsh chemicals that can damage pets, wildlife, and beneficial insects look first to preventive measures. Bad environmental conditions predispose the plant to both diseases and insects. Guard against poor nutrition, excesses or deficiencies of light or moisture, and extremes including reflected heat. Purchase seeds, plants, shrubs, and trees that are adapted to this particular area and which are resistant to local insects and diseases. Your nurseryman can help you. Control weeds, which are reservoirs of insects, water your garden with care; feed your plants properly; and inspect them frequently for signs of harmful invaders. To rid your garden of pests without sprays or dusts, hand remove them in small areas; apply paper collars and tar-paper discs to plants; or use sticky bands on tree trunks in early spring.

Start to appreciate the contribution of the pollinators (e.g., honey bee), the predators (e.g., praying mantis, ladybugs, wasps), soil conditioners (e.g., the earthworm) and the lowly toad who can eat 10,000 insects in a three month span. Protect these friends by spraying or dusting when they are most likely to be inactive. Educate yourself. Learn who and what the enemies are and how best to rid your garden of them.

It is not true that the majority of insects are harmful to man, despite the fact that we frequently kill the insects without thought of discrimination between the obnoxious and beneficial ones. The great benefits derived from some insects are easily overlooked because they may not be so obvious as compared to the harm done by other species. Less than 10% of insects are considered pests.

I suppose that the honey bee is the best known beneficial insect, and the majority of people know the part it plays in the pollination of our fruit trees and other flowering plants many of which are important to horticulture. Sometimes, in order to eliminate insect pests, we use insecticides injudiciously with the result that we not only kill the harmful species, but may at times defeat our purpose by killing the beneficial pollinators that make production of more seed possible. Therefore, it is wise when spraying fruit trees and other garden plants, to select some time during the day when there is the least activity of the insect pollinators.

Today we are using many insects in the biological control of other insects, which means that we use "bugs to fight bugs." These beneficial warriors include: parasite wasps that lay their eggs either on or in the bodies of their hosts; the hemispherical-shaped ladybugs that feed upon plant lice (aphids) and scale insects; the praying mantis; dragon-flies; and ground beetles.

Insects are also beneficial in their role as scavengers, increasing the organic content of the soil, aeration of soil, and food for animal life. Man will always wage a war against insects, but strange as it may seem, he will use with increasing efficiency the beneficial insects to combat the harmful ones.

## PEST AND DISEASE CONTROL

The current definition of insecticide is anything that kills, weakens, or repels insects. Home remedies with hot pepper, beer or environmentally harsh chemicals are under that category. All measures should be tested on flora first to see if the plant is sensitive in that season. Spray in the cool of the day.

### ORGANIC METHODS

Insecticides should be a last resort. Try these home recipes, first. They are natural, effective, and easy to make.

**Bug Burn** ▪ Use for White Flies, Aphids, June Bugs, Squash Bugs, Loopers, and Spider Mites.

Cut 1 whole head of garlic into 8 pieces. Discard tough root end. Place garlic parts into a blender with 2 cups of water, 1 teaspoon of ground Cayenne Pepper, and 2 teaspoons Mineral Oil. Blend until it is liquid and smooth. Let stand 2 hours and blend again. Strain into a 1 gallon container. Fill with water and refrigerate. To use, pour off 1/4 cup into a 1 quart spray jar and fill to top with water.

**Soda Spray** ▪ Use in a sprayer to fight Black spot on Roses and Powdery Mildew on Crape Myrtle.

1 teaspoon baking soda                    1 quart water
2 drops liquid detergent

**Potato Flour Spray** ▪ This is a milder treatment to fight Scale, Aphids, and Spider Mites. Apply in spray jar.

4 tablespoons potato flour                    1 quart water
1 teaspoon mineral oil

**Alcohol Spray** ▪ Use with caution for Aphids and Scale.

1 cup rubbing alcohol                    1 quart water

**Tobacco Tea** ▪ Use as spray to control Aphids, Fungus, Gnat, Thrips, Scales, and Leaf Miners or any chewing insect such as Squash Bugs. Soak 1 cup cigarette butts (not the filters) or the same amount of tobacco in 1 gallon warm water for 1 hour. Strain into a jar and add 1 teaspoon mineral oil.

**Beer Traps** ▪ Small dishes or jar lids placed in ground and filled with stale beer. Will attract and catch Snails, Slugs, and Pill Bugs.

**Logan's Scale Spray** ▪ Spray on scale-infested plants:

2 tablespoons cooking oil         1 gallon water
1/2 teaspoon natural soap, not detergent

**Lucinda's Fishy Food** ▪ Use on plants twice a month instead of chemical fertilizers.

1 tablespoon fish emulsion         1 tablespoon liquid seaweed
1 gallon water

Try sprays on several leaves first. Wait at least two days before spraying the whole plant. Always spray in the evening or cool of the morning.

# DUSTING AND SPRAYING CHEMICALS

Sulfur, dusting or wettable, becomes an all purpose remedy, combating leaf spot, chewing insects, or fungus. Treat both sides of the leaves with dust. A nylon stocking bag filled with dust and lightly tapped with a stick while the bag is held under and over the leaves is an easy and satisfactory method of application. A rotating hand duster is on the market which is efficient but expensive. A dust gun is best. Do not dust with sulfur in extremely hot weather. Do not use oil spray within 30 days of applying sulfur because of plant burn potiential.

### CHEMICAL SPRAY MIXTURES

Though not as toxic as many insecticides, sulfur and the following spray formulas should be treated as poisons. **Whether using chemical or organic sprays, always take precaution: guard eyes, use plastic gloves, wash skin well if touched by spray.** Do not spray on a windy day or in heat over 90°.

This list is given to assist you in mixing small quantities of most-needed sprays for home gardening. When you purchase your ingredients check for concentration and follow the specific instructions on the bottle as chemical percentages change under different trade names.

Bordeaux, Summer, or Winter (Dormant) Oil sprays may be purchased commercially.

**Bordeaux Mixture** ▪ (All purpose to use regularly as preventive)

3 gallons water         4 tablespoons copper sulfate
6 tablespoons hydrated lime

Dormant sprays are useful in our area, and will prevent some troubles.

Use on all shrubs before the buds burst or spring growth begins, especially on Azaleas, Camellias, Euonymus, Japanese Quince, Pyracantha and all fruit trees, to control over-wintering eggs and insects such as scale. Never use Oil Sprays in temperatures below 40° or over 90°. No pesticides are added to summer or winter oil sprays. The oil itself smothers the insect. Dormant oils contain no chemical pesticide. However the oil is toxic to Japanese Maples and some other plants. Test on small portion of leaf first, wait several days before proceeding.

**Winter Oil Spray** ▪ Mix two ingredients in a jar. Save. When ready to use, add 2-1/2 teaspoons of mixture to 1 cup of water. Spray.

1 cup cooking oil          1 tablespoon liquid dish soap

# INSECTICIDES, PESTICIDES, AND FUNGICIDES

Insecticides, soil fumigants and fungicides, alone or combined, should be used only when needed. Most of these products are potentially toxic and should be treated as such. Read all product labels carefully. Check carefully for percentage concentration of chemicals, as it varies with trade names. Use them only according to specific instructions of the manufacturers; never use in stronger solution than recommended; and never use on plants not named on the label. Never pour left-over sprays or unlabeled chemicals down the drain. This is water pollution. Take all to the hazardous waste drop off *(see telephone number below)*. Keep all products out of reach of children and pets; familiarize yourself with specific antidotes; protect eyes and skin, and avoid inhalation by using face masks. Wash your hands and any exposed skin area with soap upon completion of dusting or spraying. A shower is highly recommended. Remember that some insecticides will kill fish and birds, so take precautionary measures. Do not spray on windy days or near water sources.

# RECYCLING & DISPOSING OF USED GARDEN CHEMICALS

Dallas Area Household Hazardous Waste Network has a Co-op Program for Dallas County free for participating cities. Call for information 214-904-3017, hours and locations vary.

# IDENTIFICATION OF PESTS

### CATEGORIES

Know thy enemy. Proper identification means proper treatment. If you are in doubt about the culprit, take one in a plastic bag to your nurseryman. He will help you to identify it and to find which preparation to use.

To simplify the identification process, we have grouped the most common pests and their treatment as follows:

1. **Chewing Insects** ■ Those which eat leaf, stem and root.

| | | |
|---|---|---|
| Beetles | Cutworms | Leaf Rollers |
| Borers | Grasshoppers | Snails |
| Casebearers | Grubs | Sowbugs |
| Caterpillars | Leaf Miners | Webworms |

**Recommended Commercial Treatments**

| | | |
|---|---|---|
| *Bacillus thuringiensis* | Malathion | Pyrethrins |
| Diazinon | Metaldehyde | Sevin (Carbaryl) |
| Dursban | Methoxychlor | |
| Lime-sulfur | Perinethrin | |

**NOTE:** Vegetables should receive treatment relatively harmless to humans. *Bacillus thuringiensis*, Pyrethrum

2. **Sucking Insects** ■ Those which draw juices out of plant surfaces.

| | | |
|---|---|---|
| Aphids | Stink Bugs | Thrips |
| Chinch Bugs | Red Spider | White Flies |
| Leaf Hoppers | Scales | Mealy/Squash Bugs |

**Recommended Commercial Treatments**

| | | |
|---|---|---|
| Dursban | Kelthane | Sevin |
| Horticultural Oil | Malathion | Soap |

3. **Diseases** ■ Disorders caused by different types of bacteria, fungi or viruses.

| | | |
|---|---|---|
| Black Spot | Leaf Gall & Curls | Rust |
| Blights | Leaf Spot | Scab |
| Crown Rot | Mosaics | Sooty Molds |
| Dieback | Ring Spots | Wilt |

**Recommended Commercial Treatments**

| | | |
|---|---|---|
| Benomyl | Dithane M22 | Sulfur |
| Bordeaux Mixture | Dormant Oil | Summer Oil |
| Captan | Ferbam | Thiram |

# SPECIFIC PESTS

**Ants** ■ Leave granular soil mounds, chewing insects. Some can sting. Spray or dust mounds with Diazinon, Dursban, Sevin or Permethrin.

**Fire Ants** ■ Terrestrial. Build nests deep in ground. Mounds appear after rains. Small black or brown ants "boil" out of hills if disturbed. Most effective controls are broadcast bait application including Amdro, Logic or commercial fire ant killer baits. See Extension Service leaflets on two-step method. Organically, one can carefully pour one gallon of boiling water into each mound. Repeat every day until no more live ants are seen.

**Aphids** ▪ Minute green, brown, gray, or white lice. Found on most plants on stems, buds, under leaves. They reduce plant vigor, ruin bloom. Spray or dust with Malathion, Orthene, insecticide soap or horticultural oil. Indoors use Pyrethrum or use a soap spray indoors or outdoors. *(See p. 15).*

**Bacterial Diseases** ▪ Use Bordeaux Mixture for black spot and fruit rot. Use Agri-strep for fire blight and cankers.

**Bagworms** ▪ Spindle-shaped bags or cocoons on twig ends of conifers, mainly. Appear early summer. Hand pick, burn. Spray in May with Diazinon, Permethrin, or Malathion before new larva constructs its own case. *Bacillus thuringiensis* will attack the larva.

**Beetles** ▪ See Cucumber Beetle and June Bugs.

**Black Spot** ▪ Black spots with fringed margins on rose leaves. The foliage yellows and falls – may defoliate. A mildew-like fungus. Spray regularly every week with Bordeaux Mixture, lime-sulfur and dormant oil, or other fungicides.

**Borers** ▪ Make holes, spilling sawdust from newly-planted trees. Metroplex fruit and pecan trees are especially vulnerable to these. Can kill a healthy tree. Apply preventive sprays to stressed or slightly damaged trees to prevent further attack. Use sprays containing Dursban, Lindane, Permethrin, Rotenone/Pyrethrum (which is organic). Apply every four to six weeks to trunks and larger limbs. Borers may also affect Amaryllis, Dahlia, and Iris.

**Botrytis Blight** ▪ Orange or brown spots on Lilies, Peonies, Tulips, Pansies, etc., caused by dampness. Improve ventilation around plants to prevent. Destroy infected plants, control aphids (they transmit disease), spray with Bordeaux Mixture, or other fungicides.

**Caterpillars** ▪ See Bagworms, Leaf Rollers, Webworms, etc.

**Chiggers** ▪ Nearly invisible mites that infest soil. Irritating bite to humans and pets. Sulfur application to lawns and use of fertilizers incorporating insecticides in early spring and beginning of summer, help control. Diatomaceous earth and pyrethrum products are additional organic preventives. Repellants provide the best protection for gardeners working in infested areas. Keep grass mowed and weeds controlled. Diazinon or Dursban sprays may help reduce chigger numbers in limited areas. Grow an Aloe Vera plant. Its leaves, rubbed on chigger bites, relieve itching.

**Chinch Bugs** ▪ Very minute black bugs with white wings. Heavy feeding suckers. Kill St. Augustine grass. Two or three generations possible during season. Water grass before treating with Diazinon or Dursban. Repeat if it rains soon after application.

**Cotton Root Rot** ▪ Soil fungus. Kills over 2,000 kinds of plants including shrubs and large trees. Choose resistant plants.

**Crown Gall** ▪ Rough mass on surface at base of plants, at soil line. Affects trees, roses, many others. Carefully inspect all plants purchased. Destroy infected plants; abandon area affected for at least 2 years. Agri-strep is the only remedy.

**Cucumber Beetle** ▪ Looks like a green Ladybug, chews leaves of vegetables and ornamentals like roses, chrysanthemums, daisies, cosmos, etc. Control with Malathion, Pyrethrum or Sevin.

**Cutworms** ▪ Night-feeding, larva, sleep rolled up just under soil in day time. Terrific destroyers of newly set out bedding plants, cutting them at soil line. Place cups or paper rings around new transplants or seedlings to protect or spray with permethrin.

**Dieback** ▪ Progressive death of plant from tip backward. Fungi or bacteria enter through bud scars in spring, young buds or pruning wounds. Prune out dead and dying twigs and limbs. Sterilize pruning shears with bleach water between cuts. Paint cuts with Bordeaux or other wound dressing.

**Earwigs** ▪ Thin brown, chewing, beetle-like insects with forceps-like tail. Attack small plants. Spray or dust with Diazinon around plants and house foundations.

**Fire Blight** ▪ A disease caused by bacterium, characterized by twig and fruit blight, giving a burnt look to foliage. Cut off infected branches. Sterilize pruning shears with bleach water between cuts. (See Dieback.)

**Fungal Diseases** ▪ Cause Black Spot, Leaf Curl, and Blights. Spray with fungicides such as Benomyl, Captan, Funginex, or Daconil.

**Grasshoppers** ▪ Chew anything growing. Spray foliage with Sevin or Orthene.

**Grubs** ▪ See June Bugs.

**June Bugs** (Japanese Beetles) ▪ Brown, erratic flying, hard-shell, chewing beetles. The larval stage over-winters as grub worms, small white curved insects. At 3" to 6" deep they eat roots doing major damage to grasses. With Fescue lawn grass, eradicate in early summer. For St. Augustine, treat 6 weeks after main June Bug flight, with Dursban as recommended on container.

**Lace Bugs** ▪ Flat dark sucking insects that cause leaves to look bleached or stippled or have brown specks on underside. Attack Azaleas, Pyracantha, other plants. Summer oil is the preferred preventive choice. If infested, spray with Malathion, Diazinon, or Orthene. Repeat, taking care to reach underside of leaves.

**Leaf Hoppers** ▪ Thin wedge-shaped chewing bugs that stay underneath leaves. Will stipple foliage and make it yellow. Most plants affected. Spray with Malathion under leaves. Rarely a serious pest on turf or ornamentals in our area.

**Leaf Miners** ▪ Chewers that tunnel between upper and lower leaf surfaces. Affect Yaupon Holly, Boxwood, many others. Spray with Diazinon, Malathion, or Lindane when leaves are half mature, when mature, and again 6 weeks later, taking care to reach underside of leaves.

**Leaf Rollers** ▪ Caterpillars which feed inside the rolled up leaf of host plant. Some eat bugs or make webs. Affect Redbud, Caladiums, Cannas, and others. Spray with Malathion, Orthene, or Diazinon; dust with *Bacillus thuringiensis*.

**Leaf Spots** ▪ Dark spots on leaves. Bad enemy of Chrysanthemums, Indian Hawthorn and Photinia. Keep leaves dry by watering early in the day and improving air circulation. Rake fallen leaves to reduce chance of re-infestation. Apply fungicide.

**Mealy Bugs** ▪ Soft-oval, waxy cottony insects; often cluster at axils or at branch crotches. Suck juices from plants; real menace to indoor plants, particularly African violets. For mild infestation, remove bugs with toothpick wrapped in cotton, then dipped into alcohol or soapy water. Spray with horticultural oil, insecticide soap, or Diazinon.

**Midges** ▪ Gnats or flies which cause fungus on house plants. Nuisance insect. Spray with Diazinon or Methoxychlor for 2 days in succession, wetting soil around plants with spray.

**Mildew** ▪ White, powdery growth causing deformed leaves, buds. Affects Crape Myrtle, Roses, many other plants. Use lime-sulfur during winter dormancy. Spray with Benomyl, Funginex, Daconil, Phaltan, Actidone PM (none on edible crops) or summer oil.

**Mistletoe** (Parasitic plant) ▪ Prune before berries ripen so birds will not spread seeds. Prune branch at least one foot back from attachment site to completely remove embedded roots. If growing on trunk or limb larger than 2" or more in diameter, cut out repeatedly until it stops growing. Paint wounds with tree dressing to protect against oak wilt. Disinfect tools after pruning to prohibit spreading any fungus or disease.

**Mites** ▪ Tiny, spider-like. Stunt growth and web foliage, which has yellow or rusty look. Affects Arborvitae, Roses, fruit trees, Bermudagrass, Violets, Tomatoes, Marigolds, nearly all plants. Many miticides on market. Drench plants with spray of Kelthane, summer oil, insecticidal soaps, or other labeled insecticides. Mites love weeds — get rid of them. Do not compost infected plants as this can spread infestations.

**Moths** ▪ Like butterflies, but active at night. Moth caterpillars can damage plants.

**Nematodes** ▪ Microscopic roundworms. Make plants weak, lose color, die. Affect roots of Chrysanthemums, bulbs, Begonias, 1400 others. Plant cereal Ryegrass in the fall as a trap crop. Nematodes become entangled in hair-like roots and die.

**Pecan Casebearer** ▪ May destroy crop of Texas Pecans. However, case bearer doesn't hurt tree, only fruit. Spray with Dursban. Because spray dates depend upon the year's weather, always check with the local County Extension office for more precise timing. Generally late May in the Dallas area.

**Pecan Scab** ▪ Destroys crop; leaves blacken and drop; lesions on nuts. Plant resistant varieties recommended by nursery. Treat as Casebearers.

**Pecan Weevil** ▪ Young nuts shrivel and die; grubs in mature nuts. Treat as Casebearers.

**Pill Bugs** ▪ See Sowbugs.

**Pine Tip Moth** ▪ Until recently only in Southeastern forest. Now in Metroplex. Attacks growing tip of pines. Sign of infestation is die back. Treatment - spray with dormant oil, lime-sulfur spray, Lindane, Dursban, or Permethrin.

**Plant Bugs** ▪ Varieties include the Four-lined plant bug and the Tarnished plant bug. Chew foliage of everything, leaving darkened buds, spotted leaves. Spray with Malathion.

**Red Spider** ▪ See Mites.

**Roly-Poly** ▪ See Sowbugs.

**Root Rot** ▪ See Cotton Root Rot.

**Rust** ▪ Fungi that cause brownish or orange pustules or gall affects Junipers, Roses, and Crabapple. Dust with sulfur or spray with Bayleton or Daconil. Rust remedy is not to plant Junipers near Rose family members.

**Scale Insects** ▪ Thin white males, brown females. Sucking insects.

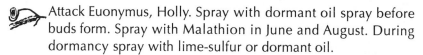Attack Euonymus, Holly. Spray with dormant oil spray before buds form. Spray with Malathion in June and August. During dormancy spray with lime-sulfur or dormant oil.

**Slugs and Snails ▪** A slug is a snail without a shell. They are night feeders that eat holes in plant leaves near the ground. Best controlled by use of baits containing Metaldehyde. Try a home made trap: cut a tin can in half lengthwise, fasten to a piece of thin scrap lumber. Put the bait under the can and it will lure the snails. Protect pets.

**Soft Rot ▪** Horrible-smelling bacteria following insect damage. Bad nuisance to rhizome-type flowers as Iris, Calla Lilies, vegetables. To control borers, plant Iris in sunny spots, divide when too thick. Burn affected roots and rhizomes. Treat rhizomes with sulfur during transplant.

**Sowbugs ▪** Not really insects but Crustaceans. Segmented bodies roll up into balls. 7 pairs of legs. Love damp spots. Found in all flower beds and around house foundations. When abundant they will eat tender plants and flowers. Use bait or spray plants with Permethrin.

**Tent Caterpillars ▪** 2" long, black with white stripe down back, spots, long hairs. Make weblike nests in branches of most trees. Cut out webs before caterpillars leave. Wrap in paper and burn. Do not burn in trees which is harmful and dangerous. Spray with Dursban, Permethrin, Malathion, Sevin, *Bacillus thuringiensis*.

**Ticks ▪** Pests to man and beast. Sucking insects. Spray yard with Diazinon, Malathion or Dursban.

**Thrips ▪** Slender, rasping insects, black or yellow, winged or wingless. Leaves on plants are silvered, streaked, spotted. Affect Gladiolus, Privet. Difficult to control. Spray with Diazinon or Orthene.

**Webworms ▪** Pale yellow worms with black spots, hairy. Make webs on tree branches, fill webs with black pellets of excrement. Treat with spray of Malathion, *Bacillus thuringiensis*, Diazinon, Sevin. Cut off infected branches and burn.

**Whiteflies ▪** Tiny white moths that suck under foliage, leave black mold. Affect Gardenias and other plants. Use dormant spray before budding. Spray with summer oil or Orthene.

**Wilt ▪** A soil fungus that works through roots. Yellows foliage of Tomato, Gladiolus, Snapdragons, Petunias. Buy wilt-resistant kinds. Use new planting locations. Burn affected plants. No known control.

# ANIMAL REPELLENTS

**Armadillos** ▪ Blood meal
**Birds** ▪ Netting material
**Cats & Dogs** ▪ Commercial dry or liquid repellent - Sulfur dust
**Deer** ▪ Lemon oil, moth crystals, dry mustard
**Field Mice** ▪ Lemon oil, camphor, moth crystals
**Rabbits** ▪ Lemon oil, kerosene, moth crystals, blood meal
**Raccoons** ▪ Trap and release
**Squirrels** ▪ Trap and release

# TRAPS & ANIMAL PICKUP

**Wild animal traps may be borrowed** from Texas Animal Damage Control Specialists at Texas Agricultural Extension Service (214) 904-3053.

**Traps and animal pickup** can be arranged with City of Dallas Animal Control.

**City of Dallas: East District; Oak Cliff**
(214) 670-7430
525 Shelter Place, Dallas, TX 75203
Hours: 8 a.m.-5 p.m. Monday -Saturday

**City of Dallas: West District; Pleasant Grove**
(214) 670-8226
8414 Forney Road, Dallas, TX 75227
Hours: 8 a.m.- 5 p.m. Monday-Saturday

**Highland Park:**
(214) 521-5000
Hours: 7:30 a.m. - 5:00 p.m. Monday-Friday (except Wednesday)
        7:30 a.m. - 12:30 p.m. Wednesday and Saturday

**University Park:**
(214) 987-5371
Hours: 8:00 a.m. - 4:00 p.m. Monday-Friday

# Chapter 7

# T R E E S

*Planting* ❧ *Fertilizing* ❧ *Protecting* ❧ *Pruning*
*Deciduous* ❧ *Evergreen* ❧ *Flowering*

Plant trees for beauty, grace, the future, shade and for cleaner air. Plant trees to enhance your property value. Plant trees for wildlife habitats. Plant small trees, medium trees. Love trees. Protect trees. Enjoy trees.

In this section following general hints, Trees are divided into Deciduous, Evergreen and Flowering.

## PLANTING

Buy trees from a reputable nurseryman, preferably one who is Texas Certified. Roadside tree peddlers may offer lower prices, but you get no assurance of the quality, or even the species of the plant. A tree may live 40 years or longer in the landscape: Make sure the one you plant is a good one. Trees are sold as bare root, balled-and-burlapped or grown in containers of various sizes.

**Bare-rooted** deciduous trees with all soil removed from roots are sold in the dormant season, which is the only time it is safe to plant them *(see p. 6)*. The roots may be dry, so soak overnight in a bucket of water, then heel it into a vacant bed until you are ready to plant. To heel it in, store it on its side in a trench and cover it with soil. When ready to plant your tree, prune broken and dead roots and place it in a hole just large enough to accommodate it. Root stimulators *(see p. 172)* are recommended. Fill the hole with topsoil to the crown level of the plant and water in well. The plant should bud out and put on new growth in the spring.

**Balled-and-burlapped (B&B)** trees can be planted anytime during the year, but are most successfully dug and planted during mid to late winter. The hole should be large enough for the tree to fit in easily. If secured with twine or wire, clip and remove to prevent girdling later as the trunk expands. Do not remove the burlap, as it holds the ball intact and will decay naturally. In the dense soils of the Metroplex, testing the hole for drainage may be useful. Before planting, fill the hole with water and allow it to drain for 24 hours. If drainage is incomplete, add several inches of gravel at the bottom of the hole. After planting, fill with topsoil and water in thoroughly. A B&B tree must be kept moist (not wet) for two full growing seasons before it can be expected to regenerate severed roots and penetrate the burlap.

**Container grown** trees also can be planted anytime during the year. Simply remove the plastic containers and place the trees in the ground. They suffer no transplant shock, as they have been container-grown from seeds and they will begin to grow as soon as the soil is warm and watered. Always purchase a guaranteed tree because if the nursery fails to increase the container size as a tree grows, its roots may begin to circle inside the container. This will delay or prevent its establishment in the landscape. If the roots are simply crowded, it may be beneficial to make several vertical cuts into the root ball, then the roots can be straightened and loosened by pulling them apart.

The following suggestions for staking come from the Master Gardeners class notes provided by the Dallas County Agent. **Staking** — A general rule of thumb is to provide support for all bare-root trees over 8' in height. Also trees 6" or more in diameter should be supported. Smaller B&B or container grown trees do not usually need support. A single stake three-quarters the height of the bare-root tree should be driven 2" to 4" from the center of the planting hole so that the stake will be on the southwest side of the tree trunk. This should be done before the tree is placed in the hole. Fasten the tree to the stake with wire inserted into a rubber hose to prevent injury to the bark as the tree moves in the wind. Another method of supporting small trees is to use two parallel stakes driven at least 18" into firm soil on opposite sides of the tree about 1' from the planting hole. The height above ground should be two-thirds the height of the tree. The tree is then supported by wires attached to the stakes and then inserted into a piece of rubber hose and looped around the trunk of the tree. A third method is to fasten three guy wires to stakes and then the wire is fastened two-thirds up the trunk by a loose loop covered with a rubber hose. All support should be removed from the small trees within 1 year after planting. Remember: a staked tree becomes a weak tree.

Soil Amendments (such as peat moss, loam, sand) are expensive and may be detrimental to plant growth. The tree must establish itself in local soils if it is to survive here. Fill the hole with the best possible amendment for your tree — the topsoil removed when the hole was dug.

## FERTILIZING

The feeder roots of trees lie near the soil surface. Eighty percent of a tree's root system will lie in the top 10" of the soil. Therefore, root fertilizers that are drilled more than 10" into the soil may be burrowed too deeply. Perhaps the best way to fertilize trees is with a conventional broadcast lawn fertilizer spreader, providing surface application. Using a complete fertilizer (12-12-12), apply 1 to 2 pounds per inch of trunk diameter at breast height. It is not necessary to feed trees for the first year after installation. Commercial tree "spikes" are a simplified way to add nutrients. Many trees (Mesquite, Desert Willow, and others suited for xeriphytic landscapes) may not thrive in heavily fertilized lawns. Other trees (Pecan) may put on soft, vegetative growth and become susceptible to early freeze damage if irrigated and fertilized late in the growing season. Sweet Gums and Maples often become chlorotic because they are unable to take up iron from the high pH (alkaline) soils of the Metroplex. Fertilizing with chelated iron and soil-acidifying sulfur is sometimes recommended, but these additives are insufficient to correct the problem for poorly adapted species and, at best, will have only a temporary effect. The Rules for Fertilizing Trees should be (1) Select well adapted species that will not become chlorotic; and (2) Don't fertilize unless the tree shows nutrient deficiency symptoms.

## PROTECT EXISTING TREES

Tree survival depends on its root system. Two-thirds of the ground under the tree's leaf canopy radius must not be disturbed. Do not dig flower beds or cover above ground level roots of old, beloved trees. If changing the soil grade of the site for other reasons, leave a circle of original level soil around the base of tree. During construction do not allow machine access or storage of materials within this magic radius. Install temporary fencing to protect valued, irreplaceable trees.

## PRUNING

Pruning is done for the following reasons: to train the plant, maintain plant health, restrict growth, and to improve quality of flowers, fruit, foliage and stems.

### WHEN TO PRUNE

**Winter** ▪ December 1 to February 15. This is the most important one when all summer blooming shrubs may be trimmed heavily. Do not start too early; wait for the dormant period. Valentine's Day is the time for pruning roses. Coniferous evergreens including the families of Juniper, Cypress, and Arborvitae may be trimmed in time for Christmas decorations.

**Spring** ▪ Just after the bloom, prune spring-flowering trees and shrubs (Spireas, Japanese Quince, Climbing Roses, etc.) which should be pruned only once a year, just after they have finished blooming.

**Summer** ▪ June 15 to August 31. This is the time to shape up formal broadleaf evergreens and hedges. It should not be done later than August so that the new growth which comes on after pruning may have a chance to harden before cold weather.

## HOW TO PRUNE

1. Take out all dead wood, making a clean cut. Tools must be sharp. Cuts can be sealed with latex house paint.
2. Branches that cross each other causing friction should be taken out. Preserve only the strongest and healthiest branches.
3. Cut suckers/adventitious branches, awkward branches.
4. Do not top. Topping is the cuttingtops off of the tall leader branches.
5. When cutting consider views trees hide such as neighbor's garage, telephone wires, and leave blocking branches where appropriate.
6. When old and scraggly, cut shrubs to the ground. New growth will return to add life, beauty, foliage, and blossom.

## REFERENCES

Brooklyn Botanic Garden *Pruning Handbook*
*Sunset Pruning Handbook*

## DECIDUOUS SHADE TREES

**Ash** *Fraxinus spp.* ▪ The **Texas Ash** F. *texensis* escarpment, shallow soil, fast growing. Small 30-45' native tree. Good fall color. Low water requirement. The **Green Ash** F. *pennsylvanica* grows to 80' along streams and the **White Ash** F. *americana* to 100', drought tolerant natives. The **Arizona Ash** F. *velutina* is not recommended.

**Bois D'Arc** *Maclura pomifera* ▪ Height to 40', thorns, large green fruit, spreading root system. A very tough tree. Dioecious, so select a tree with male flowers to prevent fruiting. Also a thornless cultivar "White Shield". Glorious old shade trees beautify our city.

**Catalpa** *Catalpa bignonioides* (Indian Bean Tree) ▪ An irregularly shaped, spreading tree to 50', the Catalpa has large leaves, orchid-like blooms, and long, persistent seed pods. Limbs are weak. Not acceptable for a home landscape.

**Chinaberry** *Melia azedarach* ▪ Fast-growing tree to 40', dark green foliage and fragrant lilac flowers in the spring, followed by clusters of translucent yellow berries. Grows in any soil. Like the Catalpa (see above) a messy tree with weak branches. Frequently seen along roadsides, fence rows, and disturbed areas. The variety "Umbraculiformis" is sold as the Texas Umbrella tree. Oriental native.

**Cottonwood** *Populus deltoides* ▪ Refer to Poplars *(See p. 70).*

**Cypress, Bald** *Taxodium distichum* ▪ Height to 50', open pyramidal growth when mature. Good in variety of moisture conditions. Attractive in well-manicured lawns. Bagworms. Fairly drought tolerant once established.

**Elm** *Ulmus spp.* ∎ The **Cedar Elm** U. *crassifolia,* and the nearly identical **Winged Elm** U. *alata,* are attractive and hardy shade trees well-adapted in the Metroplex. Few insect or disease problems. Height to 50', yellow fall color. The stately **American Elm** U. *americana,* also does well, but is much larger, to about 80' when mature. Not for small landscapes. Because Dutch Elm Disease may be halted by Texas heat, this grand tree is recommended. Yellow fall color. The true **Chinese, or Lacebark Elm** U. *parvifolia,* is a lovely small tree to about 30' with pinkish bark — remarkably drought tolerant. No serious pests. One of our better introduced trees. However, the **Siberian Elm** U. *pumila,* widely planted in West Texas, is a nuisance tree that is occasionally planted in the Dallas area. Although achieving great height to 80' and providing good shade, it is very susceptible to the elm leaf beetle which causes defoliation in mid to late summer. Many people confuse the Lacebark and the Siberian Elm, considering both the "Chinese" Elm. The **Japanese Zelkova**, *Zelkova serrata,* a member of the Elm family, occasionally is used as a substitute for elms. It has a more erect habit, grows to about 40', has few pest problems, yellow fall foliage color and is drought tolerant.

**Ginkgo** *Ginkgo biloba* ∎ The ginkgo is not widely planted in our area; it is slow growing and not particularly drought hardy. In the East it grows to 100', but in the Metroplex rarely reaches 40'. Attractive, spreading tree. Interesting fan-shaped leaves, nearly pest free. Plant male-flowering tree, as the fruit is very messy. "Autumn Gold" has yellow fall color; "Pendula" is a weeping form; "Fairmount" is upright.

**Golden Rain Tree** *Koelreuteria paniculata* ∎ Winter hardy and drought-tolerant, this 30' tree flowers yellow in the spring and provides attractive fruit pods through the fall. Menaced by the Box Elder bug. K. *bipinnata,* found in Houston landscapes, is not as cold hardy.

**Hackberry** *Celtis laevigata* (Sugarberry) ∎ Easily propagated by birds, a common existing tree in the Blackland Prairie. the shade it gives to the parched land allows shallow roots to receive moisture and other plants to exist. Can stand severe drought and low fertility. If watered, a fast growing shade tree. Short life span.

**Honey Locust** *Gleditsia triacanthos* ∎ A drought-tolerant spreading tree which reaches 60'. Select only the thornless and fruitless cultivars. Several new introductions are available.

**Maples** *Acer spp.* ∎ Several of the Southwestern native Maples have shown tolerance to basic Dallas soils: the Rubrum (red) Maples, "Drummond" and "October Glory". Other species do well in the

Metroplex: the **Bigtooth** A.*grandidentatum* from the Guadalupe Mountains, the **Caddo** A. *saccharum subsp.saccharum* native to Limestone out cropping and **Trident Maple** (*buergeranum*). Most other maples suffer from iron chlorosis and the heat of the summer sun in the metroplex. The **Silver Maple** A. *saccharinum* is a weak-branched tree that is susceptible to borers and other pests. It should not be planted. The **Box Elder** A. *negundo* a native maple that grows to the Tarrant County Line. Dallasites who attempt to landscape with cultivars of the lovely **Japanese Maples** A. *palmatum* generally are successful only when they plant in acid amended soils in shady locations *(See p. 32)*. The sugar Maples of the East will not thrive in Dallas.

**Mesquite** *Prosopis spp.* ▪ Native, drought-tolerant, many-branched small tree to about 25'. Early spring leaves are lime in color and lacy in appearance, and the yellow flowers are attractive. Old trees provide a picturesque form. An excellent choice for Southwestern landscapes. Does not survive in heavily watered and fertilized locations.

**Mimosa** *Albizia julibrissin* ▪ Attractive in spring when it flushes with fragrant pink flowers, it produces a great number of brown seed pods and harbors the Mimosa webworm and disease (vascular wilt). The Mimosa is also brittle and comes apart in windstorms and under ice and snow loads. Grows to 25'.

**Mulberry** *Morus spp.* ▪ **White Mulberry** M. *alba* brought into Texas from the Orient to start a silk industry. The fruitless variety is generally grown, because like its native Texas relative, the **Red Mulberry** M. *rubra* its fruit is very messy. A weeping form is sometimes planted. Another native, the **Texas Mulberry** M. *microphylla* is more attractive with smaller leaves and a more compact growth form but has not been adequately tested as a shade tree for the Metroplex.

**Oaks** *Quercus spp.* ▪ The **Shumard Red Oak** Q. *shumardii* is the most popular deciduous Oak grown in the Metroplex. Native to the upland escarpment it is found along White Rock Creek and its tributaries. A stately, spreading tree which reaches about 50', it colors brilliantly red in the fall. A close kin, the Texas Hill Country native **Texas Red Oak** Q. *texana* is a preferred tree to plant. The **Bur Oak** Q. *macrocarpa* so named for the ring of stiff hairs that surround its large acorn cup, is a tough bottomlands Blackland Prairie native. It grows to 75' and will withstand nearby foot and automobile traffic. A xeric Oak, **Blackjack Oak** Q. *marilandica* found in Cross Timbers soils grows only 30' and does well in neutral soils. The **Chinkapin Oak** Q. *muhlenbergii* a native to Dallas area creek bottoms, is a lovely spreading tree that may reach 50' or greater. In more acid areas the **Water Oak** Q. *nigra*, **Laurel Oak** Q. *laurifolia*, **Post Oak** Q. *stelatta*, **Southern Red Oak** Q. *falcata* and **Willow Oak**

*Q. phellos* may do well. Choose local grown or species that have been adapted to our environment. Look for several introductions in nurseries including the **Sierra Oak** Q. *cannbyi*, **Monterrey Oak** Q. *polymorpha* and the Texas Hill Country's **Lacey Oak** Q. *laceyi*. A word of warning about the Oaks: The Red Oaks are susceptible to the oak wilt disease which is epidemic in Texas. The White Oaks (Bur, Chinkapin) are resistant. *(See the Oak Wilt Hot Line at end of this chapter and Live Oaks "Evergreen Trees".)*

**Pecan** *Carya illinoinensis* ■ The State Tree of Texas. In the Dallas area, the cultivars "Desirable", "Cheyenne", "Choctaw", "Cape Fear", "Shawnee", "Oconee", and "Caddo" are among those recommended by the Texas Agricultural Extension Service. Can be planted as bare root, B&B or directly out of a container. Several pests (aphids, web-webworms, case bearer, pecan weevil, phylloxera) and diseases (scab, cotton root rot, zinc deficiency, mildew) plague the Pecan. *(See p. 61)*. For shade alone no spraying is needed. For an abundance of pecans, a spraying schedule must be followed. Contact the County Agent for dates.

**Pistache** *Pistacia spp.* (Pistachio) ■ Attractive drought-tolerant trees. Good fall color, leaf color and red seed pods, like alkaline soil with good drainage. *P. chinensis* (30-60') dark leaflets — stake new trees. *P. texana* smaller, multitrunked tree — feathery texture.

**Poplars** *Populus spp.* ■ Most of the poplars are generally considered unstately and pestiferous. The **Cottonwood Tree** *Populus deltoides* is planted in parks along water features and occasionally appears in landscapes. Fast-growing, it reaches 75' and is very susceptible to borers and diseases. The female-flowering tree produces the infamous "cotton" on its seed that stops up air-conditioning systems. Its roots are invasive and may get into water and sewer lines, surface in the yard and heave sidewalks. Its large leaves drop under drought conditions. The **White Poplar** *P. alba* grows to equal height and has impressive white bark, but is no better as a landscape plant. The **Lombardy Poplar** *P. nigra italica* has a very upright growth habit to 70'. Not attractive in winter.

**Possumhaw Holly** *Ilex decidua* (Deciduous Yaupon) ■ This shrub to small tree, reaching 15', is found throughout Texas. The female-flowering tree produces berries of red or orange which remain in the winter, providing a lovely display. Excellent in native soils.

**Smoke Tree, American** *Cotinus obovatus* and **European** *C. coggygria* ■ Good fall color. Appear to be shrouded in clouds when in flower. Good as accent plants and in groupings. The Texas native variety grows larger, to 30'. Drought tolerant. Do not irrigate.

**Soapberry, Western** *Sapindus drummondi* ▪ Native to Central and West Texas, this medium to small tree may reach 40' in height, and is drought tolerant and nearly pest free. Its foliage is similar to that of the Chinese Pistache. Colors in the fall. Good for small, xeriphytic landscapes. Prone to suckering.

**Sycamore and Plane Tree** *Platanus spp.* ▪ Large, upright trees reaching 50' with leaves the size of a lumberman's hand. These trees have vigorous root systems which find their way into sewer and water lines. They drop their large leaves at the slightest drought and make a mess of a yard. Their most serious problem, however, is a complex of foliar diseases, particularly "anthrax", a bacterial infection which can kill a tree in two growing seasons. Found in older landscapes, not presently recommended.

**Sweet Gum** *Liquidambar styraciflua* ▪ This East Texas favorite grows to 50' in the Metroplex. Its star-shaped leaves provide brilliant scarlet fall color. It unfortunately needs abundant water and becomes chlorotic in the caliche soils found in many Metroplex locations. It produces abundant spiny fruit. Also fruitless variety.

**Tallow, Chinese** *Sapium sebiferum* ▪ To 25 feet. Fast-growing, but short-lived. Recommended for its brilliant reddish fall color. Has wonderful white berries to use in flower arrangements. It suckers badly and its abundant seed will insure many little progeny appearing wherever it is planted. Not cold hardy in the Metroplex and may freeze back every 2-3 years.

**Willow, Desert** *Chilopsis linearis* ▪ Similar in appearance to the Mesquite, but thornless, the Desert Willow produces large flowers of white to burgundy throughout the growing season. Does well in dry, sunny landscapes. Several of the Texas A&M varieties have excellent flower color. To 25'.

**Willow** *Salix spp.* ▪ Willows do well in wet locations. In home landscapes, their roots are very invasive and grow into water and sewer lines. Like the poplars, they drop their leaves in drought and take on an unsightly appearance. Not long lived. S. *babylonica cv. Pendula* (**Weeping Willow**): Will grow in any soil. S. *Matsudana cv. Tortuosa* (**Corkscrew Willow**) has interesting branches for flower arrangements, whether they are fresh or dry. S. *nigra* (**Black Willow**) will be found growing along our stream banks. All subject to borers.

**Vitex** *Vitex agnus-castus* ▪ Sometimes called the **Chaste Tree**, this is a small tree with aromatic leaves and fruit. Flowers attractive to bees and is widely planted where honey is marketed. The Vitex produces flowers of lilac, white, or rose color throughout the growing season. Popular in xeriphytic West Texas and in small landscapes in many locations. Grows to 15'-20'.

# EVERGREEN TREES

**Cedars, Atlas** *Cedrus atlantica* and **Deodar** C. *deodara* ▪ **Note:** The name "cedar" is misapplied to several different Junipers; there are no native cedars in the U.S. Similar in appearance, both pyramidal, large, reach 75' and spreading 30'. The Deodar may be fuller, denser, and faster growing. Some Deodar tops froze in 1983. Bagworms. Not for small landscapes.

**Cherry Laurel** *Prunus caroliniana* ▪ Evergreen, height 8-20', tall hedge or small tree with shiny green leaves, fragrant white flowers in racemes. Sun or semi-shade. Responds to rich soil. Keep trimmed. Spray for borers.

**Cypress, Arizona** *Cupressus arizonica* ▪ The cultivar "Blue Ice" has a strong blue color. "Carolina Sapphire" is a North Carolina state introduction which can take Dallas humidity. Good living Christmas tree. 30'-40' high.

**Cypress, Italian** *Cupressus sempervirens* ▪ A very slender upright tree to 50'. Rarely used in home landscapes, more appropriate among tall buildings and in cemeteries. Bagworms, spider mites and fungal disease.

**Holly** *Ilex attenuata* (Savannah) ▪ Large, conifer shaped habit, 15-25' tall. Tolerates lime soil, especially well drained. Red berries, smaller spines on leaves. Good planted singularly or as a screen. I. *opaca Fosteri* **Foster's Holly** recommended also, narrow upright. More hollies listed in Shrubs *(see p. 79)*.

**Junipers** *Juniperus spp.* ▪ Many junipers are drought tolerant and require little attention except bagworm infestation. *J. ashei* **Ashe Juniper, Mexican** or **Mountain Cedar** is the namesake plant of Cedar Hill. *Juniper virginiana* The **Eastern Red Cedar** is the tree often growing on old homesites. These two trees are the coniferous plants original settlers found when they came to this area. 40'-50' high.

**Live Oaks** *Quercus spp.* ▪ Among the 20 "live" (or evergreen) species of oaks native to Texas, the most popularly grown are the **Southern Live Oak** Q. *virginiana,* native to extreme Southeast Texas and the **Escarpment** or **Hill Country Live Oak** Q. *fusiformis* found throughout the limestone spine of the state. Unfortunately, many of the planted Live Oaks in the Dallas area are Q. *virginiana* and are not as winter hardy as the Hill Country Live Oak. Many Live Oaks were lost in Dallas after the 1983 freeze. Live Oaks are very susceptible to oak wilt disease, but are resistant to cotton root rot. Few other pests. Mealy-oak galls are harmless. The most popular shade trees in Dallas, they grow to 50' or greater. Very stately.

**Pine** *Pinus spp.* ▪ Pines are not well adapted to soils of high alkalinity. However with acid soil ammendments, the following varieties may be grown (in order of adaptability): the **Alepo** *P. halepensis*; **Austrian** *P. nigra*; **Japanese Black Pine** *P. thunbergiana* the most common choice of local gardeners, irregular shape, not pyramidal, often used as a point of interest, grows to 25'. Also, the **Scotch** *P. sylvestris*; **Loblolly** *P. taeda*; **Slash** *P. elliott*; and **Remote Pinon** *P. remota*.

**Southern Magnolia** *Magnolia grandiflora* ▪ Large, spreading pyramidal tree reaching 60' in height and 30' in width, famed for large, dark-green leaves and white flowers. Not for small landscapes. Requires abundant water to thrive well. Many good cultivars available. As the smaller, "Little Gem", with rusty-colored leaf undersurfaces, which may reach 20' in 20 years. Columnar habit.

**Wax-Myrtle** *Myrica cerifera* ▪ An understory shrub in much of the Southeastern U.S., the Wax-Myrtle has found a new home in Dallas landscapes when trained as a small tree or used as a shrub. Similar in appearance to the Yaupon *(see below)*, it is hardy to our winters and soils. Grows to 20'. Bay scented leaves.

**Yaupon Holly** *Ilex vomitoria* ▪ Native to Central Texas, this small tree, to 25', may be the most popular landscape plant in Texas. It is hardy, drought-tolerant, nearly pest-free and attractive with small red berries on the female-flowering plant. Suited to small landscapes. Good varieties: Pride of Houston and Jewel Ornamental. For minature Yaupons, refer to Shrubs *(see p. 79)*.

## FLOWERING TREES

**Apricots** and **Peaches** *Prunus spp.* ▪ There are many cultivars of these small trees which flower from red to white and pink to peppermint, beginning in February. Most require well-drained soils and occasional pruning. To 20'. **A Note of Caution:** *Prunus spp.* are susceptible to cotton root rot and borers.

**Crabapple** *Malus spp.* ▪ Many varieties of these red-rose-white-flowering small trees. To about 15'. Watch for borers. Susceptible to cotton root rot. Fruit makes good jelly.

**Crape Myrtle** *Lagerstroemia indica* ▪ *(See pp. 77-78)*.

**Dogwood** *Cornus florida* ▪ Much-heralded, white-to-pink-flowering small tree of the South, plant only in amended, well-drained soils. A beautiful, showy tree in the spring with its flowers and the winter with its red fruit which attract birds. May reach 20' in Dallas. *C. drummondii* (**Rough-leafed Dogwood**) Dallas Native, thrives in unammended soil, small white spring blooms, good berries.

**Eve's Necklace** *Sophora affinis* ▪ Small tree native to Dallas County, pendulous pale pink flowers in the spring, chain like seed pod. Needs well-drained soil.

**Fringe Tree** *Chionanthus virginicus* ▪ (Grancy Graybeard) Narrow head, fragrant white flowers, blue-black fruit. Requires rich, moist soil, prefers shade. 15-25'.

**Hawthorn** *Crataegus spp.* ▪ Several native varieties suited for Metroplex soils. C. *mollis*, C. *reverchonii*, C. *virdis* and C. *crus-galli* — small to 30', attractive white flowers, small fall fruit, thorns. Best grown in xeriphitic conditions. C. *phaenopyrum* — least prone to fire blight.

**Magnolias** *Magnolia spp.* ▪ Oriental is the common name for the deciduous flowering small tree. **Saucer Magnolia** M. *x soulangiana* has purple, pink or white blooms before leafing out. **Star Magnolia** M. *stellata* has star shaped fragrant flowers. Plant in protected location with ammended soil. *(See p. 73* – the evergreen Southern Magnolia).

**Pear, Callery** *Pyrus calleryana* ▪ These ornamental pears flower abundantly and put on a bright and beautiful white show early in the spring. They produce no fruit, and reach only about 25', so they are suitable for small landscapes. Due to their upright growth habit they are attractive as tree-form hedges and in groupings. The "Bradford" cultivar is widely used, but may break apart under snow or ice loads and in high winds. "Aristocrat" and "Capital" are gaining wider respect among nurserymen and landscapers.

**Persimmon** *Diospyros virginiana* (Winter Plum, Possumwood) ▪ Native good for Blackland Cross Timbers and Grand Prairie. **Japanese Persimmon** D. *kaki* many cultivars with orange fruit in fall.

**Plum, Mexican** *Prunus mexicana* ▪ Native to the area, this hardy tree produces a show of white flowers before leafing out in early spring and provides yellow to orange fall color. Scattered thorns with exfoliating bark. Small, attractive fruit. Excellent for small landscapes, reaching only about 15'.

**Plum, Purple** *Prunus cerasifera* ▪ Very popular small ornamental tree which produces bronze to purple foliage after pink spring flowers. Reaches only 15'. Susceptible to borers and may be damaged under snow or ice loads.

**Redbud, Eastern** *Cercis canadensis* ▪ Very popular small tree which flowers pink, white or double in early spring. May reach 30' in a landscape. Recently two new color forms have been introduced: the "White Texas" and the "Oklahoma". The Texas-native **Mexican Redbud** C. *canadensis* var. *mexicana* and **Texas Redbud** C. *canadensis* var. *texensis* have smaller leaves reflecting the xeric habitats of the western parts of the state. They grow only to about 20' and should be used where rainfall or irrigation is minimal. "Forest Pansy" has handsome bronze to purple foliage.

**Rusty Blackhaw** *Viburnum rufidulum* ▪ Shrub or small tree typically 15'-20', this species is native to the Dallas area. Flowers white in spring, has reddish fall color and dark blue berries in late summer. A low maintenance, hardy native. Dependable.

**Texas Mountain Laurel** *Sophora secundiflora* (Mescal Bean Tree) ▪ Handsome evergreen with fragrant blue-purple flowers in spring. Protect from cold. Stands heat and drought and likes well-drained sandy loam. S. *japonica* (**Japanese Pagoda**) has showy yellow-white blooms in summer.

## REFERENCES

*Rodale's Chemical Free, Yard & Garden* by F. Bradley, Rodale Press, 1991.

*A Field Guide to Texas Trees* by Benny Simpson, Texas Monthly Press, 1988.

## ORGANIZATIONS

**Historical Tree Coalition**
660 Preston Forest Center, Suite 407
Dallas, Texas 75230
(214) 739-5886
Fax: (972) 286-6628
e-mail address: treesavers@aol.com

**Oak Wilt Hot Line**   (512) 473-3517

**Trinity Blacklands Forestry Council**
2121 San Jacinto, Suite 820
Dallas, Texas 75201
(214) 953-1190

**Shade Keepers**
An adult citizen forestry program of the Dallas Trees and Parks Foundation
Mike Bradshaw
(214) 953-1184

# Chapter 8

## SHRUBS

*Medium size (1' to 6'), multi-stemmed, woody plants*
*whose branches remain close to the ground. Whether they are let to*
*grow naturally or pruned into hedges, shrubs give definition*
*to any landscape. Most broad leafed evergreen shrubs are not native.*
*Many have flowering phases.*

## PLANTING

In transplanting, generally dig a deeper hole than required, put sharp sand in the bottom and half-fill the hole with peat moss or leaf mold. Set the plant, water and add more soil to the level of the ground and water again. Set plants at height to allow for settling. A good practice at the time of planting is to water with a root stimulator mixed in to prevent wilting and to give plants a good start. Use mulches to add nutrients and conserve water. For pruning refer to Trees *(see p. 66)*.

## REVITALIZING LONG-PLANTED SHRUBS

Root-prune old foundation shrubs to invigorate and make them more vibrant, especially if they have been in the same location 5 or more years. Take a sharp spade and slice down to cut the roots 18" from main stalk. Good for Burford Hollies, Abelia and Nandina.

## ALPHABETIZED PLANT LIST

**Abelia** *Abelia x grandiflora* (Glossy Abelia) ▪ Evergreen, height 3-6', leaves brownish tint, flowers light pink nine months, drought resistant, sun or shade. Ordinary soil, useful as a hedge. "Edward Goucher" — pink, slightly larger flowers; "Compacta" and "Prostrata", height 1-3'. Good foliage for arrangements.

**Althea** *Hibiscus syriacus* (Rose-of-Sharon) ▪ Deciduous, height to 8', upright, coarse growth, flowers white, pink, bluish in variety, single or double. Summer bloom, easy culture, sun. Diana — white, larger flowers, 6". Woodbridge – rose colored; Ardens — light purple.

**Arborvitae** *Thuja* ▪ Evergreen, tall, narrow-leaf. Not suitable for foundation planting. Avoid. Needs lot of water. Bagworms.

**Aucuba** *Aucuba japonica* ▪ Evergreen, upright bushy growth to 8'. Glossy green leaves, bright red fruit. Needs moist well-drained clay loam. Shade necessary as leaves sun scald. "Serratifolia" — dark green leaves; "Variegata" (Gold Dust) — green leaves with gold spots.

**Azalea** ▪ Refer to Chapter 9 *(see p.84).*

**Bamboo** *Bambusa* ▪ Most varieties evergreen, grow tall in sun or shade. Better to avoid on city lots as it presents too many problems with root suckers popping up everywhere. Best if grown in container.

**Barberry** *Berberis: B. mentorensis* (Mentor barberry) ▪ Evergreen, height 3-4', leaves dark green, fruit dark dull red. Sun or semi-shade, any garden soil, withstands heat and drought. B. *Thunbergii* var. *atropurpurea* has bronzy-red foliage all summer. Prefers full sun and is deciduous. "Crimson Pigmy" — height 1-3', sun, red foliage, useful hedge material.

**Boxwood** *Buxus:* B. *microphylla* var. *japonica* ▪ Japanese or Korean box. Evergreen, height to 8', leaves light green, tips may winter-kill, ordinary soil, sun or shade. May be clipped for hedge.

**Broom** *Cytisus racemosus* (Sweet Broom) ▪ Evergreen to 6', fine foliage, inclined to sprawl, yellow spring flowers, easy culture, any good garden soil.

**Butterfly Bush** *Buddleia davidii* (Summer Lilac) ▪ Height to 10', flowers in long spikes, many colors in variety, fragrant summer bloom, sun, may freeze back in winter. Heavily prune in February to encourage growth and blooms. Attractive to bees and butterflies.

**Camellia** ▪ Refer to Chapter 9 *(see p. 88).*

**Cenizo** *Leucophyllum frutescens* (Texas Sage) ▪ Deciduous, 6-8', dry chalky soils, full sun, xeriphitic, silvery foliage, purple flowers in August. Tolerates wind and heat, but no irrigation.

**Chinese Evergreen Witch-hazel** *Loropetalum chinense* (burgundy) ▪ Purple leaf with magenta flowers. Height 8" to 4', partial shade, moisture, winter blooming November-March. Add organic material to surrounding soil.

**Cleyera** *Cleyera japonica* ▪ Evergreen, neat, small shrub up to a tree of 25', leaves glossy dark green, leathery, flowers 2-3 axillary, fruit a black berry. Cultivate as Camellia to which it is related. Excellent foliage plant. Hardy in this area.

**Cotoneaster** *Cotoneaster apiculatus* (Cranberry Coton-easter) ▪ Deciduous to 6', shiny green leaves grey underside, flowers pink in spring, fruit red berries, persist through winter. C. *glaucophyllus* — semi-evergreen to 7', leaves grey, arching branches. Will espalier. Subject to fire-blight. Other varieties under Ground Covers.

**Crape Myrtle** *Lagerstroemia indica* ▪ A favorite shrub, easy to grow, with long blooming period and foliage which has fall color. Blooms in a variety of colors: watermelon red, lavender, pink, white and salmon with new colors and cultivars yearly. Crape Myrtle is one of the most decorative accents available for landscaping.

Few nurserymen refer to the Crape Myrtle by its botanical name, but rather classify it as: Dwarf (less than 5'); semi-dwarf (less than 12'); intermediate (12' to 20'); regular (30' to 40') or weeping (less than 4').

There are no special soil requirements. Plant in full sun with good air circulation before hot weather. Fertilize occasionally and lightly with 5-10-5. Super-phosphate made available to the tree or shrub before bloom-time will reward you with much larger flowers. Mulch generously. Keep well-watered while flowering.

To keep a fresh look to your garden, after blooming prune back just below the withered bloom or the seed pod that forms after the bloom. This will achieve a more continuous bloom.

After leaves have gone in the winter, prune for shape. Crape Myrtle blooms on new wood each year, therefore do not be afraid to prune severely. This is especially true for Tree Crape Myrtle. Prune all the present year's growth back if you wish to keep the same size. Current styles cancel major topiary or blunt branch pruning as they weaken the tree. Pencil size twigs are recommended pruning.

If there is too much rain or if water spray is allowed to get on the leaves of the plant or tree, you may have mildew. Watch for it and use the proper control. Treat immediately with Soda Spray *(see p. 54)*. It is wiser to spray for prevention of mildew. Aphid control *(see p. 15)*.

Whether used as a border, background or tree, Crape Myrtle gives a lacy effect and softens the lines of any garden.

**Deutzia** *Deutzia gracilis* ▪ Deciduous to 8'. Vase-like growth, floriferous (flowers white through red in panicles) in early summer. Short-lived in our heat and blackland soil.

**Elaeagnus** *Elaeagnus pungens* (Silverberry) ▪ Evergreen, height 4-8', grey-green leaves, hedges well, useful as espalier if tied to wires. Prune and use exuberant spikes in flower arrangements. Ordinary soil. Disease and pest free. Fragrant small flowers.

E. *macrophylla*: More compact.

**Euonymus** *Euonymus*: E. *japonica* ▪ Evergreen, height 6-20', many varieties *(see p. 96)*. Hedges well, full sun or shade. Scale is a problem, also powdery mildew. Avoid unless prepared to keep these pests under control.

E. *alata*: Deciduous, height to 8', bushy, likes deep soil. Beautiful fall color if planted in full sun.

**Forsythia** *Forsythia*: F. *suspensa* ■ Deciduous, height to 6', yellow flowers, on long sprays in very early spring. Sun, loamy soil, short-lived. Prune only after bloom. New cultivars: "Lynwood Gold", "Spring Glory", and "Beatrix Farrand".

**Gardenia** *Gardenia jasminoides* ■ Set out B&B plants in mid-March to be well-established before winter. Need a rich, porous, acid soil, and a large free space to attain their proper growth. Gardenias suffer in extreme cold. Local nurserymen now advise considering them as an annual. The tops may look frozen but if left untrimmed, often produce a wealth of bloom in late May.
Feed in late November with a generous top dressing of manure. Keep well-soaked in the dry summer months. Feed acid fertilizer for blooming. Watch and spray for the great enemy, the white fly, on the back of the leaves. Spray 2 or 3 times at ten-day intervals to remove mold that grows on the "honey" the fly deposits on the foliage. Use soap spray *(not detergent)*. Rinse with plain water under pressure. Varieties — Mystery has large 6-8" blooms in late spring, and August Beauty has 4-6" blooms in summer. Tolerates heat well.

**Hardy Hibiscus, Rose Mallow** *Hibiscus moscheutos* ■ Sun or light shade, height 2-5', 12" flowers white, pink, or red *(see p. 76 – Althea).*
H. *Coccineus* (Texas Star):  Height 4-5', single red flowers.
H. *Mutabilis* (Confederate Rose):  Height 4-8', large double white or pink blooms.

**Hardy Orange** *Poncirus trifoliata* ■ Evergreen, height to 10', bright green leaves, thorny, white flowers, non-edible orange fruit in fall. Sun, garden soil, useful as barrier hedge.

**Hawthorn, Indian** *Raphiolepis indica* ■ Evergreen, low, spreading to 3' or more. Flowers white or pale to deep pink in spring. Light, loamy soil in sun or shade; useful as border, in planting boxes and across foundation. Many varieties. Usually disease free, but have recently suffered freeze damage.

**Holly** *Ilex*: I. *cornuta* (**Chinese Holly**) ■ Evergreen, sizes dwarf up to small tree, thorny leaves, sun or shade, loamy soil, showy red berry, no diseases. Good protective hedge.
I. *cornuta Burfordii* (**Burford Holly**) ■ Evergreen, height 3-20', leaves not as thorny as Chinese. Many varieties including dwarf. Good hedge, background, or specimen. Showy red berries on female. No diseases.
I. *vomitoria* (**Yaupon Holly**) ■ Miniature shrub form, sheers well. Hearty variety to replace boxwood. "Nana" variety low to 4'. Keep clipped. See growth habits in Trees *(see p. 73).*

**Honeysuckle** *Lonicera* fragrantissima (White Honeysuckle Bush) ∎ Large, old fashioned winter blooming shade shrub, hearty drought resistant, easy to root, oval leaves, early spring blooming, short flowers, good for force, red berries. Deciduous 6' to 10'.

*L. maachii* (Amure Bush or Maacks Honeysuckle) ∎ Sharp pointed leaves, larger, later blooms, large background shrub for sun or shade and tolerates poor drainage.

For Honeysuckle Vines *(see p. 93)* or Ground Covers *(see p. 97)*.

**Hydrangea** *Hydrangea macrophylla hortensis* ∎ This is the florist's hydrangea which does well here when planted outside. Deciduous, rounded form, upright branching habit, rich green leaves, large globular flower heads, color varying with acidity of soil. In our alkaline soil they are pink, but if aluminum sulfate is added (1 tbl. per plant watered in) before buds appear, they will be blue (some times white). Hydrangeas are hardy, require much water, partial shade and a protected site, growing best on north against the house. Prune after blooming, for new growth will furnish next year's flowers. Feed manure in the winter and a complete commercial fertilizer after blooming. Good plants can be grown from hardwood cuttings. Do all transplanting in the fall.

*H. macrophylla* ∎ "Silver variegated Mariesii" (Lace-cap hydrangea) is a good substitute for caladium. Its green and white leaves and, sometimes, its tips, freeze back in winter, but return for summer satisfaction.

*H. paniculata grandiflora* ∎ Usually shortened to "Pee-Gee", will not take the heat in this area.

*H. quercifolia* ∎ (Oak Leaf Hydrangea) Good in shaded areas. Large white flowers remain dried on shrub until fall. Deciduous.

**Hypericum** *Hypericum* (St. John's-wort) ∎ *H. patulum* "Sun-Gold" is deciduous, low, with fragrant yellow flowers and spreading growth in the sun or semi-shade. Easy.

**Japanese Fatsia** *F. japonica* ∎ Evergreen tall deeply cut glossy dark green leaves. Tropical look. Not cold tolerant. Partial shade.

**Japonica** *Chaenomeles* also *Pyrus japonica* and *Cydonia* (Flowering Quince or Burning Bush) ∎ Hardy shrub. Favorite ornamental for hedge. Early blooming, often flowers appear on bare branches for Valentine's Day. Several varieties available: white, pink, crimson, salmon and double. Prune after blooming, for new growth will furnish next year's bloom. Acid soil. Fertilize with cottonseed meal (one cupful to a medium sized plant) and commercial fertilizer. May lose leaves late in summer. Enemies – scale and aphids.

**Jasmine** *Jasminum* ∎ Several varieties having green stems, otherwise deciduous, with spreading growth to 4'. Ordinary soil, sun or semi-shade. Will espalier.

**Jessamine, Night** *Cestrum nocturnum* ∎ Bushy 6-9', creamy-yellow flowers, very fragrant by night. Likes shade.

**Juniper** *Juniperus chinensis* ∎ Very tolerant of our cold, heat and drought. Many varieties — "Pfitzerana" is evergreen, fine needles, spreads to 10', height 4'-6', dry soil, sun; "Procumbens" is prostrate.

J. *excelsa Stricta* (Spiny Greek) ∎ An interesting specimen plant. All are subject to red spider.

**Kerria** *Kerria japonica* ∎ Varieties are single and double, yellow flowers in spring, deciduous, height 4-6', slender branches.

**Ligustrum Privets** *Ligustrum* ∎ Heat tolerant but cold problems; susceptible to cotton root rot and iron deficiency.

L. *japonicum* (Japanese Ligustrum) ∎ Evergreen, 6-20', white flowers , black seed heads. Good screening hedge or small tree. Roots objectionable, crowding out other plants. Ordinary soil, sun or shade.

L. *lucidum* (Wax-leaf or Glossy Privet) ∎ Evergreen, 4-6', glossy leaves, white flowers in summer. Sun or shade, ordinary soil, wide spread, fast growing background or hedge.

L. *vulgare* (Common Privet) ∎ Evergreen, hardy, but better to avoid its voracious feeding roots. Great for topiary.

**Lilac** *Syringa vulgaris* and S. *x persica* ∎ The common and Persian lilac, deciduous, growing to 8'. Mildew and scale. Hybrid lilacs need more care and do not relish our hot summers. Other plants are better adapted to this area.

**Loquat** *Eriobotrya japonica* ∎ Evergreen 15-20', tender (many winterkill). Large leaf, useful in flower arrangements. Good background or specimen. Sun or part shade.

**Loropetalum** ∎ Refer to Chinese Evergreen Witch-hazel (see p. 77).

**Mahonia** *Mahonia:* M. *Bealei* (Leatherleaf Hollygrape) ∎ Evergreen 3-8', upright. Any soil, but requires shade. Flowers yellow in winter. Excellent specimen plant; fruit steel blue.

M. *Aquifolium* (Oregon Grape) ∎ Evergreen, height to 3', flowers yellow in spring, less shade required. Coppery red when young.

**Mock Orange** *Philadelphus* ∎ Deciduous, height 4 - 8'.

P. *Coronarius,* fragrant.

P. *x virginalis,* has large white flowers in late spring.

P. texensis, native species, small glossy leaves, small white fragrant blooms.

**Nandina** *Nandina domestica* (Heavenly Bamboo) ∎ Bamboo-like evergreen, height 4-6', flowers white, red berries in fall. Shade or full sun.

Sun gives red color to leaves, disease free. Cut back two or three canes at ground level each year to keep from being top-heavy and bare-legged. "Compacta", 4 - 5' narrower lacy leaf. "Gulf Stream", slow growing dense mound. "Harbor Dwarf" 15-20' ground cover.

**Oleander** *Nerium oleander* ▪ Evergreen but tender in this area (severely damaged 100 miles N.). Winter protect. Upright growth to 20', flowers white, red, salmon, pink, single and double. Requires sun to bloom. Good in pots. Leaves and stems extremely poisonous.

**Parkinsonia** *Parkinsonia aculeata:* (Jerusalem Thorn, Ratama or Horse Bean) ▪ Deciduous, hedge or small tree, showy spring bloom, clustered yellow flowers, drooping long leaf. Not winter hardy in Metroplex.

**Photinia** *Photinia:* P. *serrulata* (Chinese Photinia) ▪ Height 6'-20'. Can be small tree with white flowers in spring, red berries in fall. Needs well-drained loam in sun or shade. Screening shrub, too tall for foundation planting. Excessive pruning can cause disease and decline which encourages black spot and leaf drop. Watch for aphids. P. x *fraseri* (Japanese Photinia) has bright red foliage on new growth. Fungal leaf spot prevalent.

**Pieris** *Pieris japonica* ▪ (Andromedia, Lily of the Valley shrub) Rounded dense shrub that likes acid amended soil. Whorls of leathery lana shaped leaves, dainty spike flowers in spring that resemble a string of pearls.

**Pittosporum** *Pittosporum:* P. *Tobira* ▪ Evergreen broad spreading growth to 8', fragrant cream flowers in spring, dense background or specimen. Our past freezing winters have decimated Pittosporum in this area. No longer recommended.

**Podocarpus** *Podocarpus macrophyllus* var. *Maki* (Japanese Yew) ▪ Evergreen upright rigid specimen, height to 15'; ordinary soil, semi-shade, winter tender.

**Pomegranate** *Punica Granatum* ▪ Deciduous, height 5-15', upright growth. Flowers single, double, white to orange red in summer, red fruit in fall. Ordinary soil, likes sun, dry feet. Winter tender. Dwarf variety available.

**Privet** ▪ Refer to Ligustrum *(see p. 81).*

**Pussy Willow** *Salix discolor* ▪ Deciduous, upright, height to 20'. Catkins in early spring (grown for these, not the foliage), not a pretty shrub or tree. Cut for dried arrangements before catkins bloom. Do not put in water unless you want them to flower. May be forced by cutting early and placing stems in water. Sun.

**Pyracantha** *Pyracantha*: P. *coccinea* (Fire Thorn) "Lalandei" ■ Evergreen, bush-type, height to 10'.˙ Flowers white in early spring, fruit red or orange in winter, thorny. Good hedge, vine, specimen or espalier. Many varieties, including dwarf and variegated. All subject to fire-blight (cut out diseased limbs), lace bugs, aphids and red spider. *(see p. 56)* for control. Cardinals love to nest in these plants. Sun.

**Quince** ■ Refer to Japonica *(see p. 80)*.

**Rhododendron** *Rhododendron* ■ Evergreen, large cluster blossoms. Acid soil required. Must be planted in raised beds or large pots as they cannot tolerate ground water. Refer to Azalea *(see p. 84)*.

**Rose-Of-Sharon** ■ Refer to Althea *(see p. 76)*.

**Spirea** *Spiraea* ■ Many varieties either spring blooming white or summer blooming pink. These flowerful shade shrubs may have winter kill.
S. *bumalda* ■ Height to 2 - 2-1/2' almost a perennial, summer bloom shaded pink.
S. *cantoniensis* ■ Height to 4 - 5', bridal wreath style with arching brances.
S. *prunifolia* ■ Height to 6', cascading bare branches with fall color.

**Thevetia** *Thevetia neriifolia* (Yellow Oleander) ■ Oleander-like foliage, yellow flowers, sandy soil. Winter protect.

**Viburnum** *Viburnum* (Snowball): V. *x carlcephalum* ■ Deciduous, hardy to -10° F. Excellent branching habit, height 6-7', can be pruned to any size. Large cluster white flowers, fragrant. Brilliant color in fall. Avoid sulphur on all viburnum as it blackens leaves.
V. *plicatum* var. *Mariesii* ■ Compact habit, fine foliage which colors in fall, large white flowers, red berries. Free of insect troubles. Many other varieties — check with nurseryman.

**Weigela** *Weigela rosea* ■ Deciduous upright, 6-8', flowers pink to red. Ordinary soil, in full sun or partial shade. Short-lived.

**Yew** ■ Refer to Podocarpus *(see p. 82)*.

**Yucca** *Yucca spp.* (Spanish Dagger) ■ Evergreen; tall white flower spears; upright growth. Leaves pointed and rigid, good as barricade planting or specimen. Frequently used with cacti and succulents. Sun.

## REFERENCES

*Flowering Shrubs*, James Underwood Crockett and Editors of Time Life Books, Time Life Book, N.Y., 1972.
*Pruning Ornamental Shrubs: A Wisely Handbook*, by John Clayton, The Royal Horticultural Society, 1973, 1986.

# Chapter 9

## AZALEAS & CAMELLIAS

*Preparation* ❧ *Maintenance* ❧ *Varieties*

Azaleas produce a profusion of brilliant early spring blooms and make a year-round evergreen foundation shrub. If you have partial shade, they are one of the easier plants to grow — Find or make a woodland-like site, construct the azalea bed with correct medium, plant healthy specimen, water, and re-plant every 7 years. You'll be delighted with the maintenance ease after the initial installation.

The Dallas chapter of the Azalea Society of America has tested and affirmed this new style of Azalea preparation detailed below. The Dallas Arboretum and Botanical Society has grown 2000 varieties using the following instructions since the fall of 1989. Take time to visit this world class collection, and note each family's attributes of bloom, leaf color, plant shape and size. Joe Lambert introduced azaleas to our area in the late 1930's. Since then, azaleas in bloom have become the sign of Spring to many area residents.

## AZALEAS

### SITE

1. Plant on east-facing exposure or against north-facing walls. Plants should be protected from hot afternoon sun by trees, shrubs, buildings, fences, etc. See Chapter Three for other planting recommendations.
2. Azaleas require light for flower development. Dense shade is not recommended, but high shade and filtered sunlight afforded by tall, well-pruned trees is especially desirable.
3. Winds can desiccate the moisture in Azalea leaves. Plant in a wind-blocked location.

### PLANT MEDIUM

1. Dallas alkaline clay-based soil will not support Azaleas. Once excavation and total soil replacement was the accepted method. Today, raised beds are advised.
2. In sandy, well-drained soils, amendments with well-composted organic materials may be the only change necessary.
3. For clay based soils, mix planting medium with 60% finely-milled Pine bark or Pecan shells, 40% coarse Canadian peat moss, and

add one pound micro-nutrient fertilizer per cubic yard. Pre-mixed,pre-wet mixes are available and recommended. Pine bark has a chemical that prevents root rot. Pecan hulls can be used instead of pine bark. Avoid Walnut hulls, which are poisonous to Azaleas, and hardwood bark containing Walnut.

4. When hand-mixing the planting medium, do not skimp on any mixing or moisture. If peat is not completely wet, your plants will not live.

## BED PREPARATION

1. Buy or mix Azalea planting medium. Remove turf and leaves from the ground. Bermudagrass is especially tough and will continue to grow through the beds if present.
2. The pine and peat moss mixture can be laid directly on existing soil without need for excavation.
3. Put 15 to 18 compacted inches of prepared azalea mix on bed location. Water, then let settle, then add more to achieve minimal 15 inches.
4. Edging, rock, or ground covers can hold bed shape and rise of soil.
5. Suggested ground covers are Dwarf Mondo Grass, Strawberry Begonia or Louisiana Phlox.

## PLANT AND TRANSPLANT

1. Initial planting and transplanting can be done year round so long as the root ball does not dry out in the process.
2. Do not raise the crown of a plant. Place new plants at the same surface level in a bed as they were in the container.
3. Place Azaleas close together. Tight plantings shade root systems with the plants' own canopies. Widely spaced plants should be mulched.
4. Cultivation of the soil near plants is damaging since Azaleas are shallow rooted with a profusion of tiny feeders near the surface.
5. Refer to Chapter Five Propagation and Planting *(see pp. 51-52)*.
6. Every seven years Azaleas should be excavated, planting medium replaced, and plants repositioned for artistic effect.

## WATER

Azaleas need fifty inches of water a year. Use foliar irrigation *(wetting of leaves is preferred to watering at the base of plants)*. Azaleas require well-drained planting medium capable of retaining some moisture.

1. Drainage is the worst problem for azaleas. With raised beds, drainage will occur naturally at the soil level.
2. If you have azaleas in excavated beds, be sure no pockets of dry

peat moss exist.

3. Root rot is the most common reason of azalea loss in excavated beds. Be sure the water is not being held in the bathtub effect, but see that drainage is available.
4. Water in the shade of the morning to avoid flower blight and leaf fungus.
5. With a sprinkler system, use above the plant foliar irrigation.
6. During summer months and bloom period, extra water is usually required.

## PRUNE

After blooming, prune Azaleas. Blooms are set by July 15th so don't prune after that date. Remove sucker foliage, often called water sprout growth, in November. Flower arrangers prune tall and erratic branches during bloom to use inside.

## DISEASE CONTROL

The fungus commonly called "die back" has been very prevalent in this area. Signs of this progressive disease is the wilting of leaves on individual branches. This fungus is easily transferable through infected garden shears. Thorough cleaning with rubbing alcohol between individual cuts discourages spreading of fungus. For "root rot" and wilt (phytophthora) use Subdue. For petal blight use Benomyl. For lace bugs use Orthene.

## CARE FOR EXISTING AZALEAS

1. For older plants, an acid-enhancing fertilizer for blooming plants (often titled Rose-Azalea mix) can be applied monthly from the end of blooming through July.
2. Topdress beds yearly after bloom with 1 to 2" of mulch.
3. Some add micronutrients into the mulch.
4. Fertilizer is not necessary for new bed cultivation (see p. 84-85).
5. If leaves turn yellow, more acid is needed. Dressings of peat moss, pine bark or chelated iron can be added for acidity. If commercial fertilizer is used, begin after blooming. Add monthly until the summer.
6. Every seven years the planting medium should be totally replaced. The original level of the Azalea root and stem should be kept constant in the new planting, but plants can be arranged differently.

## GROUPS AND SPECIES

Check with local dealers and the Dallas Arboretum & Botanical Society for newer cultivars and other hybrids grown here. Foliage color on red blooms is bronze, white bloom foliage is yellow-green.

The **Kurume** (Japanese) ■ Always attractive with dense evergreen foliage, compact growth covered with small flowers when in bloom. It is the hardiest for our area. The red Hinodegiri and Coral Bells are the varieties on Preston Road.

**Bloom Colors:**
**Red** ■ Hinodegiri, Hino Crimson, Christmas Cheer.
**Pink** ■ Hinomayo, Pink Pearl, Coral Bells, Salmon Beauty
**White** ■Snow

The **Southern Indica Hybrids** (Indian) ■ A taller informally shaped plant with large evergreen leaves. Less cold resistant and a later bloom than the Kurume.

**Bloom Colors:**
**Deep Rose Pink** ■ Pride of Mobile, Judge Solomon
**Fuchsia** ■Formosa
**Orchid** ■ George Lindley Tabor
**Salmon pink** ■Daphne Salmon, Duc de Rohan
**White** ■ Mrs. G.G. Gerbing, Fielder's White

The **Satsuki Hybrids** ■ Beautiful full oval landscape shaped plant. Large blooms come in late spring.

**Bloom Colors:**
**White** ■ Gumpo White
**Pale Pink** ■ Gumpo Pink, Wakebisui
**Salmon Red** ■ Macrantha Red

The **Encore** (American): A new group of fall flowering Azaleas that also show spring and summer color. Tested for North Texas seasons.

**Bloom Colors:**
**Strong pink-red** ■Autumn Rouge
**Orange-red** ■Autumn Embers
**Soft purple** ■Autumn Amethyst

The **Fashion** (American): An extended bloomer of coral blossoms.

# REFERENCE

*Azaleas* by Fred C. Galle, Timber Press, 1985.

# SOCIETY

**Azalea Society of America, Dallas Chapter**
Roy Odom, President
6161 Preston Haven
Dallas, Texas 75218
(214) 960-2945

# CAMELLIAS

During the past decade, there has been a great resurgence of interest in Camellias and they are being grown successfully in many Dallas gardens, including the Dallas Arboretum & Botanical Society. *Camellia Sasanqua* and *Camellia Japonica*, the two species which grow well in our area, fill different roles in the garden although their culture is the same. The C. *sasanqua* is a fall blooming landscape plant with abundant ephemeral flowers. The early spring C. *japonica* has larger elegant, single flowers suitable for indoor display.

## SITE

Choose a location away from icy winter winds and blazing afternoon sun. Container-grown Camellias must be protected from summer drafts, e.g. breezeways. Provide semi-shade. A northern exposure is considered best. Special beds must be prepared. Use formula for acid beds *(see p. 39)* or a mixture of 50% pine bark (shredded) and 50% good loam with drainage provided by rocks and gravel at the bottom of the bed. Individual beds may be prepared by digging a hole twice as large as the root ball and 1-1/2 times as deep. Allow extra depth for sufficient drainage. Drainage cannot be overemphasized. Root rot occurs from standing water.

## PLANT

In early spring. Set the plant so the top of the root ball is 1" above the soil level after tamping down. Then mound additional soil 3" high in a circle on the outside rim of the planting hole in the form of a cup. Fill with water. Some Camellias should be staked when small. Drive the stake close to the main trunk about 6" into the ground and tie loosely using as many ties as necessary to keep the plant upright. The stake may be removed when plant matures. Mulch is a must for Camellias. Use compost, peat moss or pine bark.

## WATER

At all times, keep moist but never wet. Water deep and well as needed. Large amounts of water are required during the summer growing period and during the flowering period. In addition, syringing of leaves is helpful. Use fogging nozzle on garden hose, but NOT when the sun is on the foliage. Keep Camellias mulched to prevent drying the roots which are near the surface. Drying out causes small blooms and bud drop.

## FERTILIZE

Start with the first sign of new growth even if plant is still blooming. Cotton seed meal or special commercial acid fertilizer should be used. Follow directions on package. Three light feedings are recommended — in late March, June, and September. Remember to soak the day before feeding. Never feed a dry plant. If your plant looks sick (yellow veins, dropping of leaves, etc.) check with your nurseryman before feeding as special measures may be required.

For container-grown Camellias, fertilize more often but use only 1/2 the amount suggested for those in the ground. Increase the number of feedings to 4, spaced equally through September.

## PRUNE

Seldom required except for shaping. Remove any dead wood. For C. *japonica* disbudding to produce large full blooms should start as soon as you are able to distinguish between flower and growth buds. Leave one bud to a terminal. Smaller but more blooms will result from leaving all buds on stems; this is especially true of varieties that have cluster blooms. Do not disbud C. *sasanqua.*

## PROBLEMS

### Dieback

A fungal disease, systemic to Camellias. Is a condition where the tips of the branches actually die back. It is easily spread by contaminated clippers. After each cut rinse clippers in diluted Clorox water or a fungicide solution. For your clippers' longevity, rinse and dry shears after use. Place commercial tree wound dressing or water-based white glue on the cut surface of each branch.

### Specific Remedies

Generally, Camellias rarely need spraying. Malathion will control mites and Sevin on the soil will control ants and beetles. Apply Winter-Dormant oil (or dormant oil) spray in cool weather after plants have bloomed. If applied in fall before blooming, it will ruin the buds *(see p. 56).* Remember oil emulsion should never be applied when temperature is under 40° or over 90° or within 30 days of using sulfur as an acidifier.

If you aren't getting good new growth in the spring, your problem is basically with the root system. Your local nurseryman will help you with that and other problems which may arise such as tea scale infection, chewing insects and bugs.

## CAMELLIA SASANQUA

*Camellia sasanqua* has smaller leaves and flowers than C. *japonica*; but its rapid, hardy growth and free-flowering, spreading forms make it particularly valuable in landscape planting as hedges, mass or foundation planting and espaliered specimens.

### VARIETIES

**White ▪** Snow and Yae-arare (with pink tip)
**Pink ▪** Maiden's Blush, Jean May, Autumn Surprise, Pink Snow
**Bright Pink ▪** Chansonette (large, formal, and double)
**Rose ▪** Cleopatra
**Red ▪** Sparkling Burgundy and Hiryu

## CAMELLIA JAPONICA

*Camellia japonica* produces flowers of many sizes in a variation of colors. The flowers may be single, semi-double, peony type, anemone or formal double. According to variety, C. *japonica* blooms from October 1 to April 15. Those blooming very late (April) or very early (October) are most successful here.

### VARIETIES

**White to Blush Pink ▪** Alba Plena, Sept. Morn., Betty Sheffield, Magnoliaeflora, Snow White
**Pink ▪** Debutante, Pink Perfection, Dr. Tinsley, Daikagura, Chandler Elegans
**Rose to Red ▪** Drama Girl, Rose Dawn, Purple Dawn, Methotiana, Prof. C.S. Sargent

# CAMELLIA ORGANIZATION

**The Camellia Society**, Clair Gothard
P.O. Box 38669
Dallas, Texas 75235-0669
(214) 343-0881

# Chapter 10

## VINES

*Evergreen* ❧ *Deciduous* ❧ *Climbing* ❧ *Trailing*
*Woody* ❧ *Annual* ❧ *Perennial*

Trailing, climbing plants can be evergreen or deciduous, annual, perennial or flowering. The plants' tendencies are such that they climb upward toward sunlight to bloom. Growing up on walls, fences, decorative screens and arbors, vines will bring an elegant vertical addition to many garden designs. Vines prefer to have their roots cool and damp. Try to plant on the north or east side of the wall or fence to allow them to drape toward the sun. Cover roots with a large rock to protect from heat of the sun if needed.

**Allamanda** *Allamanda cathartica nobilis* ▪ Not hardy, but vigorous climber, leaves 4", flowers yellow 4" diameter, magnolia fragrance; good pot plant, sunny window in winter, garden in summer, avoid west sun; heavy feeders; take cuttings in spring, keep on dry side through March, cut back before growth starts.

**Balsam Apple** *Momordica balsamina* ▪ Annual, tendril climbing to 10'; leaves lobed, 4" wide, bright green; flowers yellow 1" diameter; fruit orange, cucumber family.

**Black-Eyed Susan** *Thunbergia alata* ▪ Annual, lovely trailer; leaves triangular; flowers yellow, orange, or white with black centers, June to October. Use in baskets, urns in sun, rich soil. Sow seed March indoors, harden off before planting outdoors.

**Bougainvillea** *Bougainvillea spectabilis* (Paper-flower) ▪ Tropical *(not winter hardy here)*, evergreen, long thorny canes with heart-shaped leaves; flowers small. Requires fertile, acid soil in sun; can use on patio in tub.

**Cardinal Climber** *Ipomoea quamoclit* ▪ Annual, rapid growth to 15'; fern-like foliage a rich glossy green. Flowers scarlet, similar to tubular miniature morning glories, late Summer - Fall bloom, sun, light soil. Seed must be soaked in warm water before planting outdoors when trees begin to leaf.

**Clematis** *Clematis* (Virgins-Bower) ▪ Hardy perennial herbs or woody vines, flowers solitary or panicled, vase-shaped or open flat. All require fertile loamy soil, good drainage and cool roots (achieved either by shading or an airy mulch). When planting, use plenty of humus, a handful of commercial fertilizer and ground limestone; crowns 2" below surface, tilted in direction of growth; protect from damage. Will grow toward sun, but large flowered varieties prefer light shade from west sun during extremely high temperatures. Correct pruning is essential and is based on time of bloom (spring, summer or those that bloom in both!) and type of growth. Listed below are a few species, hybrids, and cultivars.

C. *x Jackmanii*: Deciduous, strong grower to 20'; flowers violet-purple, June to September bloom. "Purpurea Superba" a new improved form, larger, fuller and more rounded. Once fully established, prune back hard in early spring.

C. x *Lawsoniana Henryi*: Flowers 6-7" over-lapping petals, white, dark stamens, June. Prune to shape only.

C. *montana* var. *alba* (Anemone Clematis): Deciduous, rampant grower to 20'; flowers waxy white or pink, anemone-like with yellow staminodes. Cut back after flowering. While young, start vine to grow horizontally on fence or pergola.

C. *chrysocoma* var.*sericea* (C. Spooneri): The white Dogwood clematis. Deciduous, strong grower to 20'; flowers 3" white in clusters, May bloom. Downy bronze-tinted leaves; prune after blooming. Also pink variety.

C. *maximowcziana*, once C. paniculata (Sweet Autumn Clematis): Rampant grower, flowers white in clusters, small, very fragrant August bloom. Prune to 18-24" after bloom. Perennial, old fashioned — semi-evergreen.

C. *texensis* (Red Bell Clematis): Semi-herbaceous, generally dies to ground each year — no pruning necessary. Grows to 12'. Flowers long lasting fleshy bells, June to October. "Duchess of Albany" — apple-blossom-pink bells, deeper pink bars on outside; "Etoile Rose" — cerise.

**Climbing Prairie Rose** *Rosa setigera* ▪ Recommended for Blackland Prairies and Post Oak forests. Part shade to full sun, blooms on old growth in May, deep-pink flowers that fade to white. Nearly thornless, plant will sucker. Abundant purple fruit called rose hips. For other climbing Roses (see p. 140).

**Clitoria** *Clitoria Ternatea* (Butterfly Pea) ▪ Annual, to 15'; flowers dark blue, similar to Sweet Pea, also pink, white, double forms, summer; sow seed early in year.

**Coral Honeysuckle** *Lonicera sempervirens* ▪ Perennial twining vines reaching 8-12 feet, tolerates pruning, good for small patio gardens. Coral-red trumpet shaped flowers with blue green foliage, evergreen to semi-evergreen, prefers sunny location and well-drained soil. Needs support to start on fence, arbor, or decorative screens, excellent choice for attracting hummingbirds. L.*x Brownii* variety *Dropmore Scarlet* — hardy, flowers long-lobed, brilliant orange-scarlet cover vine; long blooming. Attracts hummingbirds. Refer to Shrub Honeysuckle *(see p. 80)*.

**Coral Vine** ▪ Refer to Queen's Wreath *(see p. 94)*.

**Crossvine** *Anisostichus capreolata* ▪ Evergreen native vine, long tubular flowers yellow or orange-red. Durable, needs sun, few pests.

**Cypressvine** ▪ Refer to Cardinal Climber *(see p. 91)*.

**Gourds, Ornamental** *Cucurbita pepo* var.*ovifera* ▪ Annual, native, running vines; flowers yellow; hard-shelled fruit take many forms, colors. Must be dried before using. Plant seed in spring. Fun for children.

**Grapevine** *Vitis x champinii* ▪ Hardy, native, robust climber with support; leaves dark glossy green; fruit 1/2" black. A few of the varieties recommended for this area are Carman, Fredonia, Golden Muscat. Cut each shoot of last year's growth back to one or two buds.

**Honeysuckle** *Lonicera*: L. *japonica* var. *Halliana* (Japanese Honeysuckle) ▪ Naturalized, evergreen twining to 50', rampant; flowers white turning buff, fragrant; it will take over.

**Hyacinth Bean** *Dolichos lablab* ▪ Annual, tall, will spread, purple flowers in late summer, fast growing, very easy to grow, seed in spring, good for shade arbors or trellis.

**Ivy, Boston** *Parthenocissus tricuspidata* ▪ Hardy, deciduous, leaves large, shiny, turning red to purple in fall, overlapping leaves will cover wall. Prepare soil before setting small plants, pinch any runners back, keep damp. "Lowii" dwarf variety — leaves 1-1/2" long, smaller, does not grow as high.

**English** *Hedera helix*: Evergreen, many varieties including dwarf; plant in spring, preparing soil with lots of humus and keep damp until growth starts. Makes excellent hedge when trained on chain-link fence. Leaves scald in full sun in summer; watch for aphids, red spider. Do not advise foundation planting as it tends to rot wood and displace shingles. Poisonous to eat.

**Fig** *Ficus pumila*: Not winter hardy here. Used in topiaries but must be kept moist.

**Tree** *X Fatshedera Lizei*: Evergreen, beautiful large leaf; plant in protected spot, needs support, grows to 7'.

**Jack Bean** *Canavalia ensiformis* ▪ Annual, twining vine to 4', pea-shaped purple flowers in racemes; seed pods to 12"; edible, useful in flower arrangements.

**Jasmine, Confederate** or **Star** *Trachelospermum jasminoides* ▪ Evergreen,leaves 3" long, dark green, leathery; flowers, white, petals twisted, very fragrant; needs protection in severe and freezing weather, good tub plant; keep watered when in bloom, enjoys filtered sun. Watch for red spider. Propagate by layering.

**Jessamine, Carolina** *Gelsemium sempervirens* ▪ Evergreen, light green leaves, flowers yellow, in early spring. Plant spring or fall, more effective planted behind and growing over a wall or fence; drought resistant. Poisonous. "Plena double" — evergreen glossy leaves, flowers double yellow 1" across, fragrant, heavier bloomer, lasting longer.

**Mandevilla** *Mandevilla splendens* or *Diplidena* ▪ Summer annual, best in sunny patio pot or hanging basket; large oval dark green leaves; large hot pink flowers. Bring in for winter or put in greenhouse. Attracts hummingbirds.

**Moon Vine** *Ipomoea alba* also *I. bona-nox* and *Calonyction aculeatum* (Moon Flower) ▪ Annual, leaves heart-shaped; relative of Morning Glory; sun or light shade — flowers pure white opening in evening and remaining until sunrise, delightful fragrance and beautiful when lighted at night.

**Morning Glory** *Ipomoea purpurea* ▪ Annual, fast growth, blooming in late summer and fall. Soak seeds or notch before planting. Various colors and white. Poisonous.

**Passion Vine** *Passiflora incarnata* (Maypop) ▪ Native, hardy, strong grower; leaves 3", deep-lobed; flowers white with purple or pink-brown; needs sun.

**Pea, Perennial Sweet** *Lathyrus latifolius* ▪ Hardy, beautiful if good varieties are used. White Pearl, Pink Beauty, or Appleblossom instead of the old magenta one. Large flowers on 1' stem; bloom summer to frost, growing to 8' in sun or high shade in garden soil.

**Sweet Pea** *Lathyrus odoratus*: Annual, many colors, spring bloom. Plant in trench 6" deep in rich soil in December. When seedlings reach 2", begin to fill trench with more mixed soil until trench is full as growth advances. Support vines. Be prepared to protect from frost if necessary.

**Queen's Wreath** *Antigonon leptopus* (Mexican Love Vine) ▪ Deciduous, roots tuberous, tendril climbers, liking sun and plenty of water when in bloom. Pink flowers resemble begonias in long trailing sprays. Need thick mulch in winter.

**Scarlet Runner Bean** *Phaseolus multiflorus* ▪ Annual. Beautiful prolific bloomer all summer, produced in racemes, 10-30 flowers each. Easy to grow, needs sun, water. Sow seed in April when soil is dry, keep damp but an excess of water will rot seed. Great for covering unsightly buildings or fences. When seed pods are green, pick, shell beans as they are edible.

**Silver Lace Vine** *Polygonum aubertii* ∎ Hardy, dies to ground in fall, new shoots in spring. Tiny cream flowers in sprays cover plant in summer. Vigorous clean growth, needing no support. Reseeds.

**Sweet Potato Vine** *Ipomoea bata* ∎ Vining vegetable plant that can be used as an ornamental. Get starts in April, locally grown and distributed. Good in hanging baskets. "Blackie" – deep purple; "Mararita" – chartruse, aggressive; "Tri-color" – blushed with violet pink.

**Trumpet Vine** *Campsis radicans* ∎ Deciduous, hardy, native, rampant grower, yellow or red summer bloom; spreads rapidly and can become a pest. Hummingbirds love flowers! A cross between C. *radicans* and Chinese *grandiflora* has produced a new hybrid *x. flava* which is more refined. It is hardy, with yellow flowers in clusters, trumpet-like, blooming summer into fall. Prefers ordinary soil, not too rich, and sun. Others are "Mme. Galen" – rich apricot flowers tinted orange and "Crimson Trumpet" – a true red.

**Virginia Creeper** *Parthenocissus quinquefolia* ∎ Hardy, deciduous, prune to restrict; blue fruit in September; leaves scarlet in fall. Clings to bricks.

**Wisteria** *Wisteria floribunda* ∎ Japanese. Leaflets number 7-9 in pairs; elliptic in shape; flowers in racemes to 15' long. New cultivars are "Ivory Tower" – white; "Plena" – double blue; "Rosea" – brilliant pink flowers.

*W. sinensis*: Chinese. Leaflets less than 7 pairs; flowers lavender-blue to violet in racemes 12". All hardy, deciduous, beautiful spring bloom; likes sun, water when in bloom; fruit – long seed-pod which is poisonous. A rapid grower when established, prune to control, provide support. Prune after bloom and before growth of new wood appears; root prune for more abundant bloom; remove side runners at base. Can be trained into single-trunk tree form.

*W. macrostachya*: Texas wisteria, blooms late May, after leaves appear. Less aggressive.

## REFERENCE

*Grasses, Pods, Vines, Weeds: Decorating with Texas Naturals* by Quentin Steitz, University of Texas Press, 1987.

*Vines for Southern Landscape* by William D. Adams, Pacesetter Press, Houston Publishing Company.

# Chapter 11

# GROUND COVERS

*Evergreen ❧ Flowers ❧ Running*

Ground Covers give a variety of color, texture and height to foundation landscaping. In the Metroplex the choice is exceptional. Many consider an area of ground cover to require less maintenance than grass which must be mowed. The well chosen ground cover may thrive where grass will not. The initial installation must be properly cleared of weeds and grasses. Thorough weeding and mulching are the prime procedures with early ground cover plantings.

**Ajuga** *Ajuga reptans* (Carpet Bugle) ▪ Hardy, evergreen most years here, sun or shade; well-drained soil but not dry; best results with adequate water; keep fertilized during growing season. Many new cultivars listed: some green foliage, some bronze. If you wish a change, try "Burgundy Glow", a tricolor or A. *pyramidalis* with richer, larger green leaves. Rich blue spikes 10" high.

**Bearberry** *Arctostaphylos uva-ursi* ▪ Hardy, evergreen, tiny glossy green leaves. Form dense mat on sandy acid soils. Pale pink flowers in spring, followed by persistent red berries. Sun or shade. Hard to transplant — better to purchase already established in pots.

**Cotoneaster** *Cotoneaster salicifolius* var. (Scarlet Leader) ▪ Vigorous new variety spreading several feet but only 6" tall; in sun or shade. Leaves glossy dark green, red berries in autumn. Hardy. For larger area, there is the familiar C. *horizontalis* — semi-evergreen which needs pruning occasionally to maintain a neat growth pattern.

**Dichondra** *Dichondra repens* ▪ Difficult here as it is damaged by the cold.

**Euonymus** *Euonymus fortunei* (Wintercreeper) ▪ "Acuta" — a hardy evergreen prostrate spreading vine, soon makes a dark green carpet; sun or semi-shade; excellent for problem slopes and banks. "Longwood" also dark green miniature leaf, flat, growing very close to ground.

E. *fortunei* var. *colorata* (Purpleleaf Wintercreeper) has foliage turning red in fall. Young plants must be deeply watered. Scale attacks all varieties. *(See p. 56).*

**Ferns** ▪ Various wood ferns may be used, some evergreen, others not.

Good used in shade. *(See p. 119).*

**Herniary** *Herniaria glabra* ▪ "Green Carpet" a hardy perennial, ideal for planting between stepping stones, low mounds, around pools, where a thick mat-like 2-3" carpet is desired; bright green, bronzy red in winter.

**Honeysuckle** *Lonicera japonica* var. *chinensis* ▪ Evergreen low shrub 18-24" with vine tendencies; dry soil, sun or shade; keep trimmed or sheared. Use in large areas only. Avoid "halliana" as it is difficult to control.

**Indian Strawberry** *Duchesnea indica* ▪ Hardy, fast growing with runners rooting at each node. Small yellow flowers in spring and summer, followed by red fruit(inedible); shade or semi-shade, under trees and shrubs; appreciates moisture but is drought tolerant; grows 6" tall; plant 12-18" apart.

**Ivy, English** *Hedera helix* ▪ Evergreen, shade loving; needs porous, rich soil (humus), use commercial fertilizer, not manure. When plants are about to flower, the leaves change shape and if these shoots are rooted, they produce plants that do not climb (H. *arborescens*). For small areas, other ivies include: "Baltica", leaves smaller, more closely set giving compact effect, hardier; "Green Ripples" with fan-shaped leaves, desirable in patio areas; "Hahn's Self-branching" with long pointed leaves, lighter green, sun as well as shade; "Needle point" still smaller leaves than "Hahn's", more miniature growth.

**Jap Grass** ▪ See Mondo Grass and Liriope, following.

**Jasmine, Asian** *Trachelospermum asiaticum* (Japanese Star Jasmine) ▪ Evergreen, vine-like to mounding low shrub 6-18"; sun or semi-shade, garden loam. Good for edging, keep sheared. Keep cut to 6" for best look. Several varieties.

**Lamium** *Lamium*: L. *maculatum* var. *Variegatum* (Dead Nettle) ▪ Hardy, excellent as cover for shade or semi-shade with ground-hugging stems, rooting at nodes; leaves deep green, edged with silver; flowers yellow, spring. Also used in hanging baskets. Another variety "Chequers" — hardy, 6-8" plants, smaller leaves; flowers pink in April.

**Liriope** *Liriope muscari* ▪ Variety "Grandiflora" has evergreen wide-leaf 8-12"; flowers white or violet in spikes; fruit blue; sun or shade; moisture and open porous soil, fast spreading by underground runners. Clip new shoots to control. "Silver dragon"bi-color, with white muting as matures. "Variegata" has yellow-striped leaves, 18" tall, pruning same as for Ophiopogon *(see below)*. Many varieties.

**Mondo Grass or Monkey Grass** *Ophiopogon japonicus* ▪ Evergreen, sod-forming stemless perennial, 6-9" tall; dark green, fine grass-like leaves, heavy texture; porous soil, acid conditions, shade recommended but will grow in garden soil and in sun with adequate moisture. If planted in small area you may cut back each plant to about 1" from ground before buds form in early March. Kyoto, dwarf cultivar plus several other varieties.

**Moneywort** *Lysimachia nummularia* (Creeping Jenny) ▪ Hardy, low trailing green plants; sun or shade; will grow in moist conditions. Flowers yellow, late spring and summer. "Aurea" — golden yellow leaves. May be used as edging, hanging baskets, window boxes; excellent as ground cover under shrubs. If planted in a protected spot, will remain green all winter. Roots at joints.

**Pachysandra** *Pachysandra terminalis* (Green Carpet) ▪ Growth low and compact, retains its beauty under adverse conditions. Bright evergreen leaves, 6-8" high. No direct sun. Plant where ground retains moisture.

**Periwinkle** ▪ Refer to Vinca *(see below)*.

**Phlox** ▪ *(See p. 120)* all varieties in Perennials.

**Santolina** *Santolina chamaecyparissus* ▪ Hardy, grey-green evergreen foliage. See under Perennials S. *virens* (green santolina) same culture.

**Strawberry, Barren** *Waldsteinia fragarioides* ▪ Evergreen low, waxy foliage; sun or semi-shade; flowers yellow; any garden soil. New to area. Try it.

**Strawberry Begonia** *Saxifraga stolonifera* (Mother of Thousands) ▪ Excellent year round plant for total shade loving rockeries where soil is amended and sprinkled. Rosettes send red runners of new plants. White bloom spikes in spring. Pinch back larger leaves to give small plants light to grow.

**Veronica** *Veronica repens* (Creeping Speedwell) ▪ Rich green moss-like leaves, 1-2" high, good between flagstones in sunny spots. Heat and drought resistant in well-drained sandy soil; flowers blue in May and June.

**Vinca** *Vinca major* ▪ Evergreen trailing; leaves oval, glossy; flowers blue; 12" high. Any garden soil, better in loam. Good for large shaded areas and slopes. Also likes sun, withstands heat. Spray in summer with all purpose spray.

*Vinca minor* ▪ Evergreen trailing; mound to 6-8"; leaves small, flowers blue or white in spring. Any garden soil, better in loam; resists drought but likes moisture. Newer improvements over species are "Bowles Variety" with rich green leaves heavy textured, spreads less rapidly, large flowers 1" across, deeper blue and prolific bloomer, and "Miss Jekyll's White" with small leaves, very dwarf, dense low carpet of deepest green, pure white flowers in spring.

# Chapter 12

# GRASSES: LAWNS & ORNAMENTALS

*Lawns ❧ Varieties ❧ Maintenance*
*Care ❧ Ornamentals*

## LAWNS

The lawn is an integral part of the Dallas landscape and is often the largest percentage of the planted surface of the home site. Dallas is unique in geographic location with climatic conditions changing from intense summer heat to frigid winter cold, from an arid southwestern drought to a tropical monsoon. Other environmental factors that impact the quality of a lawn include the water available, the level of shading by trees and other landscape structures, and the texture and uniformity of the soil. New grass varieties, species and techniques are added in this 13th edition manual as well as the new scientific spelling style for grasses.

The first step to a successful lawn is to identify the optimum grass for our environmental conditions. For instance, Bermudagrass is well suited to sunny areas like those found in new subdivisions. However it does not thrive in older neighborhoods where the shade from mature trees and shrubs thwarts its growth. As most landscapes will have from 20-40% shade and an equal amount of sun, choose grasses that will work well in the given conditions.

Turf or lawn grasses are divided into two groups by the seasons they grow and the seasons they are dormant. Warm Season Grasses like Bermuda and St. Augustine grow and are green in warm seasons then rest and turn yellow in the winter. Cool Season Grasses like Rye and Fescue grow in the cold months and die or become dormant in the summer. In choosing a grass decide which season you most want a green lawn. To have a lawn green longer, combine warm and cool season grasses. In this area most older lawns have Bermuda and St. Augustine through choice or circumstance. In this tandem, sun and shade areas are covered. Yet other grasses should be considered.

### WARM SEASON GRASSES

**Common Bermudagrass,** *Cynodon dactylon* ▪ The most prevalent of grasses for lawns in the Metroplex. Common-type Bermudagrasses are tough, durable and very tolerant of mismanagement. The optimum environmental conditions for common-type Bermudagrasses include full-sun (no shaded areas). Due to deep rhyzome roots, poor to moderate soil conditions are acceptable with periodic irrigation. Common-type Bermudagrasses worthy of consideration include Arizona

Common (seed), Texas Common (Sod) and U-3 (Sod). New seeded types will include NuMex Sahara, Sonesta and Guymon.

**Hybrid Bermudagrass,** *Cynodon spp.* ▪ Produces a much higher quality lawn of greater density, finer texture. It one of the most popular of lawns for new landscapes. The hybrid-type Bermudagrasses also lack shade tolerance and will not survive in areas with moderate to heavy shade. They have higher maintenance requirements including frequent mowing, fertilization and irrigation. They can be mowed with a rotary mower; however, a reel mower will provide a better appearance. Tifway 419 and the newly released Baby varieties are available only as sod and are both excellent for home lawns. Baby has slightly more cold hardiness; both will tolerate the North Texas winters with little problem.

**Buffalograss,** *Buchloe dactyloides* ▪ Native to the Great Plains of the United States, is one of the most cold hardy of the warm season grasses available for home lawns. A good choice for xeriscaping, Buffalograss has little or no shade tolerance, and wants no irrigation after establishing. Seeded Buffalograss varieties include Texoka and Sharps' Improved. The most popular sod types, Prairie and 609, are both readily available in the Metroplex. These grasses are among the lowest maintenance turfs available. They can both be established by sodding, plugging or sprigging. They prefer the heavy (clay) alkaline soil types of the Metroplex.

**St. Augustine,** *Stenotaphrum secundatum* ▪ A popular wide blade grass, a sub-tropical grass native to the Southeast. If well cared for, most attractive. More shade tolerant than most grass but needs 4 to 6 hours sun. Shallow root system cannot tolerate drought. Requires supplemental water. Runner growth will not tolerate dethatching. Raleigh is disease resistant.

**Zoysiagrass – Japanese Lawn Grass,** *Zoysia japonica* ▪ Variety "Meyer" is available. New varieties require less irrigation, have more shade tolerance and grow faster with less thatching and lower nutritional needs. Varieties such as Crowne and Palisades developed specifically for the home with mixed landscapes. Shade tolerant and require little irrigation. Excellent cold hardiness and heat tolerance and are easily maintained with a rotary mower. These Zoysiagrasses will play a significant role in the shaded landscapes of north Texas as they have excellent winter hardiness.

**Zoysiagrass – Manilia Grass,** *Zoysia matrella* ▪ Is a newcomer to the Metroplex with the introduction of Omni and Cavalier. Zoysiagrasses are noted for fine texture, excellent shade tolerance and rapid recovery from traffic damage. These grasses will challenge the hybrid Bermudagrasses for quality and durability and adaptability to mixed-light landscapes. Sod, sprig or plug.

## COOL SEASON GRASSES

**Tall Fescue,** *Festuca arundinacea* ▪ Is one of the most popular of the cool season grasses and is identified by its active growth during the winter months. Tall Fescue is a bunch grass that is established from seed, but it is also available in sod from local producers. As a species, it has good drought tolerance. However, to maintain active growth during the heat of the summer, it requires frequent irrigation. Its irrigation requirements will be similar to St. Augustine grass. Grub control requires early summer pesticides as a cool season grass. Tall Fescue is easily established from seeding between 4–6 lbs. of seed per 1000 sq. ft. from mid-September to mid-October.

**Perennial Ryegrass,** *Lolium perenne* ▪ Is used exclusively for over-seeding a warm season grass base such as Bermuda or Zoysia to provide green active turf during the winter months. Grown from seed planted at relative high rates (9–25 lbs. per 1000 sq ft.) in the fall when the host grass begins to slow in growth, Perennial Ryegrass is quick to establish and will provide a dense attractive turf area.

**Annual Ryegrass,** *Lolium multiflorium* ▪ Is used for over-seeding a warm season grass in order to have a green lawn in the winter or early spring. Annual Rye Grass germinates rapidly and has a tremendous growth rate, at times requiring mowing as often as 3–4 times per week. The cheap seed cost is rapidly offset by the additional cost of mowing and general maintenance of the turf area. If over-seeding is desired, the best alternative is to use Perennial Ryegrass that is much easier to maintain and will also provide a higher quality turf.

# ESTABLISHMENT OF NEW LAWNS

## SITE PREPARATION

A properly prepared seedbed is critical to the successful establishment and maintenance of a lawn. Evaluate the site with regard to its slopes and shapes, considering the aesthetic affect desired and the drainage.

The soil should be tilled to a depth of 6-8". Regrade the site to final shape and roll to create a firm seed/soil bed that should provide good seed/sprig contact with the soil. As one of the last steps during the tillage process, incorporate a balanced fertilizer, e.g., 10-10-10 *(see p. 35)* to enhance rapid establishment. If the soil is excessively dry during preparation, apply a liberal irrigation to recharge the moisture in the soil profile 2-3 days prior to planting.

## PLANT

The method of establishing turf grasses varies by the species and often the variety.

# TABLE ONE

*Most commonly use or recommended species for use on lawns in North Texas*

| SPECIES | SHADE Tolerance | FULL SUN Tolerance | IRRIGATION Requirements | FERTILIZER Requirements |
|---------|-----------------|--------------------|-----------------------|-----------------------|
| **WARM SEASON GRASSES** | | | | |
| **St. Augustine** | Excellent | Excellent | High | Moderate-High |
| **Bermuda Common** | Poor | Excellent | Low-Moderate | Moderate |
| **Bermuda Hybrid-types** | Poor | Excellent | Moderate-High | Moderate-High |
| **Buffalograss** | Poor | Excellent | Low | Low |
| **Zoysiagrass,** *japonica* | Good-Excellent | Excellent | Low-Moderate | Low |
| **Zoysiagrass,** *matrella* | Excellent | Excellent | Low-Moderate | Low |
| **COOL SEASON GRASSES** | | | | |
| **Tall Fescue** | Excellent | Moderate-Good | Moderate-High | Moderate |
| **Ryegrass, Perennial** | Good | Good | High | Moderate-High |
| **Ryegrass, Annual** | Fair | Fair | High | High |

| COLD Tolerance | SOILS C = Clay L = Loam S = Sandy | MOW Height | MOW Frequency | PLANTING S = Seed SG = Sprig SD = Sod P - Plug |
|---|---|---|---|---|
| Poor | C, L, S | 2-2.5″ | Weekly | SD |
| Good | C, L, S | 1-1.5″ | Weekly | S, SD, SG |
| Moderate | C, L, S | 0.5-1″ | 1-2x Weekly | SD, SG |
| Excellent | C, L | 2-3″ | Infrequent | SD, P |
| Excellent | C, L, S | 1.5-2″ | Weekly-Bi-Weekly | S, SD, SG, P |
| Good-Excellent | C, L, S | 0.5-1.5″ | Weekly-Bi-Weekly | SD, SG, P |
| Excellent | C, L | 2-2.5″ | Weekly | S |
| Excellent | C, L, S | 0.5-2″ | Weekly | S |
| Excellent | L, S | 1-2″ | 1-3x Weekly | S |

**Seeding** ▪ Each species will have a recommended seeding rate and should be followed closely to promote good growth. Regardless of the species, it is important to deliver the seed to the prepared seedbed as uniformly as possible. With small seeded grasses it is often desirable to mix the seed with a carrier such as corn meal, oat meal or an organic type fertilizer. When using a drop seeder or broad cast type, apply it in multiple directions. Once the seed is delivered to the site, it should be lightly raked, smoothed and irrigated immediately. Seeding requires 1-2 lbs of PLS (Pure Live Seed) per 1000 square feet of area and may be done anytime from March through August with the optimum time April through June.

**Sodding** ▪ The fastest and most expensive means of establishing turf is to sod the area. A square foot of sod covers a square foot of lawn area. Prepare site, place sod aligned with adjacent pieces, then roll it to push the sod tightly against the soil to eliminate air pockets and promote rapid root development. The area must be watered immediately, but will require less overall irrigation as there will be less tendency to dry out. Sodding can be done any time of the year. If sodding in winter, water as needed during prolonged cold dry spells to keep the crown area from drying out.

**Plugging** ▪ Plugging is the breaking of sod pieces into smaller 'plugs' ranging in size from 1.5-3" square and distributing them uniformly across the seed bed. Keep as much soil around the root as possible to reduce drying. Ideally, a small hole will be created on a 12" to 18" interval with each plug being planted into the hole. Roll to aid in leveling and increase contact with the soil. Plugging, like sodding, requires less water to establish than sprigging or seeding. Plugging can occur throughout the year, but the optimum time is in the spring and early summer.

### IRRIGATION

Seedling, sod or sprig/plug establishment requires that light moisture continue until the root system is able to acquire water from the soil. Immediately following planting it is important to schedule multiple irrigations during the first 24-48 hours. Beginning the 2nd and 3rd days, the frequency of irrigation will only require that the soil surface does not dry out (1–2 waterings per day). Beginning approximately the 7th day (seedling growth should be obvious), the irrigation frequency should be reduced to 1 time daily, and in the next 2-3 weeks to every other day. Once the plants are established and are being clipped on a weekly basis, they should be watered every 3-4 days for the first growing season. A properly established lawn should be irrigated on a weekly basis thereafter. The irrigation needs of each of the grasses will differ.

## FERTILIZE

A newly established lawn requires adequate nutritional support for the development of a strong root system and turf canopy. A balanced starter fertilizer (10-10-10) at a rate of 1 pound per 1000 square feet prior to or immediately after planting should be followed in 6-8 weeks with a second application. Once the lawn is established, additional feeding is required to maintain a healthy weed-free turf. The recommended formulation for subsequent applications is a 3-1-2 or 4-1-2 ratio. Tall Fescue will grow primarily during the cool months of the year, the same time that fertilizer should be provided. 4 – 6 pounds of Nitrogen fertilizer should be applied between 15 September and 15 April in split applications. There is no single recommendation to cover all grasses.

# MAINTAINING THE PERENNIAL LAWN

The best weed control for the lawn is to maintain a vigorously grown turf. The magic formula for doing such is timely application of fertilizer, proper watering, aerification and mowing *(see p. 107)*.

### FERTILIZE

Three or four applications of ammonium sulphate, urea or any other form of Nitrogen will greatly enhance the beauty of the lawn. Each treatment should apply approximately 1 pound Nitrogen per 1000 square feet. Newly formulated slow release and coated fertilizers will reduce the frequency of application, but the total quantity of nutrients available to the plant on an annual basis will be the same. Periodically contact your country agent for assistance in obtaining a soil analysis to more accurately determine the formulation best for your situation.

**Warm Season Grasses** ▪ Buffalograss and Zoysiagrass generally require 1-3 pounds Nitrogen annually *(see p. 102, Table 1)* and these applications should be made in late spring (15 May-15 June) with a final application made in the late fall (15 October-15 November). The hybrid Bermudagrass and St. Augustine grass will perform better with 1 pound Nitrogen per 1000 square feet per growing month applied throughout the summer months with a maximum application of 6-8 pounds per year. As St. Augustine grass is generally more prone to fall occurrence of Brown Patch disease, an early fall application of fertilizer can be detrimental to it. Wait until after the first frost for the final application in the fall, and the turf will be conditioned for an early spring green-up and growth. If the grass appears to be deficient during the summer months, an additional application may be necessary. This summer application will be dictated by the rainfall and your irrigation practices. **Hint:** the more water applied, the more fertilizer needed.

**Cool Season Grasses** ▪ Require 3-4 pounds Nitrogen annually. These grasses do not like to grow during the summer months, so don't force them with summer fertilizer applications. Fertilize frequently during the cool season months (September-April). Regardless of when fertilizer is applied, the application should be followed immediately by a light (0.25" ) irrigation where possible to help incorporate the fertilizer prior to heavy rains which could cause fertilizer runoff.

## WATER

The precipitation patterns in the Dallas area generally do not provide sufficient quantities of moisture for grass during the hot summer months, and occasionally during the dry winter months. St. Augustine grass, hybrid Bermudagrasses and Tall Fescue have the highest water requirements, approximately 1" of water per week and in the heat of the summer time this may have to be increased to 1.5-2" in multiple applications. Fewer applications, with greater quantities applied each time will permit the recharge of the soil profile and promote a much deeper and healthier root system. This deep infrequent irrigation also permits the turf canopy to dry out, and a drier turf canopy will have less disease and insect problems. Even the most drought tolerant, Buffalograss and Zoysia, require periodic applications of moisture (rain or irrigation) every 20 days; otherwise they will go dormant.

## MOW

Mow often. A properly mowed turf will be healthy, dense and weed free. The frequency of mowing is dependent on species, fertilization and irrigation. As mentioned, the more you fertilize, the more irrigation required and the more frequently you must mow. On old established lawns mow when the grass is one-third taller than it should be. Leave clippings on lawn. One-third nutrients for lawn can come from clippings. Select the proper height *(see Table 1, p. 102)* for your species, and maintain a sharp, properly operating lawn mower. The height of cut will generally dictate the type of mower needed. Mowing heights above 1" can generally be accomplished with a sharp rotary mower, and a mulching mower is preferred to return the clippings into the landscape. For heights of cut below 1", it may be necessary to use a well-maintained reel mower and it may be necessary to mow 2-3 times weekly, again depending on the season, amount and type of fertilizer and frequency of irrigation.

## AERATION

When a lawn is much used by people or animals, or has been established for years, the soils may become very compacted in places and will not allow water, fertilizer, micro-nutrients or air to pass through to the roots.

That lawn can be rejuvenated by simply introducing more air into the soil. To do this, aeration *(see p. 33)* is needed. The simplist aeration tools puncture, tear or rip into the soil. A core-type aerifier extracts small plugs from 2-4" of the soil profile. Hollow tines on a drum or disk revolve by power or hand-energized machinery. A stiff tined garden fork inserted every 6" can achieve aeration also. A yearly aeration in spring or summer to a depth of 2" is good, though 6-7" is better. Sprinkler system pipe and heads should be marked to avoid before aeration begins.

After aerating, a light dusting of compost, including grass seed, is the perfect follow up. (3/4 cubic yards per 1000 square feet of lawn.)

A thick layer of thatch may also stop water and nutrients from reaching roots. Thatch is a layer of dead plant debris between the runners and the soil line. Thatch should not be deeper than 1/2".

**GRUB CONTROL** (June Bugs or Japanese Beetles)

These beetle larva feed on the shallow roots of grasses like Fescue and St. Augustine. Failure to control them will result in large brown areas and dead turf *(see p. 59).*

## ORNAMENTAL GRASSES

Design possibilities with ornamental grasses stir the imagination. Varieties of these currently popular landscape plants have height, hue and function. Specimen silhouettes, screenings, borders, ground covers and container grown grass may realize form and texture for formal, rock or water gardens in every season. As grasses are the dominant plant of our prairie location, they are adaptable and reliable. Sun and local precipitation are their only needs. Cut back perennial species in late February. Annual color species decorate gardens for autumn interest.

**Blue Sheep Fescue** *Festuca amethystina* ▪ Compact growth (8") of fine textured "weeping" tufts. Blue-green colors. Good for containers, ground cover or perennial beds. Plant in full sun, moist soil.

**Big Bluestem** *Andropogon gerardii* (Turkey Foot) ▪ The three branched seed head resembles the common name. 4'-7' tall. Best in drifts, mass or as a background screen. New cultivars have more color.

**Eastern Gamagrass** *Tripsacum dactyloides* ▪ 2'-3', can reach 4'. Dense, luxurious, clump, rich dark green leaf, tolerates more shade than other grasses, prefers moist soil or location with extra seasonal run-off. Cut back in spring. Seed heads popular with deer.

**Fountain Grass** *Pennisetum setaceum* ▪ Bottle-brush, foxtail like seeds. Orientalis: 'Hamlin' buff colored beads, 'Moudrey' black flower beads, tender perennial thin leaves 1/8 to 1/4" wide, tufts 2' to 3' tall and wide, flower spikes to 5'. Prefers full sun, moist, well-drained soil.

**Indiangrass** *Sorghastrum nutans* ∎ Upright clumping grass. Feathery seed heads grow 2' to 3' above foliage. Dry stiff spikes turn attractive burnt orange in fall. A most beautiful specimen or for mass.

**Inland Sea Oats** *Chasmanthium latifolium* ∎ Native perennial 24" to 36", light green spring leaves to fall bronze, big drooping oat-like seeds. Moist well-drained soil as on creek banks. A shade loving grass.

**Japanese Silver Grass** *Miscanthus sinensis* ∎ White stripped accent plant 8' to 10' perennial, prefers moist soil in full sun, fall color is good. Rusty foliage, ivory plumes.

**Lindheimer Muhly** *Muhlenbergia lindheimeri* ∎ Native perennial, 24" to 30" clumping softer leaves than pampas, soft aqua blue color, prefers well-drained soil. *(Do not cut back in early spring because it is a slow growing evergreen.)* Tidy, contained specimen plant.

**Little Bluestem** *Schizachyrium scoparium* ∎ Fraying golden grass, rampant growth. Good for sunny slope control. 2' to 5' tall.

**Maiden Grass** *Miscanthus gracillimus* ∎ 'Morning Mist' fine texture, 3' to 4' showy seed heads, full sun, moist conditions.

**Pampas Grass** *Cortaderia selloana* ∎ One of the most popular ornamental grasses and largest. Care should be given in garden placement due to eventual size. Plume heights to 10', dense clumps cut back in late winter or early spring. Full sun to part shade, prefers moist well-drained soil.

**Prairie Dropseed** *Sporobolus heterolepis* ∎ 1-1/2' to 2' tall, arching clumps of fine textured leaves. Member of the once extensive American prairies. Now, when found in the wild, it is a sign of an undisturbed prairie. In dry areas good ground cover. Delicate odor.

**Purple Fountain Grass** *Pennisetum setaceum* ∎ 'Rubrum'. Most popular annual ornamental grass. Stunning purple blades, red-purple seed heads fading to beige. Plumes 2' to 3' above foliage.

**Ravenna Grass** or **Hardy Pampas** *Erianthus ravennae* ∎ A giant in the garden with clumps 4' to 5' wide, flower stalks to 8-10'. Leaves are medium grey-green 3' to 4' long in fall turning shades of orange, tan, brown and purple. Tolerates wide range of garden conditions. Cut back to ground when plant becomes too unattractive.

**Sideoats Gramagrass** *Bouteloua curtipendula* ∎ Native perennial. Recognized by seed heads on one side of stem. 1' to 2' tall. Prefers full sun, dry, well-drained fertile soil. The Texas State grass. Use in mass.

**Switchgrass** *Panicum virgatum* (Heavy Metal) ∎ Silver blue in summer, great red color fall. Not so rampant. Native perennial, clumping 3' to 6' tall with seed heads, good fall color. Prefers moist, fertile soil in full sun, however it will tolerate a range of garden conditions.

**Zebra Grass** *Miscanthus sinensis* 'zibrinus' ▪ Horizontal chartreuse banding across arching leaf blades, 4' to 5' tall. Good for flower arrangements.

## REFERENCES

*Tallgrass Prairie* by John Madson, A Nature Conservancy Book, Falcon Press, Helena, Montana, 1993.

*Ornamental Grasses: The Amber Wave* by Carole Ottsen, McGraw-Hill, 1989.

*The Encyclopedia of Ornamental Grasses: How To Grow And Use Over 250 Beautiful and Versatile Plants* by John Greenlee, Rodale Press, 1992.

## LOCAL PRAIRIES

A few rare virgin native prairies exist for visitation: Parkhill Prairie in Collin County Park Systems is well marked with trails, shelters and facilities. Clymer Meadow near Merit has 700 acres of the highest quality Blackland Prairie remaining in Texas.

Native prairies have never been cultivated. Many ranchers have kept some acreage in native prairies for drought season grass.

**Native Prairies Association of Texas**
3503 Lafayette Avenue
Austin, Texas 78722-1807

**Cedar Hill State Park**
(1810 acres with several sections of Tallgrass Prairie)

P.O. Box 2649 — FM 1382 near Mansfield Road
Cedar Hill, Texas 75106
(972) 291-3900

**Heard Natural Science Museum and Wildlife Sancturary**
(289 acres with 48 acres under restoration plan)

2 miles east of 75 at exit 38
McKinney, Texas
Dr. Ken Steigman, Coordinator of Natural Areas
Tallgrass prairie specialist
(972) 562-5566

**For More Open Spaces:** *(see p.165).*

# Chapter 13

## ANNUALS & BIENNIALS

*Annuals and biennials are short-lived plants popular for the infusion of color they add to a garden.*

An annual is a plant which germinates, grows, flowers, fruits and dies within a single year. For a sparkle to landscape, for instant color and garden gratification, plant annuals. A biennial is a plant which completes its life cycle within the space of two years. Biennials are noted in the list below by #.

### KEY

The abbreviation in the margin states which metroplex season each annual or biennial blooms. For instance, English Summer annuals thrive best in Dallas mild winters.

**SP**= Spring    **SU** = Summer    **F** = Fall    **W** = Winter

### PLANT LIST

SP-F   **Ageratum** *Ageratum* ▪ Blue or white, fuzzy cluster, height 8-12". Spring through fall bloom. Plant in flats in January, outside in spring, spacing 12-15". Light shade preferred. Easy. Good cutting. Feed regularly for best performance.

W     **Alyssum, Sweet** *Lobularia maritima* ▪ White, purple or lavender fragrant bloom clusters. Perform better in winter and fall on 4-6" plants. Space 12", planting in November or late February and March outside. Compact and spreading. Reseeds.

SU    **Balsam** ▪ See Impatiens.

SP    **Begonia** *Begonia semperflorens* ▪ Red, pink or white flowers, bronze-foliaged varieties for sun, green-leaved types best in shade, 8-15" tall, can be planted 6-12" apart, prefer light shade. Needs well-amended soil and good drainage. Keep moist but not wet.

SP    **Bluebonnet** *Lupinus spp.* ▪ State flower of Texas. Blue or pale pink April - May bloom, 12-14". Sow in early fall outside using treated seed to aid germination. Needs full sun, good drainage and alkaline soil. Native.

W     **Calendula** *Calendula officinalis* ▪ Orange, gold and yellow daisies bloom from late winter through early summer, 12-18" height. Plant in flats in January, or buy transplants late winter, space 12-15". Good cutting. May over-winter in protected place or in mild winter. Remove faded blooms to prolong flowering.

F    **Candle Tree** *Cassia alata* ∎ Tender perennial grown as annual, height to 8', leaves large, flowers yellow in spike-like racemes, late summer to fall bloom. Any garden soil, needs plenty of space. Sun. Watch for red spider, flowers attract ants.

W    **Chard** (Bright Lights) ∎ Ruddy leaf vegetable grown for color. Blends well with dwarf Nandina.

SP   **Chinese Forget-Me-Not** *Cynoglossum amabile* ∎ Electric Blue, 12-18" with February to June bloom. Large leaf, grey-green foliage. Plant in fall outside, spacing 6-8". Light shade.

SU   **Cleome** *Cleome spinosa* (Spider Flower) ∎ Lavender, white or pink summer blooms, height 3'. Plant in spring outside, space 18-24". Endures drought and poor soil. Good cutting. Reseeds.

SU-F **Cockscomb** *Celosia spp.* ∎ Both crested and plume-like flower types — red, yellow, orange, pink hybrids, 10-36" height. Plant out side in spring, spacing 6-24" depending on variety. Summer to fall bloom, likes sun and warmth. Reseeds. Flowers dry for arrangements.

SU-F **Coleus** *Coleus* ∎ Grown for vari-colored foliage, 10-18". Plant outside in spring in partial shade. Good cutting. Keep blooms removed and pinch when needed. Roots easily.

SU-F **Copperplant** *Acalypha wilkesiana* ∎ Copper-red foliage, variety "Louisiana Red" is rich red, 18-24", plant outside in spring-summer in sun. Rapid growing, watch for spider mites.

SP   **Cornflower** *Centaurea cyanus* (Bachelor's Button) ∎ Dark blue, pink or white. Spring bloom, 18" height. Sow in fall outside for spring bloom, space 8-10". Good cutting, easy, reseeds.

SU   **Cosmos** *Cosmos* ∎ Yellow, red, white, purple or pink daisy-like blooms in summer-fall. Height 15" to 30" depending on variety. Easy from seed, plant outside in early spring or late summer for fall bloom. Space 12-24". Tolerates light shade.

W    **Cyclamen** *Cyclamen persicum spp.* ∎ Winter flowering tuber, red-stalked conspicuous orchid-like flowers, vegetated heart-shaped leaf. Does not summer well.

     **Dianthus** ∎ Refer to Carnation *(See p. 117).*

W    **English Daisy** *Bellis perennis spp.* ∎ Use as winter annual. Small daisy-like double flower heads in red, pink and white. Dead head regularly.

W    **Flowering Cabbage** or **Kale** *Brassica oleracea* ∎ Sun, 15-18",color white to pinks. Will stand cold weather but not prolonged freezes.

SP   **Forget-Me-Not** *Myosotis* ∎ Low-growing, blue and pink with spring bloom. Plant outside in spring, spacing 6". Likes moist soil, semi-shade. Reseeds. Blooms late.

SU **Geranium** *Pelargonium x hortorum* var. ▪ Perennial used as summer annual. Performs well in pots when slightly root bound. Does best in spring and fall with cool nights. Plant in rich, well-drained soil in light shade or morning sun only. Allow to become slightly dry between waterings. Feed regularly with water soluble plant food in summer.

Propagate by taking cuttings in fall before frost. Using this year's growth-end tip, cut 3-6" branch straight across below a node with a sharp knife. Leave top 3 to 5 leaves in place, strip the others. Dip in root hormone powder and tap off all excess. Plant 1-1/2 to 2" deep in moist rooting medium *(See p. 49)*. Keep slightly moist and pot up as rooted. Plant out in early spring.

SU **Globe Amaranth** *Gomphrena* ▪ Round globe flower, magenta, orange-red, to white with summer to fall bloom. 12-24" tall. Space 6-12" in sun.

SU **Heliopsis** *Heliopsis* ▪ Yellow to orange flowers resembling shasta daisy, 2 - 3'. Summer bloom provides good cutting. Needs good drainage.

SU **Hibiscus** *Hibiscus* ▪ Several species and their hybrids are perennial. Growing to 4', some to 8', with typical hibiscus flowers in red, pink, white. Some hybrids have flowers to 14" across. Flowers only last one day. Tropical hibiscus do not take our winters. Native hibiscus do. *(See p. 79.)*

SU # **Hollyhock** *Alcea rosea* ▪ Mixed colors, usually tall, but dwarf available. Alkaline soil, needs sun and water for summer bloom (single and double). Splendid for hiding unsightly places. Subject to rust, spider mites. Start in flats in mid-summer.

SU **Impatiens** *Impatiens*: I. *balsamina* (Garden Balsam) ▪ Low bush-type balsam that displays blooms of various color at the top of the plants. Ideal for edging.

I. *wallerana* provides spring to fall bloom in variety of colors 6-15" tall. Plant in early spring outside. Likes semi-shade, loose, rich soil. Roots easily. Keep moist at all times. Heat of summer may cause leaf curl, reduction in flowering, plants will perk up with return of cooler weather. Bloom profusely so feed regularly. New Guinea impatiens require morning sun or very light shade. Many of these have variegated foliage and large blooms. Foliage may be bronze, burgundy, green with yellow or white. Best in pots. Requires more water.

SP-F **Indian Blanket** *Gaillardia pulchella* ▪ Yellow to red, May to fall bloom, 10-18" tall. Sow in spring or fall, space to 12". Good cutting. Will grow in poor, rocky alkaline soil. Keep faded blooms removed to prolong flowering. Native. Sow in fall for summer bloom. Try new cultivars, some with larger flowers.

SU **Joseph's Coat** *Amaranthus tricolor* ▪ Variegated leaves in summer. Plant in spring, in sun. Tender to frost. Height and spacing depends on variety. Roots easily from cuttings.

SU **Lantana** *Lantana* ▪ Yellow, red, white, pink, and orange flowers on shrubby plants, usually less than 3'. Trailing varieties are available. Bloom spring to fall. Full sun. Easy culture. Only *Lantana horrida*, the native Lantana, is reliably hardy. Variety "New Gold" does not set seed and blooms without cycling. Trim long shoots to keep full and compact.

SP **Larkspur** *Consolida ambigua* ▪ Often confused with Delphinium, blue, white,and pink, 24-30", spring bloom from outside sowing in fall. Needs sun, humus, and fertilizing. Good cutting. Self sows. Watch for aphids.

W **Lobelia** *Lobelia erinus* (Fairy Wings) ▪ Use as winter annual. Killed by our summer heat. Dark, light blue or white blooms. Compact and trailing varieties. Plant in spring outside in sun or semi-shade, spacing 4-8". Feed regularly. A good edger. Pinch if needed.

SU **Marigold** *Tagetes* ▪ Many varieties, some dwarf, having summer to fall bloom, orange to gold to lemon. Height to 30". Sow in flats in January, early spring or late summer (fall bloom) outside. Space according to variety. Watch for spider mites.

SU **Mexican Sunflower** *Tithonia* ▪ Rich irridescent orange to 4-6'. Spectacular summer to fall bloom. Plant in spring outdoors in sun.

W# **Mullein** *Verbascum* ▪ Yellow flowers on spikes to 2-3' tall above rosette of wooly leaves, June bloom. Likes light soil, sun. Will reseed. Start in flats in mid-summer, plant outside in November. Protect tap-root when transplanting. *Chaixii* - winter annual dark green leaves and has pale yellow or peach flowers.

W **Nasturtium** *Tropaeolum* ▪ Yellow to red, spring bloom, 6-12". Plant seeds 6" apart in February outside. Hard to transplant. Good cutting. Likes alkaline soil, sun, and minimum water. Prefers cool weather. Trailing varieties good in hanging baskets.*(See p.156.)*

SU **Nicotiana** *Nicotiana* (Flowering Tobacco) ▪ Trumpet-shaped white, pink, or red flowers on plants 12-18" tall, summer - fall bloom. Plant in flats in January. Fragrant in evening. Likes semi-shade to shade. Good cutting. Requires long days to flower.

W **Pansy** *Viola wittrockiana* ▪ Significant improvements in strains have been made to make this bedding plant even more popular, with tolerance to both heat and cold. In October or November transplant in permanent beds of amended soil, made ready previously with generous quantities of organic matter. Pansies are gross feeders and need a rich bed. Set plants high, and as soon as planted, treat for pill bugs, snails, and cutworms. Water copiously. Cover plants when a hard freeze is expected, but snow doesn't bother them. A bi-weekly application of fertilizer will make fine blooms and plants. Cottonseed meal and blood meal are excellent also. Keep flowers picked for longer and better blooms. Edible Flowers.

SU   **Pentas** *Pentas lanceolata* ▪ Pink, red, white, 15-18". Set bedding plants out in spring. It is treated as an annual in Dallas as it is only half-hardy. Butterflies love it. A tropical.

SU   **Periwinkle** *Vinca*, also *Catharanthus roseus* ▪ White to rose, 12-18", also dwarf. Mass planting in spring outside is best. Endures shade, easy culture, continuous summer to fall bloom. Usually satisfactory.

SP   **Petunia** *Petunia x hybrida* ▪ Many varieties, single, double, ruffled, in every color. Low, tall and trailing, equally suitable for baskets, beds and borders, planters, tubs, and boxes. They like the sun and are not demanding as to soil. Plant in flats in January, outside in early spring. The seeds are very fine, so do not cover with soil. If the plants become spindly, cut them back and they will bloom again. New variety Purple wave, cold hardy.

W   **Phlox** *Phlox drummondii* ▪ White to purple to rose. Plant in fall where you want them to be in bloom. Good cutting. Reseeds. Native to Texas, so they like alkaline soil and sun.

    **Pinks** ▪ Refer to Carnations *(See p. 117).*

SU   **Poppy, California** *Eschsholzia* ▪ Yellow, gold, and orange, 10-12", spring bloom. Dislikes transplanting. Sow outside in fall or spring, then thin to 9". Mix fine seeds with vermiculite to spread evenly.
    **Iceland** *Papaver nudicaule* (Flanders) ▪ Various colors, deep orange to pastels to white. Plant in fall outdoors. Edible flowers.
    **Shirley** *Papaver Rhoeas* ▪ Scarlet, orange, pink, and blue spring bloom, 18" up. Plant outside in fall. This field poppy has hairy stems and buds. Edible flowers.

SU   **Portulaca** *Portulaca grandiflora* (Moss Rose) ▪ Blooms at 2"-4" in various colors. Sow outside in spring, likes sun and hot dry weather. Flowers close in afternoon. Self sows.

W   **Primrose** *Primula spp.* ▪ Sun, part sun, mostly shade, 6"-10", tremendous range of color. Requires cool weather. Best as winter-early spring annual.

W     **Primula** ▪ See Primrose

SU    **Prince's-Feather** *Amaranthus hybridus* var. *erythrostachys* ▪ Crimson, 15 - 18". Summer bloom cuts well. Sow outside in spring.

SU    **Salvia** *Salvia splendens* (Scarlet Sage) ▪ 12-18". Red, white, or purple spikes. Plant in spring outside, spacing 8-12". Blooms from June on. Needs protection from summer sun. Native salvias are perennial.

SU    **Scaevola** *Scavola aemula spp.* (Fan Flower) ▪ Creeping annual ground cover full of bloom until frost for irrigated landscapes, tested by county agent for long term color. Pink, white, light blue, and purple.

W-SP **Snapdragon** *Antirrhinum* ▪ Various colors, 10-30". Plant in flats in January, outside in spring, or purchase plants in November and spring, spacing 10-12", sun or light shade. Good cutting. Dwarf varieties available. Cutworms love them. *(See pp. 57 and 59 for treatment.)* Can be used in winter garden.

W-SP **Stock** *Matthiola* ▪ Purple, pink to white, 6-18". Fall planting outside, protect during extreme cold. Space 12", in sun in well-drained soil. Good cutting, fragrant.

SU    **Sunflower** *Helianthus* ▪ Golden, height 2-9'. Plant seed 24" apart in spring for summer bloom. Hard to transplant. Dwarf variety available. Birds love the seeds. Full sun.

SP#   **Sweet William** *Dianthus barbatus* ▪ Pink, red, and white blooms, 6-12" height Start seeds in flats in mid-summer, set out in November for following May bloom.

SU    **Torenia** *Torenia* (Wishbone Flower) ▪ Blue, 8-12". Plant in flats in January, outside in spring, spacing 6-8" in light to partial shade.

SU    **Verbena** *Verbena x hybrida* ▪ White to magenta, 6-12", summer to fall bloom. Plant in flats in January, outside in spring, spacing 12". Variety Apple Blossom has large, fragrant pink flowers. Watch for spider mites. Some species are perennial.

SP    **Johnny Jump Up** (Viola) ▪ Small blue, white, yellow, or purple pansy face. Viola tri-color can reseed. Nice bulb cover. More resistant to snails and slugs then its cousin, the Pansy.

W#    **Wallflower** *Cheiranthus* ▪ Yellow, bronze, orange, 12-18", blooming February-April. Sow in October outside, or plant purchased plants in November in full sun, well-drained soil.

SU    **Zinnia** *Zinnia* ▪ Many colors and many varieties growing from 6" to 48". Long summer to fall bloom. Plant outside all spring and summer. Remember to avoid getting water on the foliage to prevent mildew. *Zinnia linearis*, orange or white, resist powdery mildew.

# Chapter 14

## PERENNIALS

*A Perennial is a non-woody plant which lives
more than two years, but which may die down each winter and
renew growth every spring from its roots.
Perennials are the plant most likely to be divided and shared.*


In the Dallas Area, it is best to set out all perennial plants in the fall. They become established as root growth takes place during the winter. With warm spring sunshine, the plants grow rapidly. Spring planting can succeed, but the earlier it is done the better. Mulching and proper watering habits will be especially critical the first summer. If you are planting seeds, they should be sown as soon as they ripen. Carry seedlings through the summer in flats or pots in the shade then transplant to permanent quarters in the fall. Plant for a succession of blooms. Prolong bloom by removing faded flowers cut (deadheading). Most perennials like neutral soil. Prepare your bed thoroughly since the plantings will not be removed seasonally. *(See p. 38.)* Allow for yearly increase of size.

**Achillea** *Achillea* (Yarrow) ▪ Yellow, pink, some white. Flat flower head, blooms May-June. Height 12-42". Sun. Fern-like carrot leaves stay green all winter. Cut back after bloom. Flower will dry for arrangements. Dwarf variety available, but require especially good drainage. Increase by division of clumps each spring. Start seeds in flats in summer.

**Ageratum, Hardy** *Eupatorium* (Native Ageratum) ▪ Lavender blue, 8-12" with spring summer, or fall bloom. Spreads rapidly, so you may wish to contain roots with edging. Half shade or full sun (with adequate water). Propagate by stem cuttings or division of clumps.

**Anemone** *Anemone hybrida* (Windflower) ▪ White, pink, red, single and double. Height 12-15", early spring bloom. Strawberry-like leaves. Likes slightly alkaline rich soil with plenty of water but not wet feet. Shade from afternoon sun. Does not like to be disturbed. Propagate by root cuttings. Tuberous-rooted, best treated as annual in this area.

**Artemisia** *Artemisia* (Dusty Miller) ▪ Grown for its foliage of gray leaves, 2-3', but dwarf variety "Silver Brocade" available, variety "Powis Castle" also excellent. Bloom insignificant. Rapid grower, can be invasive. Propagate by seeds or division. Roots easily. Winter garden.

**Asclepias** *Asclepias tuberosa* (Butterfly Weed) ▪ Striking orange bloom all summer, some varieties pink or red. Height 18", full sun, good drainage. Flowers attract butterflies. Difficult to transplant. Watch for red spider mites. Start from seeds, stem cuttings. Native. New cultivars: Red Butterfly & Silky Gold.

**Aspidistra** *Aspidistra elatior* (Cast-iron-plant) ▪ Bloom insignificant, grown for stiff vertical evergreen foliage of 18-24", which is good in flower arrangements. Full shade, watch for spider mites. Damaged in severe winters.

**Aster** *Aster* ▪ Many varieties having blue to purple bloom, usually in fall. Cushion size to tall, most need support and sun. Divide about every three years. Watch for spider mites.

**Banana** *Musa ensete* ▪ Rapid growth in fertile porous soil with compost, much moisture, and adequate drainage. Needs sun and protection from wind. Tropical, so cut to ground after first freeze.

**Bee Balm** *Monarda didyma* ▪ Red to pale pink, 2-3' with summer bloom. Needs rich, moist soil in sun or light shade. Leaves have minty odor, attracting bees and hummingbirds. Easy. Start in flats in mid-summer or propagate by division. Can become invasive.

**Bletilla** *Bletilla striata* (Ground Orchid) ▪ Spikes of small cattleya orchid-like dark lavender flowers in mid-spring. Foliage is linear and pleated. Needs moist, slightly acid soil and morning sun. True soil-growing orchid - *Tuberous Rhizone*.

**Candytuft** *Iberis sempervirens* ▪ Low, completely covered with small white flowers in spring. Evergreen. Plant in light shade. Trim after flowering if it straggles. Resents transplanting, so start from seeds or buy container grown. A good plant for our area.

**Carnation** *Dianthus* (Pinks) ▪ Many varieties. Check catalogs for new hybrids. Good cut flowers from spring and early summer bloom. Provide good drainage in well-amended soil or mats of foliage will rot. Seeds started in mid-summer, and set out in November will bloom in May. Propagate by division. Height to 12".

**Catnip** *Nepeta cataria* ▪ An herb with grey-green foliage and lavender spike bloom about 12" tall. Easy. Sow in spring.

**Cassia** C. *lindheimeriana* (Velvet Leaf) ▪ Yellow pea flowers, sweet fragrance, late summer. Partial to full sun. Xeriphyle for well drained clay soils.

**Cheiranthus** (Bowles Mauve) ▪ Favored perennial for long-blooming, pale purple clusters of small spikes. Grey-green evergreen leaves.

**Chrysanthemum** *Chrysanthemum x morifolium* ▪ Many varieties available for fall bloom. All mums need rich, porous, slightly acid soil, in a sunny location. Make stem cuttings in March and transplant to permanent position when well-rooted. Old clumps may be divided by discarding the center section and using one rooted stem to a planting. Keep plants growing strong all summer by giving them plenty of food and water — very important to success in the fall. Stake, if necessary, early and keep tied as growth advances. When plants are 6" high, pinch out top of main stem to make bushy. Begin feeding at this stage with a light application of fertilizer well-watered in. Keep fertilizer away from stems. Continue to feed every two weeks until buds show color. Keep plants mulched. Remember they need water but not wet feet. Watch for aphids and the cucumber beetle. Disbud if you want large specimen flowers. Chrysanthemums are classified on flower formation (i.e. anemone, button, daisy, spider, etc.), as well as their growth habits (i.e. cascade, cushion, etc.). New cultivars are developed each year, white, pink, purple, yellow, red, bronze, and apricot.

**Columbine** *Aquilegia* ∎ Many and various colors with spring bloom, 10-24". Light and graceful cut flowers. Need rich, organic, acid soil and semi-shade. Keep mulched. Watch for leaf miners. Native varieties, mostly yellow, are best-adapted, especially "Texas Gold".

**Coneflower** *Echinacea purpurea* (Purple Coneflower) ∎ Rosy purple daisy-type flowers, white varieties available, on 2-3' plants. Will tolerate full sun and drought but much better with good soil, light afternoon shade, and regular water. Native.

**Coralbells** *Heuchera* ∎ Low clumps of evergreen geranium-like foliage and spikes of small pink, red, or white bell-shaped flowers in late spring-early summer. Needs partial shade, good drainage.

**Coreopsis** *Coreopsis* ∎ Yellow, daisy-like flowers in singles, doubles, and dwarf, 10-24". Easy culture, blooming in May, June. Sun, well-drained. Plant is bushy and stems are strong, making them great cut flowers. Keep faded flowers cut for longer bloom till frost. Divide annually. C. *Moonbeam* and C. *Zagreb* have fine lacy foliage on compact plants with soft yellow flowers from May to September.

**Daisy, Blackfoot** *Melampodium leucanthum* ∎ Low growing compact small daisy. White blossoms throughout growing season. Over watering rots roots. Yellow and orange varieties available.

**Daisy, Gerbera** *Gerbera jamesonii* ∎ Showy daisies in numerous colors. Height 12-18". Flower late spring-fall. Best in cool, but not cold weather. Plant in protected place with no west sun; important that crown of plant is 1/2" above soil level. Protect in winter during extreme cold but do not mulch heavily around the crown which will cause rot. These are stunning cut flowers but temperamental. They need lots of water but good drainage. Difficult to grow here.

**Daisy, Shasta** *Chrysanthemum x maximum* ▪ Many varieties: all white, dwarf to tall with June bloom. Need deep, rich, consistently moist soil, light afternoon shade and division every two years.

**Daylily** ▪ Refer to Hemerocallis *(see pp. 131-132).*

**Delphinium** *Delphinium* ▪ Often mistaken for a large larkspur. A cool climate plant. Does not like our summers. Best if planted early fall for Spring bloom and treated as biennial.

**Ferns** ▪ Perennial, hardy, flowerless, some winter hardy. Many species with simple requirements for cultivation. Adaptable to many locations. Use massed on north side of the house where flowering plants will not thrive, in rock gardens, shady corners, or bare spots under trees or where light is insufficient. They grow in fairly deep shade, diffused light, filtered and morning sun. The more sun, the more water they will need. Most prefer moist soil and good drainage plus a mulch for cool, damp root-run. In general, soil should have humus, mineral matter, and be sufficiently friable to allow penetration by fine roots. Plant 9-18" apart, with roots not too deep and the crown at surface level. In transplanting, it is imperative to prevent roots from drying out.

*Dryopteris erythrosora* (Autumn Fern) ▪ Evergreen, low border-type comes back from severe winters.

*Polystichum acrostichoides* (Christmas Fern) ▪ 2-3', evergreen, full shade.

*Cyrtomium falcatum* (Holly Fern) ▪ Glossy, thick, holly-like leaves. Give year round evergreen accent to shady areas. If damaged will return.

*Athyrium niponicum* (Japanese Painted Fern) ▪ Metallic grey to grey-green patterned fronds. Will tolerate some sun. Hardy.

*Osmunda regalis* (Royal Fern) ▪ Deciduous fern to 4', must be moist to wet throughout summer-fall.

*Thelypteris kunthii* (Wood Fern) ▪ Deciduous fern, widely adapted, also known as *Dryopteris normalis.* Can tolerate full sun.

**Feverfew** *Chrysanthemum parthenium* ▪ Double white flowers, 20" up, pungent odor. Plant outside in spring; tolerates semi-shade.

**Gaillardia** *Gaillardia x grandiflora* (Blanketflower) ▪ Red with yellow daisies, 12-15", blooms late spring through summer, sun to light shade. Adaptable but needs good drainage. *(See p.112 - Indian Blanket.)*

**Ginger Lily** *Hedychium coronarium* ▪ Plant in sun to partial shade in rich, moist soil. Feed heavily. Tropical-looking foliage (like Cannas) to 3-5' with spikes of extremely fragrant white flowers in summer. Requires two consecutive years of mild winters with above freezing temperature to bloom. Winter-hardy but best in a protected location. Cut back to ground and mulch before frost.

**Gloriosa** *Rudbeckia* ▪ Summer bloom in yellows to bronze, in sun or partial shade, 15-24". Variety "Goldstrum" reliable and long-blooming, attractive foliage.

**Grasses** (Ornamental) ▪ Grasses were the dominant plant of the Blackland Prairie and so are very well-adapted and reliable. Numerous types are available. *(See pp. 107-109.)*

**Guara** *Guara lindheimeri* (Whirling Butterfly) ▪ Tall stalks with separate flowers of pink to white like small butteflies. Blooms from spring to fall. Texas native.

**Liatris** *Liatris* (Gay-feather or Blazing Star) ▪ Native — is lavender, but new hybrids in deep pink and white. Plant in sun in well-drained soil for late summer bloom. Attracts bees.

**Lythrum** *Lythrum* (Loosestrife) ▪ Pink and purple flowers in tall spikes. Bloom June-August on plants to 4'. Watch for aphids. Likes sun and moisture. Cut to the ground in winter.

**Oxalis** *Oxalis* (Wood Sorrel) ▪ Old fashioned pink bloom nearly year round. Yellow can become invasive. Hardy border plant, leaves have tendency to disappear in hot summer. Likes semi-shade. Susceptible to spider mites; harbors pill bugs and snails under foliage.

**Penstemon** *Penstemon* (Beard-tongue) ▪ Various types, several native species. Lavender, red, pink, or white flowers on plants to 3'; some dwarf varieties. Bloom in late spring-early summer. Like rich soil, good drainage. Propagate by division, seed.

**Peony** *Paeonia Halics hybrids* ▪ Select early bloomers only. In fall, plant roots shallow, eyes barely showing. Fertilize with 1-1/2 cups bone meal in November, February and after blooming. Add 1/2 cup Super Phosphate to February feeding.

**Phlox** *Phlox* P. *divaricata* (Louisiana Phlox) ▪ Low-growing semi-ever green with lavender, blue, or pink flowers in mid-spring.
P.*maculata*, P. *carolina* ▪ Hardy phloxes to 18" that are more resistant to mildew than P. *paniculata*.
P.*paniculata* (Hardy Phlox) ▪ Pink, purple, red, white flower heads on 1-4' plants in mid to late summer. Likes rich soil and lots of water. Keep mulched. Mildews in late summer and looks rough.
P.*subulata* (Thrift) ▪ Dwarf evergreen with needle-like leaves covered with white, red, pink, or blue flowers in early spring. Needs sun. Use as edging.

**Physostegia** *Physostegia* (Obedient Plant) ▪ Pink or white summer bloom atop 3-4' stems. Good for arrangements as flowers remain at any angle turned, hence the name "Obedient Plant." Blossoms are like tiny snapdragons. Easy culture. Spreads by runners. Needs division every few years.

**Plantain Lily** *Hosta* ∎ Grown for handsome foliage but most have spikes of white to pale lavender flowers in summer. Many varieties, green or variegated foliage. Needs shade and consistent moisture. Divide roots to propagate. Watch for snails and slugs.

**Platycodon** *Platycodon* (Balloonflower) ∎ Blue or white bell-shaped flowers similar to Texas Bluebells. Height 12-24" with summer bloom. Easy culture. Prefers acid soil and consistent moisture. Good cutting. Pinch back in mid-spring to keep full. Variety "Kamachi", blooms remain balloon-like and do not open fully.

**Plumbago** *Ceratostigma plumbaginoides* ∎ Deep peacock blue flowers borne in small clusters. Low; a good plant for ground cover, spreads by underground runners. Mid-summer to fall bloom. New growth is bronzy. Prefers sandy loam, sun to light shade. Divide clumps in spring. *Plumbago auriculata* (Cape Plumbago) ∎ Pale blue flower clusters on 12-18" sprawling plant. Plant in spring in sun to light shade. Drought resistant. Winter tender but often survives if protected.

**Red Hot Poker** *Kniphofia* ∎ Spring bloom, 2-3', good cutting. Foliage is grass-like. Must have full sun and excellent drainage. Prefers sandy soil. Difficult to grow here.

**Red Champion** *Lychnis* ∎ Deep rose-red blooms in spring, 2-3". Grey felt-like leaves in a rosette. Good cutting. Needs adequate drainage. Plant seeds in flats in summer for bloom the following spring. May be propagated by stem cuttings.

**Salvia** *Salvia* ∎ Numerous perennial varieties, mostly with purple to deep blue flowers. Most need sun to light shade, somewhat drought tolerant. *(See p. 126, other native varieties.)*
S. *azurea* (Blue Sage) ∎ Slender upright stems bear small blue flowers summer to fall.
S. *farinacea* (Mealy Sage) ∎ To 2', spring to fall bloom with medium blue flower spikes; cut back in mid-summer for good fall bloom. Native.
S. *greggii* ∎ Small shrub to 2' with summer - fall bloom in reds, pinks, and whites. Needs good drainage. Native.
S. *leucantha* ∎ Fast growing shrubby plant to 4' with grey-green foliage and spectacular spikes of velvety, purple flowers from late August to October. Grows throughout Central America. Somewhat winter tender here.
S. *superba* ∎ Long, slender spikes of deep purple in early summer and occasionally through fall.

**Scabiosa** *Scabiosa* (Pincushion Flower) ∎ Many cultivars from white to blue-lilac. Early summer bloom. Prefers light shade. Divide clumps.

**Sedum** *Sedum spectabile and cultivars* (Autumn Joy) ■ Low succulents to 18" with summer or fall bloom in pink, maroon fleshy grey-green leaves, easily propagated through cuttings. Likes sun, but not hot west sun, good drainage. Keep on dry side. Start from stem cutting or division.

**Speedwell** *Veronica* ■ 1-2'. Blue, pink, and white flower spikes in summer. Many varieties including dwarf. Easy. Prefers light to semi-shade, regular moisture.

**Statice** *Limonium* ■ Lavender flowers like Baby's-breath. Height 18-24" and drying as it is everlasting. Likes sandy loam, sun or partial shade. Leathery, dark green foliage in rosettes. Start in flats in mid-summer or divide clumps in fall. Difficult to grow here.

**Stokesia** *Stokesia* (Stoke's Aster) ■ Large, frilly, lavender blooms in late spring. Prefers light or afternoon shade, consistent moisture. Attractive foliage after bloom.

**Verbena** *Verbena* ■ Several short-lived perennial types with trailing, lacy foliage and pink, lavender, or red flowers spring to fall. Prefer sun, good drainage. Watch for spider mites. *(See p. 115.)*

**Veronica** ■ *See Speedwell*

**Violets** *Viola* ■ Several species grow here. Need partial shade, moisture. Reseed themselves. Can become invasive. Watch for spider mites. V. *Sororia* - Confederate Violet.

## REFERENCES

*Perennial Garden Color* by William C. Welch, Taylor, 1989.

*Passalong Plants* by Steve Bender and Felder Rushing, University of North Carolina Press, 1993.

TAMU: Wildflowers in Bloom Web Site
http: //aggie-horticulture.tamu.edu/wildseed

## PERENNIAL SOCIETIES

**Dallas Metro Chrysanthemum Society**
Ward English
9204 Cedar Run Drive
Dallas, Texas  75227
(214) 388-9263

**Native Plant Society**
Georgia Prakhash
1905 Wm. Bruester Street
Irving, Texas 75061
(972) 259-2020

**Southwestern Fern Society**
P.O. Box 8427
Dallas, Texas 75205

# Chapter 15

# NATIVE PLANTS
*Perennials* ⁂ *Vines* ⁂ *Flowers*

It is important for every gardener to consider the loss of our natural biodiversity, the plants of Texas prairies 100 years ago, and to work toward a restoration of what once grew on the land. We are not the only creatures on earth and our interdependence with the flora and fauna that existed in nature has not yet been determined. Therefore, if you have a neglected corner or an open sunny spot in your garden area, a prairie restoration could be attempted. One of the benefits of a miniprairie is the return of some birds and butterflies you may not have seen before in the city. Many indigenous plants are not particular as to soil type, thriving throughout our metro area in the diversity of the blackland prairie, the grand prairie, and the cross timbers prairie.

As a homeowner or land owner, be a pioneer in conservation of natural resources. Experiment. Natives are marketed in seed form and containerized plants. The Lady Bird Johnson Wildflower Center in Austin has published a list of suppliers. By using the Department of Agriculture zone numbers, you can determine if the ones you choose are suitable, temperature-wise. Wildflowers are temperamental, appearing one year or not at all, or biennially, or in 5 or 10 year periods. By keeping careful records, you can contribute to the body of knowledge that is now being sought. Many of the flowers make a continuous colorful display without the benefit of a sprinkling system, fertilizer, or pesticides. Some are shy and are the harbinger of spring, opening only a few hours to announce their presence. The shoulders of our Texas highways have become an oriental carpet of colors, a running kaleidoscope of bright wildflowers, thriving on proper neglect and mowing techniques. You could achieve similar results on your own land. Sunshine is the key to success.

*Amorpha canescens* (**Lead Plant**) ∎ Shrub with gray-green leaves, purple-spikes with exserted yellow stamens. June bloom. Said to be a prairie indicator plant.

*Amsonia* (**Blue Star**) ∎ Perennial planted from root stock. Spring bloom, area species are *ciliata, illustris,* and *repens.*

*Anemopsis californica* (**Yerba Mansa**) ∎ Perennial from root stock or seed. Seed germinates in 5 weeks if kept wet. Grows in wet places. Cut flower resembles a White Anemone, lasts about 2 weeks in water. (Sepals look like petals.) Entire plant and seeds have a fragrantly herbal scent. Forms colonies with huge beautiful leaves. Dies down each year till spring comes. Tolerates a wide range of temperatures, altitude and soil conditions as long as it is a wet place. Of ancient Indian medicinal use. Not a well-known plant.

*Argemone albifiora* (**Cowboys Fried Egg, White Prickly Poppy**) ▪ Annual or biennial with deep tap root, prickly gray leaves, exuding deep yellow juice. Blooms in hot weather.

*Aristolochia tomentosa* (**Pipe Vine**) ▪ A vine with flowers shaped like a pipe. You will see the Swallowtail Butterfly laying its eggs on the leaves.

*Caesalpinia spp.* (**Dragon Flower, Bush Bird of Paradise**) ▪ Small feathery tree that casts no shade. Widely used in landscaping in the 20's. Supposedly introduced from Argentina. Showy spring flowers with long tassel-like red stamens hanging from yellow petals.

*Camassia scilloides* (**Wild Hyacinth**) ▪ Bulb. Grows easily from seed. Eminently satisfactory garden plant of tall pale blue spikes, useful in flower arrangements. Spring.

*Cardiospermum halicacabum* (**Heart Vine**) ▪ Annual. Grows readily from large beautiful seeds, that are black and white like the yin yang symbol. Delicate leaves, insignificant male and female flowers. Seed capsule an attractive heart-shaped lantern. Graceful when climbing. Will mat as a ground cover and soil binder.

*Centaurea americana* (**Basket Flower**) ▪ A tall deep pink basket-like flower. An annual that seeds readily.

*Cocculus carolinus* (**Snailseed**) ▪ Vine. Red berries festooned in trees by September.

*Cooperia drummondii* (**Rain Lily**) ▪ Bulb. Also grows easily from seed. Comes up after rainfall at various times of the year and sets seed. Grows in the lawn, too.

*Engelmannia pinnatifida* (**Cut Leaf Daisy**) ▪ Perennial with woody tap root. Long springtime bloom. Yellow flowers.

*Eryngium yuccifolium* (**Rattlesnake Master**) ▪ Medium to tall plant, best started from rooted plants. Florets clustered at top, when dry resemble thistles. A special native of the tall grass prairie.

*Erythronium albidum* (**Trout Lily**) ▪ Bulb. Grows in moist woods. Two mottled leaves appear through fallen leaf cover. Early bloomer with strongly reflexed petals. Not a good cut flower.

*Euphorbia bicolor* (**Ghost Weed**) ▪ Use annual species for white accent to the garden in fall. Grows under trees. Irritating stem hairs cause itching.

*Eustoma grandiflorum* (**Bluebell** ) ▪ Annual. Beautiful purple summer blooms. Seeds like powder but germinate in time.

*Forestiera* (**Herald of Spring**) ▪ Shrub. Small yellow clusters on bare branches the coldest day in January. Popular with bees.

*Gaillardia pulchella* (**Indian Blanket, Firewheel**) ▪ Annual. Grows easily from seed. Bright red with yellow trim, daisy-like flowers. Looks nice with our Texas state grass, *Bouteloua curtipendula*, side oats grama grass, in the wild garden.

*Gomphrena* (**Globe Amaranth**) ▪ Annual species very satisfactory. Seeds readily available. Makes a good colorful dried flower, red or rose color. Attractive alternative to periwinkles for summer blooms.

*Hedyotis spp.* (**Bluets**) ▪ Delightful tiny white or bluish flowers with four petals that may bloom continuously on or among your lawn grasses. *Sisyrinchium, Oenothera and Cooperia* may put in sudden appearances. *Hedyotis* stays around.

*Helianthus maximiliani* (**Sunflower**) ▪ Perennial, ten feet tall. Sunflower blooms are up and down the stems. Fall bloomer.

*Hymenocallis liriosme* (**White Spider Lily**) ▪ Large bulb. Striking white lily with long blooming period. Wet places. Large green leaves.

*Linum spp.* (**Flax**) ▪ Select annuals to add delicacy to the garden. Reseeds itself. Bright blue petals strewn on the ground.

*Lithospermum incisum* (**Gromwell, Puccon**) ▪ Perennial with yellow pleated flowers, among the first to bloom. It is a solitary plant. When the prairie burns, apparently long dormant seeds are released in response to fire, and the plant is abundant. From one year to the next, its appearance is sporadic, probably due to the hard-coated rock-like seed.

*Maurandia Antirrhiniflora* (**Snapdragon Vine**) ▪ Dainty vine with small snapdragon-like lavender flowers, Readily available at nurseries.

*Monarda citriodora* (**Horse Mint**) ▪ Annual. Very good in our area. Fragrant. Blue-purple bloom.

*Nemastylis gemniflora* (**Celestial Lily**) ▪ Bulb. Light blue flower lasting a few hours, another then opening, one at a time. Pleated ribbed leaves. Springtime.

*Ornithogalum* (**Star of Bethlehem**) ▪ Tiny bulbs throw up multi-flowerets of white lilies striped in green amongst the bluebonnets in spring. Rabbits eat the leaves. Repeats.

*Passiflora incarnata* (**Maypop, Passion Flower**) ▪ Annual vine. Spreads itself around. Large purple flowers in June, July and August. Medicinal use.

*Pavonia lasiopetala* (**Rock Rose**) ▪ Shrubby decidious perennial, long bloom of pink flowers. Good in a native home garden.

*Penstemon cobaea* (**Foxglove**) ▪ Perennial. Large showy pink flowers. If you can get one, it is a must. *(see p. 120.)*

*Phlox drummondii* (**Drummond Phlox**) ▪ Annual with bright red flowers. Can be seeded fall to spring. Use builder's sand to cover seeds. Will barely tolerate alkaline soils.

*Phyla nodiflora* (**Frogfruit**) ▪ A host plant for the Buckeye Butterfly. Low growing, with minature white flowers circling a central cone.

*Rivina humilis* (**Pigeon Berry**) ▪ Is happy under trees. Pink flowers and red berries at same time. Yields a dye.

*Sabatia campestris* (**Rose Gentian**) ▪ Annual. Sandy soil. Lovely pink flowers. Spring.

*Salvia coccinea* (**Scarlet Sage**) ▪ Dry area, dappled shade, colonizes. Upright perennial with red or pink flowers.

*Salvia penstemonoides* (**Big Red Sage**) ▪ Perennial. Hybridized plants available in nurseries. With lots of watering, blooms nicely in June. Good garden plant.

*Sisyrinchium ensigerum* (**Blue-Eyed Grass**) ▪ Charming blue Iris family flowers growing in little clumps in the grass. Sometimes white.

*Solidago* (**Golden Rod**) ▪ Perennial. Graceful yellow plumes. Fall bloomer. Does not cause allergies.

*Ungnadia speciosa* (**Texas or Mexican Buckeye**) ▪ Shrub. Spring fragrant pink flowers with elongated stamens. Tolerates some shade.

*Verbascum thapsus* (**Mullein**) ▪ Biennial. Found on disturbed ground. Spectacular. Was grown extensively in medieval gardens for medicinal uses. Dried flowering stalks soaked in oil were used for illumination. First year an attractive rosette of silvery soft gray leaves Second year sporadic yellow flowers on a tall stem.

# REFERENCE BOOKS

*Native Texas Plants: Landscaping Region by Region* 2nd Edition by Sally and Andy Wasowski, Gulf Publishing Co., 1997.

*Shinners Manual of North Central Texas Flora,* by the Botanical Research Institute of Texas, reprinted 1998.

*Manual of the Vascular Plants of Texas,* Texas Research Foundation, Renner, Texas, 1970.

# Chapter 16

## BULBS, CORMS, & TUBERS

*Spring Bulbs* ❧ *Summer Bulbs* ❧ *Planting*
*Naturalizing* ❧ *Resting*

The best guarantee in seasonal garden bloom comes from the first planting of bulbs, corms and tubers. Spring bloomers are the most common, but every season has its specialties. However these are usually planted a definite period before expected bloom. Repeating perennially depends on the species and the amount of sun.

**Bulb** ▪ A swollen underground stem. An encased bud, surrounded by fleshy scales. A bulb encases food and plant potential, e.g., Tulip; whereas a seed encloses plant potential only.

**Corm** ▪ A swollen short bulb without scales, e.g., Crocus, Gladiolus.

**Rhizome** ▪ A horizontal underground stem that sends out shoots and roots from nodes, e.g., Iris, Canna.

**Tuber** ▪ A swollen stem, usually underground, bearing buds or eyes, e.g., Irish Potato, Caladium.

**Tuberous Root** ▪ A thick underground food storage root with buds at the base of the plant stem. A true root, e.g., Dahlia, Sweet Potato, Day Lily and Ranunculus.

## PLANTING

The depth of planting depends on the size of the bulb. Check alphabetical listing under Bulbs, Corms and Tubers. At the bottom of the hole, use bone meal and a handful of commercial fertilizer well dug in and mixed with the soil. Above this, place a layer of sharp or play sand and/or perlite. Generally the depth should lower the bulb to within three times its diameter measuring from the shoulder of the bulb to the soil surface. Press the bulb into the sand, add more sand, humus, and soil to the level of the bed. All bulbs which are planted dry should be dusted with sulphur before planting. Those planted after soaking are Anemones, Gladiolus and Ranunculus.

## HOW TO REST BULBS

Simply avoid watering for two or three months after blooming season. They will begin to grow again when watering is resumed.

## HOW TO NATURALIZE BULBS

Naturalizing bulbs, e.g., to scatter and plant where they fall with-

out any formality, is very effective in grass, on sloping banks or nest-
ling here and there around trees. Make irregular plantings in drifts of
one kind of spring flowering bulb for the best effect. Try Anemones,
Crocus, and Narcissus (Divisions 6, 7 & 8).

For information on Bulbs for indoor bloom *(See pp. 156-157).*

**Agapanthus** *Agapanthus* (Blue Lily of the Nile) ▪ Showy flowers of blue
or white. Hardy out of doors in mild winters if placed in protected
area and mulched. Excellent for container culture and cutting. Vigorous grower needing supplemental feeding.

**Alstroemeria** *Alstroemeria* ▪ Dainty, rust red, purple, and yellow flowers in clusters spotted and tipped with chartreuse and other colors.
The tubers may be transplanted anytime after bloom. They are vigorous growers and need to be divided annually. Alkaline soil is tol-
erated. The foliage, as dainty as the flowers, is a distinctive color of
green and makes a beautiful house plant. Disease and pest free.

**Amaryllis** *Amaryllis* and related plants:
*Cooperia drummondii* (Evening Star) ▪ 10", native. White with reddish tinge outside.
*Hippeastrum* ▪ Many hybrids — white to pink to red. Will survive
mild winters outdoors.
> **Plant varieties** listed above in early fall with tops covered 2".
> Mulch well before winter. These are heavy feeders.

*Hymenocallis galvestonensis* ▪ Native white "Swamp Lily".
H. *Narcissiflora* (Peruvian Daffodil) ▪ A white Spider Lily.
*Sprekelia formosissima* ▪ A bright crimson exotic bloom.
> **Plant varieties** listed above in the spring as all have tender
> roots requiring care in handling. Summer bloomers.

*Lycoris radiata* (Spider Lily) ▪ Foliage comes after red or pale yellow
bloom to stay green all winter, disappearing in late spring. Avoid
watering when dormant during summer. Leave undisturbed for best
results. Entire plant is POISONOUS to eat.
*Nerine sarniensis* (Guernsey Lily) ▪ Leaves appear after bloom of
rose pink to deeper scarlet.
*Zephyranthes drummondii* (Rain Lily) ▪ Native, 10", white.
Z. *Texana* (Copper Lily) ▪ 6-12". Blooms in August to September.
> **Plant varieties** listed above in June.

**How To Grow Amaryllis in Containers** ▪ For Dutch hybrids, use
deep 7-8" pots which have been soaked overnight. Provide drainage in form of pebbles, broken pots, or charcoal. Place some sphagnum moss over this. Use good potting soil. Dip base of bulb in

root-hormone mixture. Place bulb in pot, the soil covering only 2/3 its depth. Water thoroughly and set in a warm dark spot. Supply a minimum amount of water until growth appears. Bring plant gradually to the light. Water with liquid fertilizer added to it every ten days. Cut the first flower stalk when faded and the second one will appear. 8-10 weeks required to produce bloom. Plant in October for Christmas bloom.

**Summer Care** ▪ Sink pot in shaded spot, level with the ground. Use fertilizer solution twice a month during summer. Withhold water beginning September 1 for 90-day rest period.

**Anemones** *Anemone* ▪ Range in color — red, pink, white, and blue. No yellow. Good cutting. Flowers are poppy-shaped and follow Narcissus in bloom. Good in rock garden. Like sun and rich soil with humus. Soak 1/2" bulb which resembles a tiny Dahlia tuber in water for at least 4 hours before planting. Examine closely to find hairlike remains of roots. Plant these down. If still in doubt, you can plant slanted. Plant in December 3" deep and 6" apart. Keep ground moist but not soggy.

**Arum** *Arum italicum* ▪ Grown primarily for mottled, arrow-shaped leaves. Produces small white flowers on fleshy stalk followed by red berries. Needs rich moist soil.

**Begonia** *Begonia* ▪ Tuberous-rooted does not do well in our climate. Fibrous Begonias are successful here *(see p. 110)*.

**Caladium** *Caladium* ▪ Of the Arum family. Ornamental leaves. The tuberous roots may be started outside after all danger of frost is over. If planted outside too early, the bulb will rot. May is an ideal time when the temperature is about 80°. They may be started inside in peat moss or vermiculite with sand at the base of the pot for drainage. When growth appears, transplant to a rich soil, well-composted. Plant 2" deep. Heat and moisture are their requisites. Plant outside in shade 1' apart and in two or more rows for staggered arrangement. Group planting is effective. Will do fairly well in semi-shade but avoid full sun. As Caladiums feed from the top, put fertilizer on top of beds. They like acid-plant food. Water frequently and keep calla-like blooms removed. Lift tubers in fall after frost. Dry in warm place about 40 days and when tops die back, clip off. Clean tubers gently, dust with sulfur and store where they will not freeze. Try newer, more sun-tolerant varieties. Strap or lower growing types make best container specimens. A very large-leafed variety is named "Elephant's Ear" up to super Jumbo in size. Exotic green. Poisonous.

**Calla Lily** *Zantedeschia spp.* ▪ These tuberous rooted plants require plenty of food, water, and light. The yellow variety is hardier than the white and is often grown half-immersed in pool water. They need a rest period after blooming and when the leaves have matured.

**Camassia** C. *quamash* ▪ A native wild Hyacinth with edible bulb. Grassy foliage and tall graceful wands of pale blue flowerets. A nice cut flower. Can be transplanted any time after bloom. Good drainage is the only soil requirement. *(See p. 124.)*

**Cannas** *Canna* ▪ No other class of rhizome is so easily grown. They increase rapidly, have wonderful foliage for flower arrangements. Plant in March or April, covered 3-4". They are heavy feeders, liking manure and bone meal. Check with your nursery for new hybrids which can be spectacular. The Dallas Park Department plants "The President" — a strong-red dwarf variety.

**Colchicum** *Colchicum* (Meadow Saffron or Autumn Crocus) ▪ Plant in summer, 2" deep for fall bloom. Flowers before leafing out. All colors.

**Crinum** *Crinum* ▪ Refer to Amaryllis *(see p. 128)*. Bulbous plants to be set out in April with bulbs just covered. They require rich soil, much water, partial sun, shallow planting, and resent being moved. The leaves are thick and strap-shaped. The colors are white, pink to red. Good cutting. As they multiply, provide enough space for the groups to form. The foliage will freeze and new growth begins in spring. Water well before May and June bloom. Off-shoots will bloom later.

**Crocus** *Crocus* ▪ Of easy culture, tend to increase rapidly. Color varies according to variety. Some bloom in spring, very early; others in the fall. Plant Dutch Crocus 4" deep; Species 2-3". Good for naturalizing. Sun or very light shade. October planting.

**Daffodil** ▪ Refer to Narcissus *(See pp. 134-136)*.

**Dahlias** *Dahlia* ▪ April is early enough to plant Dahlia tubers. They prefer a rich porous soil and are always hungry. To plant: Dig a hole 12" deep and twice the diameter of the tuber, add a trowel of sharp sand, place a stake firmly, and put the tuber 2" from it, 8" deep on its side with the eye or sprout end up. Never plant tubers on end! Put 4-6" of rich soil on top of tuber, and continue to fill hole as the Dahlia grows. Water. Label at time of planting.

**Culture** ▪ Cultivation is important. Soil should be kept loose and not permitted to bake. When bloom comes, the roots are nearer the surface and should not be disturbed. Irrigation is the best method of watering. Keep plant tied to stake as it grows. Add super-phosphate in August. Dahlias like cow manure spaded in their bed in the winter. The tuber may remain in the ground here during winter, but must be separated every two or three years. Each tuber must have a portion of the stem or it will not grow.

**Classification** ▪ 1) Incurved Cactus, 2) Recurved and straight Cactus, 3) Peony, 4) Semi-Cactus, 5) Formal Decorative, 6) Informal Decorative, 7) Ball, 8) Anemone, 9) Single, 10) Duplex, 11) Pompom, 12) Collarette and 13) Miniature Decorative.

**Disease** ▪ Watch for red spider, thrips and cucumber beetles. *(see p. 57)* for spraying tips.

**Erythronium** E. *dens-cansis* (Dog-Tooth Violet) ▪ This native plant is first to bloom, having nodding Lily-like flowers, whitish pink or yellow, with two interesting spotted fleshy leaves. A good accent plant for the rock garden. Will grow under trees. *(see p. 124.)*

**Eucharis** *Eucharis grandiflora* (Amazon Lily) ▪ Popular bulb for greenhouse culture. Six bulbs can be planted in 10" bulb pan with good potting soil mix similar to Amaryllis mix. Heavy feeder. Evergreen foliage. Slender leaf-stalk produces umbel of several Daffodil-type white, fragrant flowers. Blooms best when pot-bound.

**Galanthus** *Galanthus* (Snowdrop) ▪ Has early bell-like white flowers. Tuck anywhere in sun or shade. Plant 3" deep, in fall, in groups or drifts.

**Gladiola** *Gladiolus* ▪ Plant these corms (see p. 127) 6" deep and 6" apart in soil that has been well-forked, following instructions on planting bulbs. Begin to plant February 22 and plant every two weeks for continuous bloom. Tall varieties may need staking. Can be planted among Iris and are effective with Baby's-Breath, Petunias, and Poppies. Spray for thrips every two weeks. Take up when foliage begins to die down but before it readily pulls away from the corm, by carefully loosening the soil and removing corm with small corms clinging to it. Dry in a single layer with plenty of air space between each corm so they will not rot. When thoroughly dry, separate and store. Try some of the new miniatures. They need no staking.

**Gloriosa** *Gloriosa rothschildiana* (Climbing Lily) ▪ Exotic Lily-like flower, usually bright red and yellow, borne on a climbing vine needing support. Excellent for pot culture and as cut flower. Plant tuber horizontally in spring after "eye" is evident. Growth will continue in direction of "eye". Feed and water regularly during growing season. Lift and store in bed of dry peat.

**Hemerocallis** *Hemerocallis* (Daylily) ▪ This tuberous root flowering perennial, made up of a group of small tubers, is called "lily" because of the shape of the bloom and "Day" because the flower lasts only one day. Every color is available except true blue and pure white. With careful selection of varieties, flowers may be had from May to September. Plants are disease free, adaptable to all soils but multiply better in good beds with regular fertilization and water.

Avoid over-watering in heat of summer as they can rot. Bloom well in sun or light shade. Withstand freezing. Plant same depth as originally grown, 12-18" apart. Keep mulched. Divide after blooming when branches in the crown become crowded and the central part somewhat elevated. It takes about three years to make a large clump. In late September separate into sections of convenient size, except that the smallest should include at least one bud of the crown with the roots attached to it. Remove accumulation of dead roots and replant. Many new varieties are appearing on the market — from large (5') to small (12") — with ruffled, wide-petaled flowers in a diverse array of colors. Buy name varieties to get the type, color, and time of bloom you want. Check with Dallas Hemerocallis Society for varieties that do well in this area.

**Pests** ▪ Snails, slugs, aphids.

**Hyacinth** *Hyacinth* ▪ Different varieties for white, blue, pink and/or yellow spring bloom. Plant in December at a depth 3 times the diameter of bulb. Dig out 8-10" of soil. Mix well in composted cow manure at 10-12" level. Follow instructions on bulbs. Not easy to dig and hold over winter. They need cold storage in your refrigerator. Better to plant new bulbs each year. Like full sun. Entire plant poisonous to eat.

**Hyacinth, Grape** *Muscari* ▪ Grows anywhere. Plant in fall, 3-4" deep and apart. Will naturalize. Low.

**Iris** *Iris* **I. Bearded Iris** (Pogoniris Group) ▪ Has beard-like growth along the center line of the fall. They are best planted 3 fans to a group, rhizomes pointing outside the circle, and covered 1" with soil. It is better to plant after blooming period, but Iris may be moved or planted at any time. They like good drainage — use sharp sand or small gravel under them when planting. Full sun. Give a light feeding with commercial fertilizer and not much water. Visit a good Iris garden at bloom-time and choose your varieties.

**II. Beardless Iris** (Apogon Group) ▪ Should be planted in the fall, require rich, moist soil at all times, and can stand any amount of fertilization. Plant in partial shade or open sun, roots or rhizomes covered with 1-2" of soil.

A. Japanese I. *kaempferi* are most gorgeous. Require bog conditions and acid soil identical with Azaleas and Camellias, but even richer in manure as they are gross feeders. If planted in pockets by a pool, the planting pockets should be an inch higher than the water in the pool so that water will not stand in them continuously. However, they like water over crowns as long as 24 hours at a time. Plant new roots in the fall, but divide old plants after blooming.

B. Siberian I. *sibirica* makes a thick clump of narrow strap leaves with dainty butterfly-like blooms. Variety of tones. Like fertilizer and water. Good around pools, but do not need swamp conditions.

C. Spuria I. *spuria* tall, narrow leaf, all season foliage. Culture like Louisiana and Siberian.

D. Louisiana are gorgeous hybrids, almost like Orchids, in many colors and heights. Does not require swamp conditions as Japanese, but responds to fertilizer and water.

E. Vesper I. *dichotoma* many-branched with dainty dark spotted lavender blooms lasting one day. Blooms in late summer. Flowers attractive to hummingbirds. Easily grown from seed.

F. Pseudacorus I. *pseudacorus* grown mostly in pools. Yellow except for one white variety I. *p.alba.*

G. Miscellaneous I. *unguicularis* (Christmas Iris), lilac blue and white, blooming in November and through Christmas. 6-8", an old time favorite. Flowers will be bigger if evergreen leaves are cut half-way back in September. Flowers close at night when cut.

**III. Bulbous Iris ▪** A true bulb, to be planted in October and November and treated like Narcissus. Follow instructions for planting bulbs. Hardy. May be left undisturbed for several years. Fine for cutting. Of the Species, the Dutch and some Spanish are grown successfully here.

**IV. Crested Iris** I. *tectorum* ▪ Clear blue. Temperamental.

**Note ▪** The first Iris to bloom are those listed as Dwarf, then the Intermediates, followed by the Talls, the Siberian, and the Spurias. Make your selections for continuous bloom. Watch for root rot, borers, snails, slugs, and pill bugs.

**To Divide Iris ▪** Dig an old clump when it is through blooming and wash all soil from the roots. Cut off strong new rhizomes and throw away the old root. Remove dead leaves; those remaining may be cut back to 5-6". Prune the roots of the rhizomes you are to replant. Set in groups, spacing about 10" apart.

**Jonquil ▪** Refer to Narcissus *(See pp. 134-136).*

**Leucojum** *Leucojum* (Snowflake) ▪ This is Texas' "Lily-of-the-Valley", leafy, with white bloom having a green spot at tip of each flower. Plant in early fall. Pick a spot not in full sun. Multiplies.

**Lilies** *Lilium* ▪ Lilies are somewhat difficult since they like their heads in the sun and their feet shaded by good growth! Keep moist but not wet. Most lilies need acid soil.

**Two Kinds of Lilies ▪ A)** Base-rooters have roots only at the base and are planted not more than 2" deep.

**B)** Stem-rooters have circular masses of roots above the bulb as well as the base and are planted 4-6" below the surface. Dig holes the proper depth and follow instructions on planting bulbs. Plant as soon after flowers fade as bulbs can be obtained.

**Area Lilies** ▪ *Lilium auratum*, white but crimson-spotted; L. *brownii*, white inside of rose purple; L. *candidum*, the "Madonna Lily", white; L. *elegans*, crimson red and black-spotted; L. *hansonii*, orange but purple-spotted; L. *longiflorum*, the "Easter Lily"; L. *philippinese*, white but green-tinged; L. *regale* "Royal Lily", white inside, purple outside, yellow at base; L. *speciosum* "Japanese Lily"; L. *x testaceum*, apricot; and L. *tigrinum*, the "Tiger Lily" black-spotted salmon to orange red.

The Madonna Lily, the best suited for our area, can be divided in August and September, if crowded. It is a base-rooter and needs sunlight and heat.

**Montbretia** ▪ Refer to Tritonia *(See p. 136)*.

**Narcissus** ▪ The Daffodil is a member of the Amaryllidaceae family. The genus is Narcissus (Latin) and the English name is Daffodil. Only Daffodils which belong to Division 7 are properly called Jonquils.

**Plant Daffodils** ▪ In the fall only after the soil has cooled — (54° F at a 6" depth). Plant at a depth 3 times the diameter.

**In A New Bed** ▪ Dig soil 12-18" deep to encourage root penetration. Consider using pine bark mulch as a soil amendment. It breaks down at a slower rate than peat and is cheaper. Mix fertilizer throughout area. Apply at the rate of 3 lbs. per 100 sq. ft. using a 3-10-6-ratio. Follow instructions on planting bulbs *(see p. 127)*, remembering that all bulbs need good drainage. Bone meal may attract "animals". In a new bed, use only a low-nitrogen commercial fertilizer well-dug in and mixed with soil at the bottom of the hole. Above this, place a layer of sand and/or perlite to serve as a rooting medium and a protection for the Daffodil's sensitive basal plate.

**Established Bulb Beds** ▪ Should be fed with a low-nitrogen fertilizer as top dressing — in the fall, at spring emergence and after flowering. Try the newer instant bulb foods for the latter two applications. Dallas' Daffodils need supplemental moisture — one inch per week during their growing season. Select early and mid-season bloomers for this area. Plant all divisions to extend season of bloom and to learn variety of forms. Place Daffodils in the back of border. After blooming, foliage must allowed to die naturally to insure blooms next year. Do not braid foliage or use rubber bands. Bulbs may be left in the same spot until crowded, then lifted, divided, and replanted. Need rest period. The entire plant is poisonous to eat. Mulch!

**Classification Of Daffodils** ▪ There are two parts to the bloom; the perianth (background segments) and the central portion called cup or trumpet or corona depending on its form. Miniatures come in all divisions. The Classification will consist of a division number and color code (e.g.,1Y-Y, 2YW-Y). The colors and equivalent code letters which may be used to describe a Daffodil cultivar are: **W**-white or whitish, **G**-green, **Y**-yellow, **P**-pink, **O**-orange, and **R**-red. The color code will consist of two letters or two groups of letters separated by a hyphen: the letter(s) before the hyphen will describe the perianth segments — outer zone, mid-zone, and base; the letters following the hyphen will describe the cup-eye-zone, mid-zone, and rim.

**Division 1** ▪ Trumpet Daffodils of Garden Origin.
One flower to a stem; trumpet as long or longer than the perianth segments, e.g., Artic Gold 1Y-Y, Downpatrick 2W-Y.

**Division 2** ▪ Long-Cupped Daffodils of Garden Origin.
One flower to a stem; cup more than one-third, but less than equal to the length of the perianth segments, e.g., Butterscotch 2Y-Y, Festivity 2W-Y, Ice Follies 2W-W, Daydream 2Y-W.

**Division 3** ▪ Short-Cupped Daffodils of Garden Origin.
One flower to a stem; cup not more than one-third the length of the perianth segments, e.g., Aircastle 3W-Y, Audubon 3W-P.

**Division 4** ▪ Double Daffodils of Garden Origin.
One or more flowers to a stem, with doubling of the perianth segments or the cup or both, e.g., Tahiti 4Y-O, Erlicheer 4W-W.

**Division 5** ▪ Triandrus Daffodils of Garden Origin.
Usually two or more pendent flowers to a stem, perianth segments reflexed, e.g., Thalia 5W-W, Liberty Bells 5Y-Y.

**Division 6** ▪ Cyclamineus Daffodils of Garden Origin.
One flower to a stem (few exceptions), with a very short pedicle, perianth segments reflexed; flower at acute angle to stem, e.g., Charity May 6Y-Y, Dove Wings 6W-Y.

**Division 7** ▪ Jonquilla Daffodils of Garden Origin.
Usually one to three flowers to a rounded stem, leaves narrow, dark green; perianth segments spreading not reflexed; flowers fragrant, e.g., Trevithian 7Y-Y, Suzy 7Y-O, Stratosphere 7Y-O, Pueblo 7W-W.

**Division 8** ▪ Tazetta Daffodils of Garden Origin.
Usually 3 to 20 flowers to a stout stem, leaves broad, perianth segments spreading not reflexed, flowers fragrant, e.g., Geranium 8W-O, Silver Chimes 8W-W.

**Division 9** ▪ Poeticus Daffodils of Garden Origin.
Usually one flower to a stem; perianth segments pure white; cup usually disc-shaped, with a green or yellow center and red rim; flowers fragrant, e.g., Actaea 9W-GRR.

**Division 10** ▪ Species, Wild Variants and Wild Hybrids.
All species and wild or reputedly wild variants and hybrids, including those with double flowers, e.g., Jonquilla 10Y-Y, Bulbocodium conspicuus 10Y-Y.

**Division 11** ▪ Split Corona Daffodils of Garden Origin.
Cup split rather than lobed for at least one-third its length, e.g., Baccarat 11Y-Y, Phantom 11 W-P.

**Division 12** ▪ Miscellaneous Daffodils.
Daffodils not falling into any of the foregoing divisions, e.g., Tete-A-Tete 12 Y-Y (miniature).

**Ranunculus** *Ranunculus* ▪ Range in color from red, pink, white to yellow, but no blue. Some are double. They like partial shade, rich soil and humus. Their claw-like roots are planted down, after having been soaked at least four hours. Plant in December, pressing down firmly and covering with 2" of soil.

**Snowdrops** ▪ Refer to Galanthus. *(See p. 131.)*

**Snowflakes** ▪ Refer to Leucojum. *(See p. 133.)*

**Spring Star Flower** *Ipheion uniflorum* (formerly *Tritelia*) ▪ Excellent multiplying delicate flower for spring gardens. Pale blue star shaped blooms 4" high. Grass like foliage. Plant under trees. Prefers dry dormant conditions and good drainage.

**Sternbergia** *Sternbergia* ▪ *S. lutea* is similar to Crocus. Yellow, often called "Autumn Daffodil". Very late blooming. Plant in Sept. 3-4" deep, 6" apart, in acid soil. Group planting suggested.

**Tigridia** *Pavonia grandiflora* (Tigerflower or Shellflower) ▪ Not to be confused with Tiger Lily L. *tigrinum*. Tigridia is of the Iris family. Plant in April, 3-4" deep, in clumps, as flowers only last one day.

**Tritonia** *Tritonia* (Montbretia) ▪ In bulb, foliage and flower like hardy glads. Plant 4-5" deep, 5-6" apart in groups of 12-24. They like well-drained, rich soil and full sun. They need moisture during growing and flowering season.

**Tuberose** *Polianthes tuberosa* ▪ Plant these tender tubers in April, 2" deep and 4" apart in rich soil. They should be lifted in the fall, but may not freeze if well-mulched. Their fragrant blooms withstand the drought of July and August.

**Tulips** *Tulipa* ▪ Plant between Thanksgiving and Christmas. Pre-cool in the refrigerator for several weeks before planting *(see p. 19)*. Plant about 3 times diameter of bulb in depth. Instructions on planting bulbs (see p. 127). Water when planting and continue to water if no rain. Long stems achieved only with plenty of water. Good drainage is essential. In our area, Tulips are treated as an annual.

**Tulips are classified** into many divisions. **Single Early Tulips** — large flowers 10-16"; **Double Early Tulips** — peony-like 4" flowers; **Darwin Hybrids** — T. *fosterana* scarlet-orange, 24-28"; **Mendel** — midseason, white, yellow; **Darwin** — most popular midstream, clear colors, purples, maroon; **Lily Flowered** — long narrow pointed petals; **Cottage Tulips** — late seasoned and the **Parrot Tulips** — large fringed, ruffled in various colors.

**Repeating tulips** in the Metroplex are the small species tulips; **Lady** or **Candy** tulips. Find sources in catalogs. T. *clusiana* — red and white and T. *chrysantha* — pink and yellow.

**Water Lilies** *Nymphaea* ▪ Refer to Water Gardens *(see p. 160)*.

# REFERENCES

American Daffoil Society, Inc.; *Handbook for Growing, Exhibiting, and Judging Daffodils* and the ADS Journal.

*The Complete Guide to Growing Bulbs in Houston* by Sally McQueen (Squire).

*The Little Bulbs*, *Through the Garden Gate*, and *The Southern Garden* by Elizabeth Lawrence, Univ. of N. Carolina Press, Chapel Hill.

*Lilies* by Jan de Graff.

# BULB SOCIETIES

**American Daffodil Society, Inc.**
1686 Gray Fox Trails
Milford, Ohio 45150

**Daffodil Society**
Mrs. Donald Sable
4301 Edmondson
Dallas, Texas 75205

**Dallas Hemerocallis Society**
Eloise Koonce
447 Crestover Circle
Richardson, Texas 75080
(972) 231-3516

**Iris Society**
Ferron Campbell
(214) 841-7941

# Chapter 17

## ROSES

*Planting* ❧ *Varieties* ❧ *Pruning*
*Climbers* ❧ *Old Garden Roses*

Growing roses in the Dallas area is very rewarding, with colorful blooms from April through November and often into December if the first killing frost is late.

For the rose bed, select a location on the east side away from trees and hedges where there is sun at least half of the day. Roses thrive best in a slightly acid soil.

### PLANT

Bare root roses are dormant and can be planted from the middle of December until the middle of February. Container grown roses can be planted anytime. Throughly soak all rose roots 24 hours before planting. Prepare the bed ahead of time. Remove any grass and weeds for a width of 4' for a single row of roses, 6' for a double row. Prepare the bed 15-18" deep, working in sharp sand and humus such as well rotted manure, compost, peat or ground pine bark so that the resulting soil is 1/3 soil, 1/3 humus and 1/3 sand. Super-phosphate can be worked in at the same time. The completed bed should be 3-6" higher than the surrounding area to give a well-drained bed. If replacing a rose in an existing bed, be sure to remove the old soil (3' wide x 1' deep), because the previous rose plant has released a toxin into the planting area. See the formula for an acid 12-Year bed in Soils (*see pp. 38-39*).

The distance between bushes should be 20-24" and the holes 18" deep. Optimally, plant Teas or Grandifloras on 4 to 5' centers. Place Floribundas on 3' centers and Miniatures on 12" centers. To plant good quality, bare-root roses place a mound of soil high enough under the base of the bush so the roots slant downward into the hole and the base rests at ground level. Cover the roots with the soil mixture, pack firmly around the roots, and water well. When the water drains away, fill in around the bush with more soil, and "hill up" or mound the soil around the canes to protect them from drying winter winds. Pull away the mound when growth starts. The bush should be planted so the bud union will be 1" above the soil surface. The bud union is a swelling at the base of the main stem.

In bare rooted roses, spread roots naturally in an uncrowded manner. Guide the outer roots away from the ball so they will grow out into the soil rather than circle around the bush.

Mulch in the spring with 2-3" of ground pine bark, chips, pine needles, leaves, compost or other suitable material to conserve moisture and help control weeds. Roses do not like to be cultivated because it disturbs their fine surface roots. Hand pull weeds, don't till soil for weed control and removal. Keep roses well-watered in all seasons.

## CARE

Apply an acid-type fertilizer every month beginning in the spring when growth starts. Discontinue feeding the end of August to let the bushes harden off for winter. Special rose fertilizer is best, but use no more than 1 pound for 40 bushes each application. The bushes should be thoroughly watered weekly by irrigation or the soaker hose. Avoid overhead watering unless you apply a fungicide spray within 24 hours.

A healthy plant is less affected by fungus, black spot and insects. Maintain good foliage at all times to assure abundant blooms. It is better to use preventive measures against the most common diseases of black spot and mildew. Black spot is the single most common problem with roses in Dallas gardens. Weekly spraying with Bordeaux mixture is recommended. Spray both sides of leaf. Begin spraying in the spring. Use a good fungicide every 7 days until freedom from black spot and mildew is assured. Remember the underside of the leaves! A good spray mixture (Texas Rose Research Foundation, Inc.) is 1 tbsp. "Funginex" and 1/2 tbsp. "Manzate" per gallon of water.

Reduce concentration of chemicals during extremely hot or dry weather. **Hint:** Do not use insecticides unless insects are present. Refer to section on Insects and Diseases *(see p. 57)* for treatment of aphids, beetles, caterpillars and red spider mites. Avoid sprays containing oils which might burn. Use iron chelate for yellow leaves.

New roses may be cultivated from old favorites by air-layering, *(see p. 50)*.

## PRUNE

General pruning will be necessary after the first year's growth and should be done after plants are dormant in late winter (mid-February) in the Dallas area. Prune out all dead wood and remove enough top growth to keep the bushes in size and shape. Make pruning cuts just above buds. To prune for cutting and to extend blooming, remove spent or old blooms. Always angle cut the stem below a leaflet of five leaves. At this juncture the stem has properties to re-bloom, however above this point it cannot.

## ROSE LIST

Hybrid Teas ▪ Erect bushes, large blooms, one to a stem, best cut flower:

**Red** – Avon, Mirandy, Mister Lincoln, Big Ben, Don Juan; **White** – Garden Party, Honor; **Pink** -- Royal Highness, Tiffany, Perfume Delight, First Prize; **Yellow** – King's Ransom, Orange Tropicana.

**New Hybrids ▪** Cross of Antique Roses and Hybrid Teas:
**Pale Gold** - Medallion, Peace; **Pink Gold** - Chicago Peace.

**Grandifloras ▪** Tall bushes, large blooms, several to a stem:
**Red** - John S. Armstrong; **Pink** - Queen Elizabeth, Tickled Pink; **Yellow-red** - Granada; **Orange-red** - Montezuma.

**Floribundas ▪** Blooming freely, floriferous, best for landscape show. Plant groups of the same variety for mass color. Cut any cane below the bud union. Always cut 1/4″ above a node (a place on the stem where a joint is visible). Floribundas and Miniatures should have only half of the total growth removed in pruning: **Red** - Red Pinocchio, European; **Pink** - Else Poulson, Cherish; **White** - Iceberg, Summer Snow; **Yellow** - Sunsprite; **Coral Pink** - Fashion.

**Polyanthas ▪** Small, bushy with cluster of blooms, dwarf more disease resistant: **Pink** - Cecile Brunner, The Fairy and Pinkie.

**Miniatures ▪** Quite small, bushy, for low borders. Very small blooms, sometimes in clusters and sometimes one to a stem. Very popular, ideal for small gardens or apartment patio beds: **Red** - Beauty Secret, Red Imp; **Pink** - Eleanor, Starina; **White** - Cinderella, Starglo; **Yellow** - Rise and Shine, Yellow Doll.

## CLIMBERS

These are most useful in a small garden, growing up instead of out. They are prolific, have stems a good length for cutting and cover fences and trellises. Canes trained horizontally produce more blooms and longer stems. Prune once a year, removing 1/3 to 1/4 of older canes after blooming in the spring. Remove awkward, unmanageable canes.

**Varieties to try:** Pink Cameo, Dainty Bess, Don Juan, Flame, Golden Rapture, High Noon, Lady Banksia, Mermaid, Paul's Scarlet, Peace, Picture, Show Girl, Silver Moon, Talisman, Blaze, America, Golden Showers and Climbing Prairie.

## OLD GARDEN ROSES

A large group of roses encompassing many classes all sharing introduction into commerce prior to 1867, the date the first hybrid tea, La France, was introduced. Gardening virtues include historical interest, fragrance, color, with diversity of landscape form and increased disease resistance. We believe the following classes to be excellent choices for planting throughout Texas.

**Chinas ▪** Everblooming, colorful with a fruity fragrance, mostly shrubs. Examples are Old Blush, Mutabilis, Cramoisi Superieur.

**Teas** ∎ Everblooming, medium to large flowered, very fragrant, mostly shrubs. Examples are Duchesse de Brabant, Mrs. B.R. Cant, Sombreuil, and Mrs. Dudley Cross.

**Noisette** ∎ Repeat blooming, pastel colored, fragrant, mostly climbers. Examples are Madame Alfred Carriere, Blush Noisette, Reve D'Or, and Jaunes des Pres.

**Bourbon** ∎ Large flowered, fragrant, spreading open shrubs or climbers. Examples are Souvenir de la Malmaison, Maggie, and Gruss An Teplitz.

**Hybrid Perpetuals** ∎ Large flowered, upright shrubs (best for pegging) rich colored and very fragrant. Examples are Marquise Boccella, Paul Neyron and Frau Karl Kruschki.

**Species** (Wild Roses) ∎ Extremely healthy and vigorous. Various growth habits. Can tolerate poor soil conditions or partial shade. Good fragrance. Usually once blooming.

## REFERENCE

*The Organic Rose Garden* by Liz Druitt, Taylor Publishing Co., Dallas, 1996.

## ROSE SOCIETIES

**Dallas Rose Society**
Mr. Frank Lang
1006 Knott Place
Dallas, Texas 75208

**Collin County Rose Society**
Lynn Ellen Martin
1409 Hillside
Plano, Texas 75074

**Dallas Area Historical Rose Society**
Publication — Yellow Rose
Belinda Pavageau
P.O. Box 831448, Richardson, Texas 75083-1448

## AREA PUBLIC ROSE GARDENS

**Fort Worth Botanic Garden**
3,000 Roses including historic (1933) Ramp, and the Republic of Texas Rose Garden.

**Collin County Public Rose Garden**
On the campus of Collin County Community College, Spring Creek Campus in Plano on Jupiter Road — 800 Roses.

**Dallas Horticulture Center** — Fair Park, Dallas
Samples of many rose classes, old fashioned roses, many fragrant, displayed in garden settings.

# Chapter 18

## VEGETABLES

*Perennials* ❧ *Leaf Varieties* ❧ *Seeds*
*Vines* ❧ *Roots*

Vegetables will grow in a sunny plot all to themselves or scattered among other plants or even in pots on the patio. Decide what you want to try. Read instructions on seed packets. Then prepare the garden area following the rules for good soil preparation *(See p. 31 f.f.)*. Plant quick-maturing crops among those which take longer to mature. Plant later crops after those which mature early; for example, follow English Peas with Black-eyed Peas or Green Beans. Thin out abundant growth and enjoy lettuce or greens for dinner. Plant short rows every 10-12 days for successive harvests of many vegetables. Check on organic controls for safe eating and enjoy the fruits of your labor, for vegetable gardening is truly a labor of love. The following is a list of vegetables which do well in our area.

**Asparagus** ▪ A perennial vegetable A. *officinalis.* Roots or crowns are available from January to April. Two year old crowns will yield the following year. Crop increases in successive years. In planting, the crowns are placed in a furrow 6-8" deep, 18" apart in any good soil. Spread out the roots, cover the crowns with 4" of soil. As the top grows, the remaining soil is filled into the furrow. Use organic fertilizer on the bed in winter. Break off with a snap at just the right place for the whole stalk to be tender. Cut daily during the cutting season which is usually 8-10 weeks in the spring. Asparagus produces a tall fern after the harvest.

**Beans** ▪ All kinds of beans are easy to grow from seed. The weather in Texas presents a problem, for beans will not survive frost, yet they must reach maturity before hot weather. As the date of maturity varies from 40 to 90 days, you should plant as early as mid-February for the spring crop; in August or September after a rain for the fall crop. Make successive plantings a week apart to insure success in the spring. Plant snap beans 3" apart in rows 2' apart; pole beans 1' apart in rows 3' apart. Seeds germinate in a week. The soil should not be rich in nitrogen. This causes lots of foliage and few beans.

**Beets** ▪ A root crop. One of the oldest known vegetables. Plant 3 seeds 1" deep in rows 1' apart, from February to May, and September to

October. May be started inside in January and transplanted. Thin when 2" high and eat the greens. Pull up every other one to harvest little beets. Those left will have room to grow larger. Cultivate lightly until plants are half-grown. Beets may be grown between rows of corn.

**Blackberries ▪** Easy-to-grow natives of Texas and can be trained on your fence. Root cuttings are sold in winter and should be planted up to 3' apart at a depth of 2-4". "Brazos" and "Comanche" are varieties that are thorny and grow erect. The roots are perennial in the ground but the canes are biennial. This means that after the harvest, you cut off and discard the canes that have fruited, trim the new growth to about 5 or 6 canes to each plant and top them to encourage branching. Fertilize sparingly before harvest for maximum size fruit, and heavily after harvest to provide strength in the new canes. Rooted tips, young plants produced by layering, may be transplanted.

**Carrots ▪** A root crop. Need rich, friable soil and require much moisture for seeds to germinate, not so much afterwards. Spring and fall sowing period. Plant 1/2" deep. Thin and eat baby carrots when 3" high.

**Chard, Swiss ▪** A leaf crop. Thin to 4" apart. Later thin to 1' apart. Use leaves to eat cooked or raw. Can cut down to 3" stump from which new leaves will grow.

**Corn, Sweet or Pop ▪** Plant first in very early spring with successive plantings a week apart to insure against a killing frost. You must have at least two rows of corn to insure a crop. Don't plant sweet and pop in the same garden! Harvest when silk tassels turn brown.

**Cucumber ▪** A vine. Needs support. Plant twelve seeds in each hill (make each hill 3-4' apart in each direction) mid-March through April. Provide rich soil. Thin to 2 plants per hill when 4" high. Need continuous moisture, a complete fertilizer while growing, and shallow cultivation until vines cover the ground.

**Eggplant ▪** Seed may be started inside, transplanted in April, or planted outside in April or May. Has long growing period. Flowers (magnificent) will not set fruit if there is too much moisture.

**Garlic ▪** Refer to Herbs *(see p. 148)*.

**Greens ▪** All kinds are easy to grow and good for you. Mustard greens, turnip greens, beet greens in the spring. Collards in the fall and winter. Try some.

**Herbs ▪** Refer to chapter 19 *(see pp. 146-152)*.

**Horseradish ▪** A root crop. Roots available in early spring. Remains in ground like garlic. Has lovely large green leaf. Plant thick end up. Perennial.

**Lettuce** ▪ Leaf variety does best in Dallas. Successive plantings in small areas will provide salad greens as you keep the young plants thinned. It is harvested either by removing the entire plant or by using what's commonly called the "cut-and-come-again" technique, which is removing the outer leaves as they mature. Responds quickly to nitrogen fertilizer. Continuous moisture necessary. Needs early morning sun. Plant in fall and spring. Hot weather makes it bitter.

**Melons** ▪ Need lots of room to vine but will grow here.

**Okra** ▪ Grows well here. Plant seeds 1" apart in rows 3' apart in April and May. Thin to 8-10" apart. Matures in 90 days. Gather pods while very young. Four plants enough for a large family. Full sun. Try making pickled okra from surplus crop.

**Onions** ▪ Have a continuous crop of onions all year. Plant seeds in early spring at the same time onion sets are available. In late summer and fall, plant seed onions (small dried pearl onions). Water frequently. Onions will withstand very cold weather. Seed pods formed in summer are interesting and will dry for arrangements. Bermuda onion is a Texas staple crop.

**Parsley** ▪ Refer to Herbs *(see p. 150)*.

**Peas, Black-eyed or Purple Hull** ▪ Vines or bush forms. Plant in April and in August after a rain. Crowder, Cream and Lady peas all do well here. Make successive plantings and have peas until fall frost.

**Peas, English** ▪ Need cool weather but you can get a crop if planted early. Sugar peas have a shorter maturity date and can be grown successfully.

**Peanuts** ▪ A root crop. Plant in April in sandy soil. Take a long time to mature. Pull up in fall to find peanuts all over the roots.

**Peppers** ▪ Banana, bell, cayenne, chilies, chile pequin, jalapeno or ornamental. Sweet or hot. Red, yellow, green, purple. Plant in April or May, 18" apart each way. Full sun. Easy. Harvest before frost; will keep in the freezer. May be grown in containers. Charming plants.

**Potatoes, Irish(white), New(red)** ▪ Root crop. Plant February 14 or in August after a rain. Cut potato in large pieces, leaving a lot of potato and several eyes on each piece. The seed end of a red potato is the part away from the stem. Be sure to include a part of this in each piece. Plant 6" deep, 1' apart, in rows 2' apart. Late frost in spring or early frost in fall will not hurt as they continue to form under ground. Dig carefully and store immediately.

**Potatoes, Sweet or Yam** ▪ Plant slips. Need warm weather and sandy loam. Has long maturation. Frost kills. Vining plant. (see p. 95.)

**Pumpkin** ▪ Needs lots of room to vine, but it is fun for the children to grow their own Jack-O-Lantern. Needs water.

**Radish** ▪ A root crop. Several varieties. Hardy. Easy. Plant all year.

Need rich, porous soil well-supplied with phosphorous and plenty of moisture. Four weeks to maturity. Pull when mature or they get woody. Will grow in partial sun.

**Squash, Summer or Winter** ▪ All varieties do well, but are inclined to be bothered by squash bugs. Nicotine sprays or bulk tobacco spread on the ground around the plants help keep them off. Squashes need room to spread. Plant in hills following seed packet instructions.

**Strawberries** ▪ A perennial which increases each year with runners. Eight plants will give you a good start. They require rich, well-drained soil. The crown center of the plant should be set flush or level with the soil. Too much nitrogen makes soft berries. The fruit must be kept off the ground while ripening by the use of mulch, such as pine needles, straw, or perlite.

**Tomato** ▪ A vining plant. Not all varieties will withstand the heat of our summers. In winter you may start tomato plants from seed planted in peat pots. When all danger of frost is gone, these or purchased plants may be set out. Do not plant near potatoes or cabbage. Three plants provide enough for a family. Dig a hole large enough to accommodate some sharp sand and super-phosphate mixed. To provide a strong root system, set the plant in up to its first set of leaves. If it is leggy, turn on its side! If in full sun, mulch until plants grow enough to shade the root area. Set stakes at time of planting. Allow 3 to 4' all around each plant, or use tomato cages to provide maximum production in a limited area. Prune suckers between main stalk and leaf joint in the joint of the stem. Keep fertilized and watered (deeply) during the bearing period. When allowed to ripen on the vine, the flavor is tops. Green tomatoes are good fried with bacon.

**Tsai Shin, Chinese Cabbage** ▪ More like lettuce than cabbage. Cut 12" stems but leave a few leaves to promote new growth. Keep moist.

**Turnips** ▪ Used both for greens or roots. Can be broadcast or planted in rows. Use thinnings as well as tender leaves to eat. Turnips are a traditional Christmas dish in many Texas homes.

## REFERENCES

The Vegetable Book by Dr. Sam Cotner, Texas Gardener (Magazine) Press, Box 9005, Waco, TX 76714, 1985.

Growing Vegetables & Herbs by Southern Living Magazine staff, Oxmoor House, Box 2563, Birmingham, AL 35282, 1984.

The Field and Garden Vegetables of America by Fearing Burr in 1863; reincarnated by Keith Crotz, The American Botanist, 1103 W. Truitt Avenue, Chillicothe, IL 61523, 1988.

# Chapter 19

## HERBS

*Plants which have been proven useful to mankind.*

**Culinary Herbs** ∎ Those herbs with at least one part (such as stem or fruit) which has been proven safe for human consumption, depending, in some cases, on whether that part has been properly cooked, and assuming adherence to Nature's Law of Moderation. Example: fewer sage leaves should be consumed if raw than if cooked.

**Salad Herbs** ∎ Those culinary herbs which are considered best eaten raw. Example: Salad Burnet.

**Potherbs** ∎ A group of culinary herbs traditionally thought of as "boiled greens" and by Victorian youngsters as "spring tonic". Example: a plant with an unfortunately misleading name of "Poke Salad". To be safe to ingest, it must be prepared in a precise manner involving multiple boilings.

**Seasoning Herbs** ∎ Culinary herbs which can impart flavor to other foods. This includes tender herbs which are added toward the end of cookery, as well as robust herbs which continue to release flavor during more prolonged cookery. Included in the latter are some abrasive herbs (like lemon grass foliage and bay leaves) which could cause injury if not removed before the food is served.

### KNOW BEFORE YOU PLANT OR USE ...

1. Is any part of the plant poisonous (such as tomato foliage) or otherwise possibly harmful (such as rue on a sunny day)?

2. Which parts can be safely consumed raw or cooked in a routine manner?

3. Is the plant resistant to diseases or pests which cannot be controlled without systemic spraying, thereby rendering it unsafe for consumption (such as with a group of disease-plagued begonias known as Reiger Begonias)?

4. Before acquiring a new plant for seasoning purposes give it the following test. Firmly stroke a leaf or sprig and then smell your fingers rather than the leaf, just as you test perfume on your own skin. If it pleases your nose, it is likely to please your palate. If you don't like it, wait a while and give it another chance. One can acquire a taste for something initially detested, even Houttuynia.

5. Many herbs grow well in our area. For best results, start with plants rather than seeds. Most can be planted from April through August and will tolerate local soil and full sun. Those with unusual requirements and tolerances are so noted in the following list of culinary herbs.

6. Whether herbs are used in cooking, in fresh or dried arrangements, in fragrance crafts, or in herbscapes, their ancient symbolism can be brought into play. Most herbs have several meanings, one of which is included in parentheses with each herb listed below.

## KEY TO SYMBOLS

### Life Cycle
**A** = Annual    **A** = Treated as an Annual in the Dallas area
**B** = Biennial    **P** = Perennial    **GN** = Evergreen    **GY** = Evergrey

### Height
**L** = Low (under 15")    **M** = Medium (15" to 35")    **T** = Tall (over 35")

### Blooming Season
**SP** =Spring    **S** = Summer    **F** = Fall    **W** = Winter

P/M/S/F    **Anise Hyssop** *Agastache foeniculum* (Gratitude) ▪ Almost too beautiful to eat but too good to resist, though neither an Anise nor a Hyssop!

A/M/S/F    **Basil, Sweet** *Ocimum basilicum* (Many Good Wishes) ▪ Rhymes with dazzle. First freeze kills both green and purple leafed varieties. Loves our summers!

GN/T    **Bay Laurel** *Laurus nobilis* (Award of Merit) ▪ Tolerates some shade. Needs protection from sudden or prolonged freezes. Use to season but discard before serving.

P/M/SP S/F    **Bee Balm** *Monarda didyma* (Sweet Virtues) ▪ Also called Bergamot. Stolons spread and require thinning occasionally — semi-aggressive.

A/L/SP-F    **Begonia** *Begonia semperflorens* (Woes Be Gone) ▪ A tart, crunchy salad herb with great eye appeal in both flowers and foliage. Gorgeous garnish!

A/M/SP/S    **Borage** *Borago officinalis* (Courage) ▪ Cucumbery salad herb. Can't survive our summer heat but reseeds in autumn. White blooms rare.

P/L/SP/S    **Calamint** *Calamintha nepeta* (Dilemma) ▪ Peppermint-Savory taste causes frequent mislabeling.

<u>A</u>/L/SP/S  **Calendula** *Calendula officinalis* (Despair) ▪ Sometimes called "Pot Marigold". Flower petals make great salad confetti.

<u>A</u>/M/SP  **Caraway** *Carum carvi* (You Will Return) ▪ Requires rich soil and afternoon shade for relief from our heat.

A/L/S  **Carrot** *Daucus carota sativa* (Rooted in Sweetness) ▪ Freeze the peelings until needed to season soup stock.

<u>A</u>/L/SP  **Chervil** *Anthriscus cerefolium* (Sincerity) ▪Tolerates shade. Seasoning bouquets of this herb are called "pluches" in France.

P/L/S/F  **Chives, Garlic** *Allium tuberosum* (Moderation) ▪ Also called "Green Garlic" and "Chinese Chives".

P/L/SP  **Chives, Onion** *Allium schoenoprasum* (Usefulness) ▪ Wash and stack the hollow leaves in small bundles and freeze for ready use. Use the flowers!

<u>A</u>/M/SP  **Coriander** *Coriandrum sativum* (Hidden Worth) ▪ Flavor of foliage (called "Cilantro") is markedly different from seeds.

A/T/SP  **Dill** *Anethum graveolens* (Protection) ▪ Likely to drop seeds during hot summers and return with cooler nights. Flowers and green seeds both delicious.

P/T/S  **Epazote** *Chenopodium ambrosioides* (Go Away) ▪ Free seeding large medicinal shrub used as seasoning in many Mexican recipes. Moderation urged.

P/T/SP/S  **Fennel** *Foeniculum vulgare* (Success) ▪ One variety *'azoricum'* called "Florence Fennel" has swollen stem, dug as a vegetable, hence, an annual.

P/M/SP/S  **Garlic** *Allium sativum* (Healing) ▪ Prefers rich soil. Serves a different purpose than the large **Elephant Garlic**, A.*scorodoprasum.*

<u>A</u>/T/S  **Ginger** *Zingiber officinale* (Royal Guest) ▪ Cold-sensitive. Plant the hand (rhizome) in a container. When foliage appears, plant outside in filtered shade and rich soil. To use, cut through the soil and slice off quantity needed but replace soil.

P/L/SP/S  **Heart Mint** *Houttuynia cordata* (From the Heart) ▪ The acquired taste of the new millennium may be this beautiful Oriental ground cover which enjoys afternoon shade here as well as dampness. Not a mint, but invasive.

<u>A</u>/M/S/F  **Jasmines** *Jasminum spp.* (Elegance) ▪ The fragrant blossoms have delightful uses in the kitchen, but beware of so-called

"jasmines" which are not *Jasminums*. Some (such as Carolina "Jasmine", a *Gelsemium*) are quite poisonous. Most true jasmines are frost tender and like some shade here.

GY/M/SP/S **Lavender, English** *Lavandula angustifolia* (Good Luck) ▪ Morning sun and superb drainage are essential to success, and year-round mulch of coarse sand worth the trouble to give a good home to this gorgeous herb.

P/M/SP/S **Lemon Balm** *Melissa officinalis* (To Soothe) ▪One of few culinary herbs to tolerate shade and dampness. Its tea makes delicious ice cubes.

A̱/M **Lemon Grass** *Cymbopogon citratus* (Refreshment) ▪This tropical can survive some winters if cut back and mulched, but usually requires lifting. Adds oxygen to indoor rooms or easily over-wintered in garage. Recipes calling for this herb usually mean only the tender white base of each leaf, though the abrasive foliage is effective if discarded before serving.

P/M/S/F **Lemon Verbena** *Aloysia triphylla* (Enchantment) ▪Incredible flavor! An elegant must for the kitchen, but often incorrectly labeled as a *Lippia* or a *Verbena*. Species describing its taste (*"citriodora"*) is obsolete.

A̱/M/SP **Lovage** *Levisticum officinale* (Generosity) ▪ Prefers cooler summers than we have and may insist on it! With some luck and afternoon shade, you may enjoy its foliage, stems, and seeds.

A̱/L/S **Marjoram** *Origanum majorana* (Joy) ▪ (See **Oregano** below).

P/L/S/F **Mints** *Mentha spp.* (Hospitality) ▪ Tolerate dampness and their invasiveness can be outwitted!  Every kitchen deserves Ginger Mint.

A/L/SP/S **Nasturtium** *Tropaeolum majus* (Patriotism) ▪ Peppery foliage and flowers for salads and sandwiches. The poorer the soil, the more flowers for colorful "pepper". Protect from hot summer sun.

A̱/L/S **Onion** *Allium cepa* (Indispensable) ▪ This familiar seasoning requires rich, loose soil. Sets need months to mature.

GN/L/S **Oregano** *Origanum spp.* (Substance) ▪ **Sweet Marjoram** (or **Knotted Marjoram**) O.*majorana* has a delicate flavor but is a tender perennial. A small-leafed hybrid O. *X majoricum* has the traditional "oregano flavor" and the advantage here of being winter hardy. Many substitutes for that flavor are found in many genera other than *Origanums*, such as a *Coleus* from Cuba and a *Lippia* from Mexico. It is folly to purchase seeds which are labeled "Oregano".

A/L/SP/S **Parsley** *Petroselinum crispum* (Festivity) ▪ Contrary to popular insistence, the flat-leafed variety P. *neopolitan* does not have more flavor than the pretty curly variety when grown side by side. Space limited? Plant the curly.

GN/GY/L **Pink** *Dianthus carophyllus* (Lasting Beauty) ▪ Only clove-
SP/S scented varieties qualify as culinary herbs.

A/T/SP **Poppies** *Papaver spp.* (Extravagance) ▪ Don't eat the seeds you purchase to plant, but wait to enjoy your own crop of seeds (which only you have handled...). Most varieties have similar flavor and all add excitement to food.

A/L/S **Purslane** *Portulaca oleracea* (Persistence)▪ A delicious salad or seasoning herb long dishonored as a "weed" which now sports new varieties which are destined for success long overdue. Try the **Golden Purslane** *P. oleracea var. aurea* for vitamin-packed citrusy crunch in salads and tasty thickener for cooked dishes.

A/M/SP/S **Rocket** *Eruca vesicaria* var. *sativa* (Tantalize) ▪ Seed in porous soil in February. Both flowers and foliage are a great taste treat. Also called "Roquette", "Arugula", and "Rucola".

GN/T/W **Rosemary** *Rosmarinus officinalis* (Remembrance) ▪ There are three winter-hardy upright varieties for this area: 'Arp', with sparse grey foliage, is upstaged by 'Furneaux Hardy' and 'Hill Hardy', both of which have thick green foliage and need some protection only during most extreme cold spells. Trailing varieties are not winter hardy here.

P/LMT **Roses** *Rosa spp.* (Love) ▪ Fragrant varieties are preferred
SP-F for culinary use. *(See pp. 138-141 for special soil and care.)*

GY/M/S/F **Rue** *Ruta graveolens* (Grace) ▪ The bite in Mozzarella cheese you have enjoyed quite likely was this glorious herbscape plant, which can bite in another way on a sunny day when it acts the opposite of a sun screen!

GY/M/SP **Sage** *Salvia officinalis* (Wisdom) ▪ All varieties of sage need best possible drainage and maximum sun. In addition to this "Garden Sage", also try golden and tri-color varieties and the handsome, flavorful *'Berggarten'*.

P/L/S **Salad Burnet** *Poterium sanguisorba* (A Merry Heart) ▪ Great in salads and for cucumber-flavored garnish.

GN/L/S **Savory, Winter** *Satureja montana* (Interest) ▪ Its tender tips substitute beautifully for temperamental **Summer Savory** *S. hortensis,* and how else to season green beans at Christmas? Its relative, **Pink Savory,** *S.thymbra,* which has such a thyme flavor that it actually may be the secret of that "Wild Thyme" honey you brought home from Greece! Especially if you also detected a hint of oregano.

A/M/SP/S **Scented Geraniums** *Pelargonium spp.* (Preference) ▪ The low-growing Coconut-Scented *P. grossularioides* is winter hardy, as is the Rose-Scented, *P. graveolens* provided it is mulched. The countless others are treated as annuals here and dream of their homeland in Africa.

GN/L/S **Sorrel** *Rumex acetosa* (Affection) ▪ This vinegary herb with foot long elliptical leaves is popular but cannot compare to the French variety R. *scutatus* with smaller, more triangular leaves, and a lemony taste.

P/L/S **Sugar Leaf** *Stevia rebaudiana* (Hope) ▪ Paraguay is home to this tender perennial. May use in baking as a sugar substitute.

P/L/S/F **Sweet Leaf** *Lippia dulcis* (Sweet Surprise) ▪ Use this hardy trailing plant in small quantities to highlight the sweetness of a dish, not as a sugar substitute in baking.

P/M/F **Sweet Marigold** *Tagetes lucida* (Compassion) ▪ Strong anise flavor. Pruning for compact growth must be done before mid-summer to protect its fall color. The old-fashioned name is often lost among new "discoverers" who call it "Texas (or Mexican) Tarragon", "Mint Marigold", or "Marigold Mint" even "Sweet Mace".

P/L **Tarragon, French** *Artemisia dracunculus* (Lasting Interest) ▪ Give rich, porous soil and afternoon shade. Then try to keep alive in August. Needs winter nap under mulch. If all else fails, treat it as an annual.

GN/GY/L **Thymes** *Thymus spp.* (Activity) ▪ Every kitchen needs three
SP/S old-time varieties: **Lemon** *T. citriodorus,* **Caraway** *T. herbabarona,* and **English** *T. vulgaris* (with lamb try the new variety *'orange balsam'*).

A/T/S/F **Tomato** *Lycopersicon esculentum* (Love's Apple) ▪ How else to season sauces but with the amazing vitamin-packed low-calorie fruit of this otherwise poisonous plant which has so many poisonous relatives?

P/L/SP **Violet** *Viola odorata* (Devotion) ▪ Give filtered shade and acid soil, as well as space for spreading. The leaves are very useful in the kitchen, but it is their heavenly scented flowers, crystallized, which make a meal's finale grand.

*Herbs*                                                                                    151

# REFERENCES & IDEAS

**Herb Plants** ▪ Seasonally available at numerous area nurseries and year round in Dallas.

**Fresh-Cut Culinary Herbs** ▪ Found in virtually all Dallas supermarkets and in ethnic specialty shops (often featured in Food Section of *Dallas Morning News*).

**Area Herb Organizations** ▪ The Dallas Arboretum maintains an up-dated list of a wide variety in our area.

**Other** ▪ The national headquarters address of **The Herb Society of America** is:
9019 Kirtland Chardon Road, Kirtland, Ohio, 44094.
Fax (216) 256-0541; Phone (216) 256-0514;
E-mail herbsociet@aol.com

**For more on growing** or using herbs, visit a public library, and start acquiring a small but well-balanced library of your own, which would include: Something old; something new; something borrowed; and greenery, too!

**Something Old** ▪ English translations and modern editions of old herb-als (such as *Gerard's* from the 16th century) which will acquaint you with the romantic history and symbolism of your plants. The old uses are out of date, and some quite dangerous.

**Something New** ▪ Subscribe to a periodical (such as *The Herb Com-panion* or *The Herb Quarterly*) for up-to-date quality reading, in-cluding reviews of new books flooding the market. For herb identi-fication your will want a superior guide, such as those by *Eyewit-ness Handbooks* or the old faithful *Golden Guide*. For herb grow-ing, none are more reliable than *Hill-Barclay's* and *Rodale's Ency-clopedia*. For herb cookery, *Lucinda Hutson* and *Carole Seville* may be your authors. Regarding plant dyes, no one touches *Rita Buch-anan*, and for herbcrafts ad infinitum, *Phyllis Shaudys* has shared her collection.

**Something Borrowed** ▪ Out-of-print jewels can be acquired at estate sales and from numerous booksellers. Get on their mailing lists and learn from early 20th century English and American herb pioneers.

**And Greenery, Too** ▪ If you are as patient as your herb, your plant itself is the quintessential teacher. Let your senses, one at a time, attend class, and memorize each part of the plant. If you find the plant pleases your nose, your eyes, your palate, and your touch, then don't be surprised when you hear from it as well ... so listen and you may be filled with wonder as you become acquainted with the creative person you have become!

# Chapter 20

## SPECIALTY GARDENS

*Container* ❧ *Water* ❧ *Butterfly* ❧ *Wildlife*

## CONTAINER GARDENS

Urbanites with limited space, time, and money can reap benefits and beauty of nurturing a living plant with container gardening. The magical minature environments may be one house plant, a balcony of hanging baskets or a lavish patio garden.

### PLANTS TO CHOOSE

Anything that will grow in the ground may be container-grown. In addition, many tropicals may be added to your patio or terrace for they can be taken inside during cold weather. Most plants store up enough energy outdoors in summer to live indoors all winter.

### CONTAINER

Choose a receptacle from pots, tubs, boxes, urns, kettles, ceramics, concrete, wrought iron, hollowed-out logs, or volcanic rock. New clay pots should be soaked in acid water *(see p. 170, Glossary)* overnight before planting. Unglazed pots have good drainage, but dry out rapidly. Glazed pots must have drainage holes and do not require watering so often. In unglazed terra cotta, a water and oxygen exchange flows through the clay medium much as it would through fine top soil. Wooden tubs should be made from materials that resist decay: redwood, cedar, cypress, and others which do not require preservative treatment.

Economical and unbreakable plastic pots come in many forms and colors. Polyurethane vessels and solid non-porous containers require less water and lighter soil mixes to prevent root rot. Heat build up in non-breathing chambers can kill a plant. Choose or make shadier locations for plastic container plants.

### SOIL MIXES

**All Purpose For Pot Plants In General:**

2/3 clean Garden Loam — No Clay

1/3 Peat Moss (Canadian) or Compost

For each wheelbarrow load, add the following and mix well:

1  3" flower pot of Dolomite (1/3 manganese, 2/3 lime)

1  4" flower pot of Commercial Fertilizer (6-10 or 12-6)

1  4" flower pot of Perlite

Use a 20 gallon garbage can for storage. It takes about 3 wheelbar-rows of mixture to fill the can. Place about 6" of dry mixture in can, sprinkle with 1 pint of water. Add another layer of soil mix, sprinkle with water, and continue until all is used. Place top on can. Do not use for 10 days. (Much odor as it forms a gas). Good indefinitely. Liq-uid manure may be substituted for water.

### Special for Begonias, Tuberous Begonias, Gloxinias, etc.

1/2 good Garden Loam — No Clay
1/2 Humus (1/4 Pine Bark, 1/4 Canadian Peat or Compost)
For each wheelbarrow load, add the following:

1  3" pot of Super-phosphate
1  3" pot of Dolomite (1/3 manganese & 2/3 lime)
4  4" pots of Rotted Cow Manure
4  4" pots of Perlite

Mixture is fluffy, loose, very friable. Keep plants in 80° to 90° shade. Keep moist — never wet.

### PLANTING THE CONTAINER

When filling containers, the openings must be covered with gravel, broken pots, or plastic mesh. Over this, spread a thin layer of sphag-num moss to prevent soil from washing down and clogging the drain-age holes. High quality, lightweight commercial potting soil may be used.

### REPOTTING PLANTS

**Remove from old pot** by placing fingers over the soil ball and turn-ing pot upside down and tapping pot sharply on table edge. Eureka - it's loose!

**Soak in a bucket of water** and starter solution *(see p. 52)* to remove old soil. Prune damaged roots, if any, with a sharp knife. If you wish to replant in the same pot and think the roots are too full, prune some of them away. If you want to use a large pot, remember to use the next size larger — don't jump two or more sizes. Remember the holes in the pot must be covered with gravel or broken pieces of clay pots. If pot is deeper than 4", add a layer of sharp sand over gravel to improve drain-age. Use a good potting soil. Firm soil around plant. Water immedi-ately and keep shaded for a day or two.

### CARE

**For growing plants** in containers, watering and drainage are two of the most important considerations, followed by proper fertilization.

**Container plants** require more frequent watering than the same plants in open garden space. This is especially true during our hot, dry summers. To prevent rapid drying in the summer, a pot within a pot (the space between filled with sphagnum moss) is recommended. A cooling spray with the fogging nozzle of your hose is helpful in summer. Remember to wait for the plant to be in the shade, do not water when sun is on the leaves. On the other hand, if insufficient drainage is provided, plants in containers easily become water-logged. Maintain a happy medium *(see p. 45, Hand Watering).*

**Container-grown plants** are more sensitive to extreme heat and cold than those planted in garden soil, however they are easily shifted to a protected spot. They are subject to the same diseases and pests as garden-grown plants, and are remedied in the same way. They will need fertilizing more often but always with a light solution (1 tsp. to 1 gallon of water).

**Let the plant tell you** when it needs re-potting rather than the calendar. Re-pot as soon as roots fill the pot, but just to the next size pot. Too large a pot increases the hazard of over-watering, which upsets the equilibrium of the plant. You will need to renew the soil in small pots sooner than in large because the plant nutrients are exhausted faster.

## VACATION CARE

**House .** Before departure, water house plants and wrap entire pot in a plastic cleaners bag. Secure it around the base of the plant stalk. This will hold moisture three weeks and still allow the plant to breathe. No moisture comes through the base of the pot so it may be placed anywhere, but keep out of the sun.

**Outdoors .** Set pots in shaded trench filled with peat moss or saw dust. Soak thoroughly before departure.

### REFERENCES FOR CONTAINER GARDENS

*Illustrated Guide to Houseplants* by Anna Skalicka & Rudolf Subic, 1988.

*The Complete Houseplant Book* by Peter McHoy, 1995.

*The Indoor Potted Bulb* by Rob Proctor, 1993.

### HANGING BASKETS

## MATERIALS

Wire or plastic baskets, 10-12"; unmilled sphagnum moss; coconut basket liners; all purpose potting soil; plants; all purpose fertilizer (5-10-5).

## PLANTING SUGGESTIONS

1. For 80% shade and no more than 2 hours morning sun: Fibrous Begonia, Mints, Scaevola, Boston Fern, Wandering Jew, Ivy, and Impatiens.

2. For some afternoon sun: Asparagus Sprengeri, miniature Roses, Petunias, Geraniums, Marigolds, and trailing vegetables such as Strawberry and Sweet 100's Cherry Tomato.
3. Full day sun: Mandevilla, Geraniums, Lantana, Portulaca, Culinary Herbs: Prostrate Rosemary, Basils, Thyme, and Oregano, and Sweet Potato Vine.

## DIRECTIONS

**Put basket together, attaching the three hanging wires.** Place the moss loosely in a three gallon bucket, cover with water, and push down to get thoroughly soaked. Wring out a handful of moss at a time and pat down in the bottom, up the sides and over the top of the basket. Hold up to be sure all areas are covered. A clay pot saucer or aluminum plate between the moss lining and the soil will partially overcome drying out.

**Fill in one-third of the basket with potting soil.** Select the plants and arrange in the basket. Don't crowd too much; leave room for growth. If the plants are in pots, set in basket to see how they will look. At this point, you can tell if the soil level is enough. When finished, the soil level should be 1" from the top of the basket sides and sloping toward the center to form a cup for watering.

**Plant the center plant first, then work out.** When putting in trailing plants, set plant on side or at an angle so it will trail quickly. If you use rooted cuttings which are not in pots, take a large pencil and poke a hole about 1/2-3/4" wide and 3" deep into the basket. Gently insert the cutting and pull the moss back around it to hold in place. Be sure there is moss between the wire and the stem. Water these spots at planting time to prevent roots drying out.

**After planting, water slowly until water runs from the basket.** Hanging baskets need to be watered once daily (more often in the dry weather) and fertilized every two weeks with a light solution of fertilizer. Feed in the late afternoon or evening after the basket has had its daily watering in the morning.

**Hang baskets in appropriate sun to shade site.**

### BULBS FOR INDOOR BLOOM

## METHODS

**Water and Pebbles** ▪ Varieties best suited are either Paper-White Narcissus or the Yellow Grand Soleil d'Or. Using a glass bowl, place bulbs about an inch apart and fill in around them with small pebbles or stones. Add water until it reaches just above the base of the bulb. The roots need to be in water but not the bulb. Set bowl in a dark cool place until green shoots appear, then bring gradually to the light. Always keep in a cool room. As the roots absorb the water, add more to the same level as above. If the leaves and/or the flower stalks fall or drop, stake the plant with three to five uprights held with decorative twine, raffia, or ribbon. **Hint** – the storage of bulbs in the refrigerator for 6 weeks prior to planting gives better results. It takes about 6 weeks for leaves and buds to develop.

**Soil** ▪ Any kind of bulb may be planted in pots. The miniature varieties are especially suitable. Use clean clay pots with drainage holes covered with broken bits of pots. Fill with planting mixture (1/3 each of sand, loam, and either vermiculite or peat moss) and stir in a sprinkling of bone meal. Plant in pot so that tops of bulbs come an inch below the rim of the pot. Space bulbs about an inch apart. Set planted pot in a large container of water until thoroughly soaked. Afterwards, follow the same procedures as for water and pebbles, except add water from top when soil appears dry *(see p. 128)*.

## BROMELIADS

These tropical container plants are excellent for indoor use. They thrive outside in shade with sprinkler systems until the first frost. Many are rosettes with colorful foliage and/or long-lasting blooms. Most species withstand adverse conditions and neglect. Some common genera are Aechmea, Ananas (Pineapple), Billbergia, Cryptanthus, Guzmania, Neoregelia, Tillandsia, and Vriesea.

### LIGHTING AND WATERING

Most species require bright shade, good air circulation, and humidity. Generally, plants with soft green or pale colored leaves forming a cup that holds water need shaded, humid conditions and moisture in their cups at all times. Examples are Guzmania and Vriesea species. Be sure to water the potting medium as well as the cup. Plants with stiff or succulent leaves with little or no place to hold water can withstand more light and periods of drying. The more colorful the foliage and more prominent the leaf pattern, the less light is required. Plants profusely covered with scales such as Tillandsia species need bright light and must be misted regularly.

### PROPAGATION

The original plant blooms only once and slowly dies 1 to 2 years after flowering. Before its demise, the plant will produce 1 to several offshoots from its base or in the leaf axils. These offshoots, often colloquially called "pups", may be severed and removed with a sharp knife when they have reached a height of 6" or more, and have taken on the characteristics of the parent plant.

### POTTING

Generally, if the plant is smaller then 2-3 feet, it is probably an epiphyte and should be grown in fir or redwood bark shavings, osmunda fern fiber, or a commercial epiphyte mix. Exceptions to this rule are Ananas and Cryptanthus species which are terrestrial. Tillandsia species do best when grown in osmunda fiber, or wired to cork bark, fern slabs, or tree limbs.

## NUTRITION

Fertilize in the spring and summer with one-quarter to one-half strength 15-15-15 constant feed fertilizer or an organic equivalent at monthly or bi-monthly intervals. Do not fertilize when dry. Avoid micronutrient fertilizers containing copper or zinc. They are extremely toxic to Bromeliads.

## PESTS

Grasshoppers, scale insects, snails, and slugs are the only major problems.

### BROMELIAD SOCIETY

**Dallas Bromeliad Society**
Betty Girco
4337 Park Lane
Dallas, Texas 75220
(214) 350-7136

# WATER GARDENS

Having a water feature in your garden can be one of the most rewarding projects you will undertake in your gardening life. A water feature may be a bird bath or a rotating lawn sprinkler. Plants within the water feature create a water garden. Water brings an additional dimension and life to the garden. Water in the garden will also attract a variety of wildlife, an occasional raccoon, waterfowl, or frog. Some will come to visit and some may stay to nest. The more naturalistic your pool is, the greater chance of having a variety of wildlife visitors. The sound and movement of a fountain, the flash of goldfish or the reflection of the garden on a still pond surface, will lift any gardener's spirits. It is the greatest sensual element you can add to your garden. Consider these factors when designing your own water garden element.

**Design** ▪ Natural or geometric, whichever is better suited to the garden.

**Size** ▪ Minimum for a well balanced pool is 50 square feet of surface area, (10x5 foot rectangular or 8 foot circular).

**Depth** ▪ Any pool should be 18 to 24" – Fish pools in Racoon infested areas should be at least 3 feet deep.

**Edging** ▪ Choose materials that will blend your pool into your garden design. Rock, brick, steel edging, or wood can accent the pool.

**Construction Materials** ▪ Ponds can be lined with the following materials:

PVC (fish grade) 7 to 15 years

Butyl or Rubber (fish grade) 30 years

Fiberglass - 50 years

Concrete - lifetime, if properly installed

**View of Pond** ▪ Site the pool to achieve the most advantageous views from the deck, patios or porch.

**Site Selection** ▪ A pool should be located:

In full sun, or as much as possible

The most level site available

Within easy access of water and electricity

Where the water can reflect the beauty of the surrounding landscape

**Avoid the following site selection:**

Locating the pond where it may catch leaves falling from trees

Low spot in the garden where heavy rain could flood the pool

Where soils are prone to saturation which could cause the liner to float

**Consider having professional advice** on the design, installation and maintenance of the garden water element. A thoughtful, well-designed pool or fountain will add a long-lasting and delightful element to the garden. Ground all electrical systems.

## TUBS AND POOLS

New concrete pools must be cured. Speed up nature by the following method:

Fill with water, let it set 5 days; drain, refill, and let set another 5 days; drain; mix 1 qt. vinegar with 10 qts. water and scrub entire area with brush or old broom.

Age new wooden tubs or barrels which have held whiskey, vinegar, molasses, etc. with lime water for 2 or 3 days. *(See Glossary, p. 171).* Be sure to rinse before using. Never use receptacle which has ever been filled with gasoline, tar, oil, roofing compound, etc. Never use copper containers as they poison fish. Avoid redwood as it discolors the water.

Coat inside of iron kettle and old bathtubs with rubber-based paints to prevent rust.

## SOIL

An excellent soil to use for planting Lilies is three parts good garden loam or compost, and one part thoroughly decomposed manure. Never use fresh manure, so if rotted is not available, substitute a double handful of 10-10-10 fertilizer for each container.

## PLANT

When planting tubs or pots to use in the pool, put in fertilized soil and wet it so you can press it snugly in and around the root. N. *odoranta* root stock is planted horizontally, an inch below the surface of the soil with the growing tip extended above the surface. Weight root with a flat stone; cover soil surface with crushed stone or gravel. Do not cover the growing point with either flat stones or gravel. Lower into the pool. N. *marliacea* and hybrids are treated in a like manner but are planted perpendicularly. Do not set pots too deep until growth is sufficient to allow leaves to float naturally. Lower as necessary. Maintain proper water level after planting, for it must be deep enough to prevent curling of the stems.

## WATER LILIES
### *Nymphaea*

**Hardy Lilies** are perennials and come in all sizes and shades except blue. Shallow-water hardy Lilies are good for culture in tubs sunk in the ground and small pools. They are day bloomers and must have at least four hours of direct sun. *Nymphaea odorata minor*, N. *tetragona*, N. *helvola*, N. *mexicana* and others do well in shallow pools. Check with dealers. Hardy Lilies may be left alone for two or more years, but they do better if you lift, divide and re-fertilize them each fall. Do not uproot and replant in the middle of the growing season. If plants show signs of hunger (small leaves, small and few blooms, yellow leaves, etc.) fertilize by making "pills" from small paper sacks containing bone meal or blood meal (a good-sized handful). Thrust the bag into the soil beneath a root.

**Tropical Lilies** are annuals. They require much more pool and pot space for they are larger in bloom and leaf, and are rapid growers. The blooms are of many shades and tints including blue. Tropicals must have 5 or 6 hours of sun. Do not plant until water holds a temperature of 70°. Arrange to have no more than 12" of water above the crowns for tropicals, which include both day and night blooming varieties. Remember the night blooming lilies also need 5 or 6 hours of sun. There is no such thing as a shade-loving Water Lily. Practically all day and night blooming tropicals do well in shallow water.

## WATER PLANTS

**Arrowhead**, *Sagittaria latifolia* ■ Perennial, sun-part shade. Arrow-shaped leaves 6-12" long, on stems 2' above the water. 1 1/2" white flowers with yellow center. Blooms summer. Easy to grow. Texas native.

**Arrowleaf**, *Peltandra* ■ Glossy arrow-shaped leaf with bloom like caladium (spathiphylum). Stately, to 3'. Texas native.

**Dwarf Cattails**, *Typha spp.* ▪ Perennial, sun, 2-3'. Wonderful texture plant. Agressive. Likes wet, marshy soils.

**Floating Fern**, *Azolla spp.* ▪ Annual, sun-shade. Fern-like foliage that floats on the water. Coloration green to burgundy. Prolific.

**Horsetail**, *Equisetum hyemale* ▪ Perennail, sun-part shade. Wonderful texture for the water's edge. Tubular, jointed stems with scale-like leaves that are emerald green. Good for holding banks. Vigorous spreader. Good in flower arrangements. Texas native.

**Lizard's Tail**, *Saururus cernuus* ▪ Perennial, sun-part shade. "Viney" plant with tapering foliage 3 x 6" long, mostly at top of plant. White spiked bloom (looks like a lizard's tail) 8-10" long dropping at tips. Will make a ground cover 8-10" in moist or wet area. Texas native.

**Pennywort**, *Hydrocotyle spp.* ▪ Perennial to evergreen, sun-shade. Round, dark green foliage 8-10" above water. Infrequently blooms with tufts of white flowers. Also ground cover in wet areas. Texas native.

**Pickerel Rush**, *Pontederia cordata* ▪ Perennial, sun-part shade. 2-3" height. Deep green calla lily-like leaves. Deep blue spike flowers. Beautiful in masses or as specimen. Will grow in damp soil or to 1' deep in water. Dragonflies love to rest on this plant. Texas native.

**Umbrella Plant**, *Cyperus alternifolius* ▪ Tender perennial, sun-part shade. Erect, slender stems, with an umbrella-like crown of leaves, 3-4'.

**Water Canna**, *Thalia spp.* ▪ Perennial, sun-shade. Foliage to 4' in two forms, red or green. Striking flowers in bluish-lavender grape-like clusters.

**Water Hyacinth**, *Eichhurnia crassipes* ▪ Annual, sun. Floater. Lilac, hyacinth-like flowers, very beautiful. Great for spawning. Needs winter protection. Vigorous spreader.

**Water Sedge**, *Carex spp.* ▪ Perennial, sun-part shade. Bog plant with grass or reed-like foliage. 12-24". Interesting texture.

## REFERENCES FOR WATER GARDENS

The Water Garden by Anthony Paul & Yvonne Rees, 1986.

Rock and Water Gardens by Ogden Taylor & the Editors of Time-Life Books, 1979.

## WATER GARDEN SOCIETY

**North Texas Water Garden Society**
P. O. Box 9127
Dallas, Texas 75209-9127
(214) 956-7382

**Leftwich Reflecting Pool**
Dallas Horticulture Center
30 Species of Water Plants
Maintained by NTWGS

# BUTTERFLY GARDENS

**Five spectacular Swallowtails** reside in North Texas. Look for the Black Swallowtail, Tiger Swallowtail, Giant Swallowtail, Pipevine Swallowtail and Spicebush Swallowtail. The most common area butterflies are the American Painted Lady, Monarch, Cloudless Giant Sulfur, Red Admiral, Gulf Fritillary, Question Mark, Buckeye and Hackberry Butterfly.

**To attract the beautiful visitors**, plant food for the adult butterfly (nectar-producing plants) and the young caterpillars (foliage plants). These plants grow best in full sun and butterflies respond best to mass plantings of their favorites. Plant at least three to five of each kind of plant.

Butterflies respond to purple, yellow, orange, white and red blossoms. Among the top ten nectar producing plants are Lantana (the native L.*horrida* and the naturalized L.*camara* work best, but the new hybrids are effective too), Eupatoriums (Mistflowers), Asters, Salvias, Penta, Buddleia (Butterfly Bush), Zinnias, Globe Amaranth, Verbena and *Ascelepias tuberosa* (Butterfly Weed).

**Cultivate larval food plants.** Female butterflies spend a large portion of their time looking for specific plants on which they can lay their eggs. Provide host plants for the Gulf Fritillary Butterfly by planting Passion Vine, both native and non-native. The Black Swallowtail chooses the Carrot family, especially Parsley, Fennel and Dill. The Monarch butterfly uses the nectar and the foliage from Milkweeds. The Buckeye Butterfly has gorgeous fake "eyes" on each wing, and can be attracted with Verbena and a low growing native ground cover, Frogfruit. Hackberry Butterflies get their name because that is their larval food source. Native trees as Elm, Ash, Cottonwood and Willow also provide larval food for beautiful, local butterflies. Look carefully for eggs about the size of a pin head. Once the caterpillar hatches, it will feed on the larval plants until it is ready to form a chrysalis or pupa.

**Moisture and nutrients** are available from damp soil or shallow puddles. Butterflies do not need water to "drink", but are frequently seen around puddles that form next to fresh cow or sheep manure or manure mulch.

**Some butterflies over winter** in the Metroplex. The Red Admiral, Painted Lady, Question Mark and Hackberry Butterflies are the most common. They take shelter in crevices, the deep bark of old trees and other protected areas.

**The Dallas Horticulture Center** has annual butterfly gardening workshops in the spring where each participant receives a workbook of butterfly gardening information and a flat of plants to help them start a habitat for local butterflies. For information on the Butterfly Habitat Certification, call (214) 428-7476, ext. 22.

## REFERENCES FOR BUTTERFLY GARDENS

*Butterfly Gardens for the South* by Geyata Ajilvsgi, Taylor, 1990.

## BUTTERFLY SOCIETY

Dallas County Lepidopterist's Society
Dale Clark (214)320-9066 or
Ernie Ryan (214) 330-7315

# WILDLIFE GARDENS

**Desirable wildlife** can be attracted to any backyard that meets the basic requirements for life: food, water, shelter and space. Because birds are airborne and can easily spot good habitats, often they are the first visitors to a garden that is rich in habitat diversity. Depending on your yard, you can reasonably expect visits by of Blue Jays, Mockingbirds, Cardinals, Chickadees, Woodpeckers, Goldfinches, House Finches and Titmice. When you start sighting birds like Thrushes, Wrens, Warblers, Buntings and Hawks, you know you are offering a good habitat! With the right environment, toads, lizards and other interesting critters will reside in city gardens as well.

**Wildlife food is supplied** by gardeners raising a wide variety of plants. Native plants give birds good, year-round diversity of nutrition in the form of seeds, nuts, fruit, nectar and foliage. Large native shade trees such as Eastern Red Cedar, Hackberry, Pecan and Oak provide a good source of food, as do small native trees such as Redbud, Mexican Plum, Carolina Buckthorn, Roughleaf Dogwood, Prairie Flameleaf Sumac, Wax Myrtle, Yaupon and Possumhaw Holly. Other, non-native, plants that offer berries are Pyracantha, Mahonia and Fruiting Mulberry. Shrubs and perennials include Pigeonberry and Sumacs. If you like the look of seed clusters in the winter, Maximilian Sunflowers and Purple Coneflowers extend attractive seed sources.

**Supplemental food sources for birds** are an alternative. A bird feeder will allow you to see birds close up, but commercial food should be considered a supplement only - native food is still the best diet. Suet and peanut butter can supply high energy in the winter months, and hulled Sunflower seeds make a good, no-mess food source for the greatest diversity of birds. Other good options are black oiled sunflower, Safflower and Proso Millet. Niger Thistle will draw Goldfinch.

**Water is imperative**, if not more important for wildlife, than food. A diversity of water will encourage a diversity of animals. Although you can contract for a water feature or a pond, bird baths are an inexpensive source of water. Place basins on the ground, and rinse them out every couple of days. The water that overflows will make the surrounding soil cool and moist, a habitat inviting to toads. Birdbaths on pedestals of various heights will attract a variety of birds. Remember that most birds drink or bathe in water that goes from 1/4" to 2" deep, make the sides of the basin slope gradually, or add rocks or gravel to it. Since birds will be vulnerable to predators while bathing, put the water sources at least 5' away from places cats could hide, and introduce an open-branched shrub or small tree they can fly to and from while using the water.

**Provide shelter options for birds.** When most people think shelter, they think bird houses. Bird houses are homes for "cavity nesters" such as the Titmouse, Chickadee, Woodpecker, Bluebird and Wren. To attract Purple Martins, place their special houses 10' off the ground and 20' away from trees or structures. Evict competitive, non-native birds such as Starlings and Sparrows from any bird house immediately.

**A variety of branching structures** encourage bird life. Most of the birds you can enjoy around your yard prefer branches to birdhouses for their nests. A garden with a wider assortment of plants, will offer more numerous branching positions. Many of our birds nest from 6-10' off the ground, so small trees or shrubs supply good nesting opportunities.

**Other habitat alternatives** for wildlife include a brush pile or a loose-stacked rock walls (no mortar). Shelter belts or islands are areas of dense cover spanning the open gaps between other shelters. A good "layering" of plants (short grass, tall grass, shrubs, small trees and at least one large tree) will mimic the "edge effect" found where prairie meets woodland.

**Wildlife protection through camouflage** can be achieved by a mixture of plants and ground surfaces. One easy way to make winter cover is to leave the stubble in your perennial garden after the first frost, and then let leaves blow into the garden. Leaves are camouflage, and will keep other food (bugs and worms) close to the surface for birds to feed on.

**Space is the last component of a good habitat.** Another way to look at space is to think of the way plants are arranged in your yard. Add shelter belts, shelter islands and the edge effect. The biggest missing component of landscape in nearly every urban site is the layering effect. Think about what gets cleared out on a newly developed lot, then you have pictured what needs to be replaced to provide layering. Many urbanites clear out their understory, and live in a sea of grass with a few shade trees thrown in. It is easy to design attractive, wide swaths of large (4-6') shrubs and small trees (6-10'), to reclaim the layering so desperately needed to provide a good habitat.

**Learn more from** the Texas Parks and Wildlife Department's program to design, install and maintain an attractive urban habitat. To receive a Texas Backyard Habitat Program Wildscapes packet, send $15 to TPWD, Nongame & Urban Program; 4200 Smith School Road; Austin, Texas 78744. This packet includes books on Butterfly and Hummingbird gardening, a list of plants native to your area which will attract wildlife and an application to have your landscape certified as a Texas Wildscape.

## MASTER NATURALIST PROGRAM

The Master Naturalist Program of North Texas is a cooperative education of volunteers who want to learn more about native plants, animals, birds, and other resources in North Texas. Those seminars by experts develope knowledgeable leaders who will assist public projects on urban forests, wildscapes, native prairies and native plant collections. Most classes are held at the Texas Agricultural Extension Services Office. For information on schedules and locations call (214) 904-3053.

## URBAN OPEN SPACES WITH WILD OR NATIVE HABITATS

Open Spaces differ from native prairies, in that they have been cultivated (see p. 109).

**Fort Worth Nature Center and Refuge** — (817) 237-1111
9601 Fossil Ridge
Fort Worth, Texas 76135
Rob Denkhaus, Naturalist/Volunteer Coordinator

**Dallas Nature Center** — (972) 296-1955
7171 Mountain Creek Parkway
Dallas, Texas 75249

**Woodland Basin Nature Area**
2332 E. Miller Road
Garland, Texas 75043
Bottomlands Habitat

**Spring Creek Forest Preserve**
1770 Holford Road
Garland, Texas 75044

**Connemara Conservancy** — (214) 351-0990
Directions for Daily Use Entrance: Highway 75N to Allen - Exit at 34 McDermott Drive - Go west on McDermott to Alma - Go south on Alma through neighborhood, to Tatum (dirt road) - Go south on Tatum to bridge, park in front of ballards - Walk into meadow. Call for special event parking directions.
10000 Technology Blvd. West, Suite 117
Dallas, Texas 75220
Fields of rolling hills and creek side savanna.

# ADDENDA
*Additional tips & little known tidbits*


## POISONOUS PLANTS COMMONLY FOUND IN DALLAS GARDENS

We plant our gardens to bring enjoyment in the viewing of them. Along with beauty come some of nature's hazards. Volumes have been written on this subject so it would be impossible to compile a comprehensive list of all known plants into two groups: poisonous and non-poisonous. We think the best advice is to plant what you like and TEACH YOUR CHILDREN NOT TO PUT THINGS IN THEIR MOUTHS without knowing what they are. This is especially true for leaves and berries.

From September-October 1967 issue of the *Lone Star Gardener,* a publication of the Texas Federation of Garden Clubs, here is a partial list: Belladonna, Boxwood, Buckeye, Carolina Yellow Jessamine, Castor Bean, Crown-of-Thorns, Daffodil, Dieffenbachia, Easter Lily, Elephant Ear, English Ivy, Foxglove, Holly, Hyacinth, Hydrangea leaves, Japanese Yew, Jimson Weed, Juniper berries, Larkspur, Locust, Mistletoe berries, Narcissus, Oleander, Spider Lily, Poinsettias and Poison Ivy.

Adults and children alike have learned to avoid poison Ivy, Oak and Sumac. We can add others to this list easily. Further information may be obtained from the National Safety Council, the Texas Department of Safety Education, Agricultural Extension Agents and poison control centers.

**The Poison Hot Line Number – 1-800-POISON-1.**


## REFERENCES

*Deadly Harvest* by Dr. John Kingsbury, Holt, Rinehart Winston, 1965.

*Poisonous Plants of U.S.* by Walter Conrad Muenscher, McMillian, 1970.


## HINTS FOR THE FASTIDIOUS GARDENER

1. Scrape fingernails in a bar of soap before working in soil
2. To get the last bit of dirt from your fingernails, wash your hair.

3. Use sun screen on face, neck and hands.
4. Take a thermos into the garden so you don't have to go back inside. Don't become dehydrated.
5. Wear a brimmed hat and light color clothing during summer months.
6. Limit your time out in the heat of the day.
7. Dress in layers during cold temperature gardening, trapping layers of dead air next to the body for warmth.
8. Wear a hat in cold temperatures. Large amounts of body heat are lost from the head.
9. Wear a gardening apron to hold hand tools: a trowel, clippers, scissors, ties and a whisk broom.

## PLANTS WITH GREEN BLOOMS

**Bells of Ireland**

**Gladiolus** ▪ Small flowered - Green Dragon, Green Lace, Mint Julep
Large flowered - Emerald Queen, Green Ice, Green Waters

**Iris** ▪ Tall bearded - Green Pastures
Dwarf novelty - Snakeshead

**Lilies** ▪ Green Magic Strain - Green Dragon. Chartreuse-colored, bowl-shaped Trumpet Lilies.

**Nicotiana alata**

**Rosa chinensis** ▪ Green rose

**Tulip** ▪ Viridiflora praecox, emerald green, white edge.

**Zinnia** ▪ Envy - 3-4" Dahlia-flowered, 2-1/2" high.

## LIME OR ALKALINE-LOVING PLANTS

| | | |
|---|---|---|
| Bluebonnet | Hollyhock | Poppies |
| Candytuft | Lavender | Pomegranate |
| Cassia lindheimeri | Liatris | Salvia |
| Chinese Pistache | Lilac | Scabiosa |
| Dianthus | Purple Coneflower | Texas Pistache |
| German Iris | Possumhaw Holly | Zinnia |

# PLANT NAMES

*Genus ⋅ Species ⋅ Variety ⋅ Cultivar*

**Botanical names may be part of your current vocabulary.** Zinnia, Dahlia, and Crocus serve as the part of the botanical and the common name as well. Mrs. Belsterling, in her first edition of this manual, suggested the reader learn formal names and not be afraid to use them. It is still good advice.

**For direct information about a plant, check the index of a book for the scientific name.** Non-standard common, colloquial or regional terms are often unclear or redundant. Many locals call flowers Marigold, Daisy, and Japonica. A Marigold may be a Calendula in England, a Sweet Marigold, a Mexican Mint Marigold or a Marigold tagetes. These plants do not look alike nor have similar uses or grow under the same conditions. In the Metroplex we have several English language names for the same flower. Firewheel, Blanketflower and Indian Blanket are the identical plant with very different nicknames. They have separate listings in this index. If you look under Gaillardia the Latin name, all references are cited. Worldwide there are 800 species of Oak and 120 kinds of Poppies. For example specific names help gardeners clarify which Oak families are susceptible to Oak Wilt. This manual lists thirteen deciduous Oaks.

**Binomial nomenclature is the official term for two-named plant classification botanists use.** Each plant is given its own double Latin name. Scientific names, based on natural-like relationships that provide the most accurate means for identifying plants. Universally written in our Latin alphabet and generally italicized, this one international language serves as a worldwide communication tool. The system was developed in the 18th century by a Swedish botanist today known by the Latin derivation of his name Linaeus. He arranged plants into a huge science that organized all living things into a system called taxonomy. Plants fall into two basic categories: flowering plants and non-flowering. Each of these are divided into families then sub-divided again and again. In binomial nomenclature or standard plant names, like plants have the same first name. The first part such as Viola for Violets stands for the genus, the group to which the flower belongs. The second half is the species name and it may describe some useful detail about the plant, such as habit of growth, color, size, or even the botanist's name who recorded it.

**Genus names, the first part of botanical names,** are the most difficult to learn. Usually they are not definative in meaning and must be memorized. This first name or noun of the name is always capitalized. Many are classical words, but some have become the common name through usage: *Chrysanthemum, Hemerocallis, Ilex, Ranunculus,* etc. Genus names are used to categorize plants that are more like each other than like any other group. This name may be abbreviated after the first use of the full name — *Pyracantha coccinea* becomes *P. coccinea.* Species is a subdivision of a genus.

**Species names are descriptive names** that follow the genus names. The adjectives have several sources. Many have common root words: *compacta, deliciosa, fragrans, odorata.* Others will be recognizable from Latin translations: *florus* (-a, -um) for flower, *grandi* for large, *longus* for long or *longipetala* for long-petals, *macro* for large and *micro* for small. Many species terms are commemorative or refer to the individuals for whom they are named, ending in one or two "i's" or vowels: *davidii, drummondii, laceyi and ashei.* Some indicate the places of origin: *americana, canadensis, californica, japonica, siberica, texensis, virginica.* Species words may pertain to color: *albus* is for white, *aurea* for golden, *coelestis* for sky blue, *purpurea* for purple, *rubra* for red, *viridis* for green. In this manual species is often abbreviated to sp. for one or spp. for several. Clematis is an example with many varieties, cultivars and hybrids.

**Variety** is a division of a specie that is found in the wild or naturally occurring that differs from the remainder or basic plant. The term subspecies and variety may be used interchangeably. Variety is noted in this manual by an abbreviation, var. for the Latin name verietas. The Texas native Redbud *Cercis canadensis* is var. *mexicana.* Under shrubs the *Virburnium plicatum var. mariesii* is listed.

**Cultivar** (cv.) is a variety reflecting human intervention that began by man using cuttings, division or grafting. Cultivar is an abbreviation for cultivated variety. All individuals are geneticaly alike. In this book cultivars are capitalized and found in quotation marks. "Little Gem" Magnolia is a popular, petite form of Magnolia *grandiflora.* Both mutations and sports can be propagated asexually. Most of the _Dallas Planting Manual_ entries feature on particular specie, but the entries for Azaleas list many outstanding cultivars.

**X or x** is a hybrid or a plant that has been crossed by genetic mutation. Hybrids have been crossed or purposefully bred by pollination. A refined, non-invasive Trumpet vine hybrid, *x. flava* is a cross between *c. radicans* and Chinese *grandiflora.* In this book hybrid Tea Roses are listed by color. Occasionally the official organization that oversees plant names changes them. Some of these are mentioned in the manual.

# GLOSSARY
*A collection of terms for the metroplex gardener*

**Acclimatization** ▪ The process of preparing young plants for outdoor existance by gradually reducing the amount of water, and lowering the temperature of plants begun indoors to toughen their tissues. Colloquially termed "hardening off".

**Acid Water** ▪ A 1/2 cup natural apple cider to 1 gallon water, for aging pots and/or organic watering.

**Alkaline** ▪ A statement of acidity, particularly in substances having a pH value of more than 7. May refer to soil or water.

**Annual** ▪ A plant which germinates, grows flowers, fruits and dies within a single year.

**Anti-transpirant** ▪ A commercially available spray to protect foliage from evaporation to conserve moisture.

**Biennial** ▪ A plant that completes its life cycle within a space of two years.

**Biostimulant** ▪ A substance which activates microorganisms in the soil for optimum performances, thus creating an enriched soil for plant growth.

**Blackland Prairie** ▪ The Blackland Belt, one of the ten natural regions of Texas named for the black soil and prairie grasses it supports. Stretching from the Rio Grande to the Red River, it parallels I-35 from San Antonio through Dallas in a northeastern direction.

**Bleach water** ▪ One quart of bleach in one gallon of water.

**Bottomlands** ▪ A North Texas colloquial term for river flood plains.

**Bulb** ▪ A tight rounded storage system that contains the embryo of a plant, an encased bulb surrounded by fleshy brown scales.

**Catkin** ▪ A flower cluster typified by the Pussy Willow.

**Chlorosis** ▪ An iron deficiency in plants often diagnosed by yellow leaves or pronounced veining.

**Conifer** ▪ A cone-bearing tree or shrub such as Pine and Cedar. Junipers are the native coniferous trees in North Texas.

**Corm** ▪ A bulb-like storage system without scales.

**Crown** ▪ Often root crown, where the stem and roots meet.

**Cultivar** ▪ A term denoting a cultivated variety which is reproduced by asexual methods so that all individuals are genetically alike. The Texas native Redbud is *Cercis canadensis* var. *mexicana*.

**Cultivate** ▪ To prepare land for raising plants by plowing, planting, and fertilizing. To loosen, dig or till the soil around growing plants. In this book "do not cultivate" means do not spade the flower bed.

**Damping off** ▪ A fungus disease causing seedlings to rot at ground level.

**Deadhead** ▪ To pick off spent blooms.

**Deciduous** ▪ A plant that sheds leaves in winter; the opposite of evergreen.

**Dioecious** ▪ A plant bearing either male or female organs. When fertilized the male may bear fruit or berries, e.g., Peaches and Yaupons.

**Disbud** ▪ The removal of one or more buds, leaving a single flower to achieve all sustenance. Used with Camellias and Chrysanthemums.

**Division** ▪ The act of cutting or separating fleshy storage organs, e.g., rhizomes, tubers, root clumps to thin and make more plants.

**Dormant** ▪ A period during which a plant shows no visible growth, usually during winter.

**Escarpment** ▪ A steep slope or a long cliff formed by erosion.

**Force** ▪ Bringing a plant into a warmer climate, perhaps inside, or manipulating the hours of light to "force" earlier bloom than would naturally arrive outside.

**Foundation planting** ▪ Traditional evergreens planted around a house to hide the juncture of building materials and the bare ground. Plants close to a facade of the house give form to the basic landscape, especially in winter dormancy.

**Friable** ▪ Loose, crumbly soil as opposed to tight clay.

**Genus** ▪ The family group in the scientific name of a plant. In Latin, it is capitalized and listed first.

**Germination** ▪ When first true leaves appear in sprouting.

**Hardening off** ▪ The process of making plants ready for outdoors by gradually reducing the amount of water, and lowering the temperature of plants grown indoors to toughen their tissues.

**Heeling-in** ▪ Storing plants on their side in a trench, covered with soil until time to plant.

**Herbicides** ▪ A weed control chemical frequently used on lawns to prevent broad leaf plant growth. These are not recommended as they may kill nearby trees. Pre-emergent is a weed preventative. Post-emergent is a weed killer. Both are herbicides.

**Hybrid ▪** A variety resulting from crossing two species or cultivars.

**Indiginious Plants ▪** Plants found in an area before European immigrants arrived. Often called native plants.

**Invasive ▪** Hardy species which tend to grow out of control.

**Irrigation ▪** The application of supplemental water to augment precipitation.

**Leaching out ▪** A process where water soluble nutrients or undesirable mineral build-up is washed away.

**Lime-sulfur ▪** Calcium sulfate, a fungicide and insecticide applied during the winter months.

**Lime water ▪** One handful of slack lime to 5 gallons of water.

**Naturalizing ▪** Informal style of planting to bring about the effect of natural informal, irregular growth.

**Node ▪** The place at which a leaf or bud joins the stem to which it is attached; a joint.

**Panicle ▪** An open flower cluster.

**Perennial ▪** A plant that may live on indefinitely, die to ground in winter, but renew growth in spring.

**Pinching back ▪** The shortening of young shoots to achieve bushy form, to encourage the development of a greater quantity of buds, flowers or fruit.

**Plant association ▪** An established grouping that is traditionally found growing together as a plant community or biotic region.

**Pre-emergent ▪** (See p. 4).

**Raceme ▪** An elongated flower cluster blooming from the bottom up.

**Rhizome ▪** A horizontal underground stem that sends out shoots and roots from nodes.

**Root bound ▪** Usually a container grown plant with a mat of roots circling the outside of the ball. This wrapped root condition prohibits securing enough moisture and may prove fatal. However, some pot plants prefer to be root bound to bloom well.

**Root flare extension ▪** An aerial root that exits the soil some distance from the trunk.

**Root hormone ▪** Preparation to encourage rooting in cuttings (See p. 47).

**Root stimulant ▪** Plant nutrient that stimulates early, stronger root formation; reduces transplant shock.

**Savannas ▪** A native grassland with occasional trees. The transition between grasslands and forest.

**Separation** ∎ The man-made division of natural vegetative growth, e.g., bulbs and corms as perennial plants.

**Species** ∎ Subdivision of a genus. Second half of a two part Latin name, often descriptive.

**Sterile plant** ∎ A plant that does not seed.

**Sterile soil** ∎ Pasturized soil, free of all organisms, e.g., sharp sand.

**Succulent** ∎ A plant that stores water and becomes adapted to the lack of it.

**Sucker** ∎ A shoot arising from a subterranean stem or root; the sprout that grows in the joint of the stem between the leaf stalk and the main stalk of plants. Nutritionally sapping to structural growth, these are often pruned or eliminated.

**Top-dressing** ∎ The application of additional material, often mulch, scattered on top of and raked in, to improve the soil.

**Tree canopy** ∎ The overhanging roof-like structure of foliage. The diameter of the leaf umbrella of a tree.

**True leaves** ∎ The second set of leaves to grow on a seedling. Typical of the specific plant.

**Tuber** ∎ A swollen stem bearing buds, usually occuring underground.

**Unammended Soil** ∎ Original earth that has not been improved by tilling, adding or fertilizing.

**Variety** ∎ Subdivision of a species.

**White-frost** ∎ Not a killing frost; one damaging to tender plants.

**Xeriphite** ∎ A plant that can survive without supplemental watering.

**Xeriphitic Conditions** ∎ A horticulture style where no additional irrigation or fertilizer is given to existing planting. Native prairie plants e.g., Buffalograss and Hawthorn trees thrive with this maintenance.

# INDEX

*Dallas Planting Manual*

*Dallas Planting Manual*

Trinity River 26, 27
**Tritonia** (Montbretia) 136
*Tropae'olum* **Nasturtium** 4, 113, 149
Trout Lily 124
True leaves 50, 172
**Trumpet Vine** *Camp'sis* 95
*Tsai Shin,* **Chinese Cabbage** 145
Tuber 127, 173
**Tuberose** *Polianth'es* 8, 22, 136
Tuberous Root 127
**Tulip** *Tulipa* 7, 9, 20, 22, 58, 127, 136-137, 167
**Turk's Cap** 19
**Turnip** 4, 22, 145
Twelve Year Bed 38-39

————— **U** —————

Umbrella Plant 161
*Ungnadia* **Texas** or **Mexican Buckeye** 126

————— **V** —————

Vacation Care, for Plants 155
Variety 169, 173
Vegetables, when to plant 4, 6, 8, 12, 14, 16, 18, 22, 142
Vegetables, list of 142-145
*Verbas'cum* **Mullein** 113, 126
**Verbena** 9, 17, 19, 115, 122, 162
*Veron'ica*
  **Creeping Speedwell** (Ground Cover) 98
  **Speedwell** (Perennial) 122
*Vibur'num*
  Rusty Blackhaw 75
  Snowball 9, 83
**Vinca** 10, 12, 13, 98
Vines, list of 91-95
*Viola* 115
  Pansy 113-114
  Violet (Perennial) 122
  Violet (Herb) 151
**Violet** 5, 7, 11, 13, 61, 122, 151, 168
  African 49, 60
  Viola (Herb) 151
**Virginia Creeper** *Parthenociss'us* 95
**Virgins-Bower** *Clem'atis* 91
*Vitex agnus-castus* **Chaste Tree** 15, 71
*Vitis* **Grapevine** 93

————— **W** —————

*Waldstei'nia* **Barren Strawberry** 98
**Wallflower** *Cheiran'thus* 3, 5, 20, 115
Warm Season Grasses 99, 100, 102, 105
**Water Canna** *Thalia* 161
Water Gardens 15, 158-160, 163
**Water Hyacinth** *Eichhurnia crassipes* 161
**Water Lilies** *Nymphae'a* 10, 15, 17, 160
Water Oak 70
Water Plants, list of 160-161
**Water Sedge** *Carex* 161
**Watermelon** 8, 16
**Watering** (Water)
  Azaleas 85-86
  Bromeliads 157
  Camellias 88-89
  Container Gardens 154
  General 2, 4, 6, 8, 10, 12, 14, 16, 18,
  Lawns 42-46, 104, 106
  Wildlife Gardens 163-164
**Wax-leaf** *Ligust'rum* 81
**Wax-Myrtle** *Myrica cerifera* 73, 163
Weather 27-28
Webworm 62
**Weigela** *Weigela rosea* 83
White Rock Lake and Creek 27
**White Spider Lily** 125
Whitefly 54, 57, 62
White-frost 173
**Wild Hyacinth** *Camassia* 124
Wildflowers 4, 16, 123
Wildlife Gardens 163-164
**Willow** 5, 71, 162
  **Black** S. *nigra* 71
  **Corkscrew** S. *matsudana* 71
  **Desert** (flowering) *Chilopsis* 71
  **Pussy** S. *discolor* 82
  Oak 70
  **Weeping** S. *babylonica* 71
Wilt 62
**Windflower** *Anem'one* 116
**Wine Cup** 11
Winged Elm 68
Winter Annuals 110, 111, 113, 114, 115
Winter burned foliage 4, 79
**Winter Bush Honeysuckle** 3, 22, 80
**Wintercreeper** *Euon'ymus* 3, 81, 96
Winter-Dormant Oil 3, 55, 56
Winter Jasmine 5

# ORDER FORM

## Dallas Planting Manual
14th Edition, 2001
**Price per Book $13.95**

Please Send _____ Books          **TOTAL** _____

**SHIPPING & HANDLING** _____

$5.00 for first book _____

$1.00 for each additional book _____

Add 8.25% **SALES TAX** _____

**TOTAL AMOUNT** _____

Check or Money Order Payable To:
**DALLAS GARDEN CLUB**

**SHIP BOOKS TO:**

Name _____

Address _____

City _____ State _____ Zip _____

**MAIL FORM AND PAYMENT TO:** Dallas Planting Manual
P. O. Box 710355
Dallas, TX 75371

### TOTAL COST 1-4 BOOKS
**1 book**
$13.95 + 1.15 sales tax + 5.00 shipping & handling = $20.10
**2 books**
$27.90 + 2.30 sales tax + 6.00 shipping & handling = $36.20
**3 books**
$41.85 + 3.45 sales tax + 7.00 shipping & handling = $52.30
**4 books**
$55.80 + 4.60 sales tax + 8.00 shipping & handling = $68.40